Picturing the Artist's Studio, from Delacroix to Picasso

Northern Lights

Series Editor: Walter Melion, Asa Griggs Candler Professor of Art History, Emory University, and Foreign Member, KNAW, Royal Netherlands Academy of Arts and Sciences

The 'Northern Lights' book series profiles Northern art in its infinite variety, including paintings, sculptures, objects and architecture. Often the phrase 'Northern art' conjures iconic works of the Northern Renaissance and the 'Dutch Golden Age'. While welcoming contributions about such works, this series also looks beyond 'the usual suspects'. The extended time period – from the Middle Ages to the 19th century – invites authors to explore themes in Northern art without the constraint of conventional chronological boundaries. The expansive geographical coverage offers the potential to highlight the names and works of artists and movements that haven't been privileged in art-historical publishing up until now.

The series publishes illustrated thematic surveys, artist monographs and histories of Northern art collections in museums. It incorporates a range of volumes, from more specialised studies for scholars, to books that are accessible to art enthusiasts.

Picturing the Artist's Studio, from Delacroix to Picasso

Heather McPherson

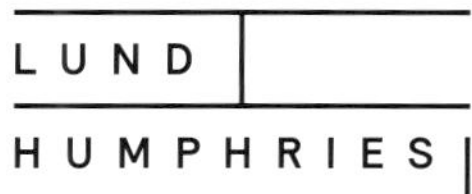

First published in 2024
by Lund Humphries
Huckletree Shoreditch
Alphabeta Building
18 Finsbury Square
London EC2A 1AH
www.lundhumphries.com

ISBN 978-1-84822-521-3

A Cataloguing-in-Publication record for this book is available from the British Library.

Copy edited by Kimberley Skelton
Project managed and designed by Crow Books
Set in Adobe Jenson Pro
Printed in Bosnia and Herzegovina

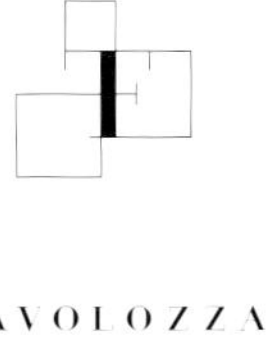

TAVOLOZZA
FOUNDATION

Front Cover: Frédéric Bazille, *Studio on the Rue La Condamine*, 1870, oil on canvas, 98 × 128.5 cm, Musée d'Orsay, Paris

Contents

Acknowledgments

In researching and writing this book, I have incurred numerous debts that I can only partially acknowledge here. A Visiting Senior Fellowship at the Center for Advanced Study in the Visual Arts, National Gallery of Art, Washington, DC, launched the project during fall 2010. A 2013 Dean's Grant from the College of Arts and Sciences at the University of Alabama, Birmingham funded archival research, and a 2020 sabbatical leave provided unencumbered time for writing. I am grateful to the Tavolozza Foundation for their generous support of my illustrations. Numerous museums, collections and archives in the United States and France were crucial for my research. Special thanks to Mary Morton, Curator and Head of the Department of French Paintings, National Gallery of Art, Washington, DC for inviting me to contribute to the exhibition catalogue *Corot: Women* (2018) – an invitation which stimulated my research on Corot's studio. At Lund Humphries, I am indebted to Erika Gaffney, Acquisitions Editor, who encouraged me to submit the project, and to Walter Melion, the Series Editor, for their unwavering support, as well as to the excellent editorial and production team, especially Rebeccah Williams, Lucie Worboys and Kimberley Skelton.

Among the numerous individuals who have provided assistance, I particularly wish to thank Therese Dolan, Jane Kromm and Mary Morton for reading preliminary drafts of individual chapters and for providing valuable feedback and suggestions. For advice and assistance with illustrations, I am grateful to John Klein, Georges Matisse, Bonhams, Jill Newhouse and Madeleine Beaufort. I also wish to thank the staff at museums, archives and libraries that facilitated my research: in Paris, Aude Gobet, Service d'étude et de documentation, Département des peintures, and the Cabinet des dessins, Musée du Louvre; the Service de documentation, Musée d'Orsay; and the Cabinet des estampes, Bibliothèque nationale de France; in Washington, DC, at the National Gallery of Art, the Department of Painting Conservation, Gregory P. J. Most and the Department of Image Collections, Yuri Long (Special Collections Librarian), as well as the National Gallery of Art Library; in New York, the Prints and Drawings Study Room of the Metropolitan Museum of Art. At the University of Alabama, Birmingham, the Mervyn H. Sterne Library and interlibrary loan service supported my research and furnished numerous books and articles. Finally, I wish to thank the students who enrolled in my artist's studio seminar and 19th-century courses for their enthusiasm and for stimulating my thinking.

I am grateful to the friends and colleagues who have sustained and encouraged me: Edie Barnes, Martha Bowden, Marilyn Brown, William C. Carter, Therese Dolan, Ellen and Fred Elsas, Mary Hart, Jane Kromm, Joan Landes, Noa Turel, Marie Weaver, Michael Yonan and Georgianna Ziegler; the Department of Art and Art History faculty at UAB; and my sister, Elspeth, her husband Owen, and my niece and nephews, Caitlin, Knut and Olav.

Some material from Chapter Two appeared in 'Corot's Studio Revisited: Theme and Variations' in *Corot: Women* (2018) as well as a paper on Corot's studio that I presented at the 2014 College Art Association Conference. I am grateful for permission to republish this material in revised form.

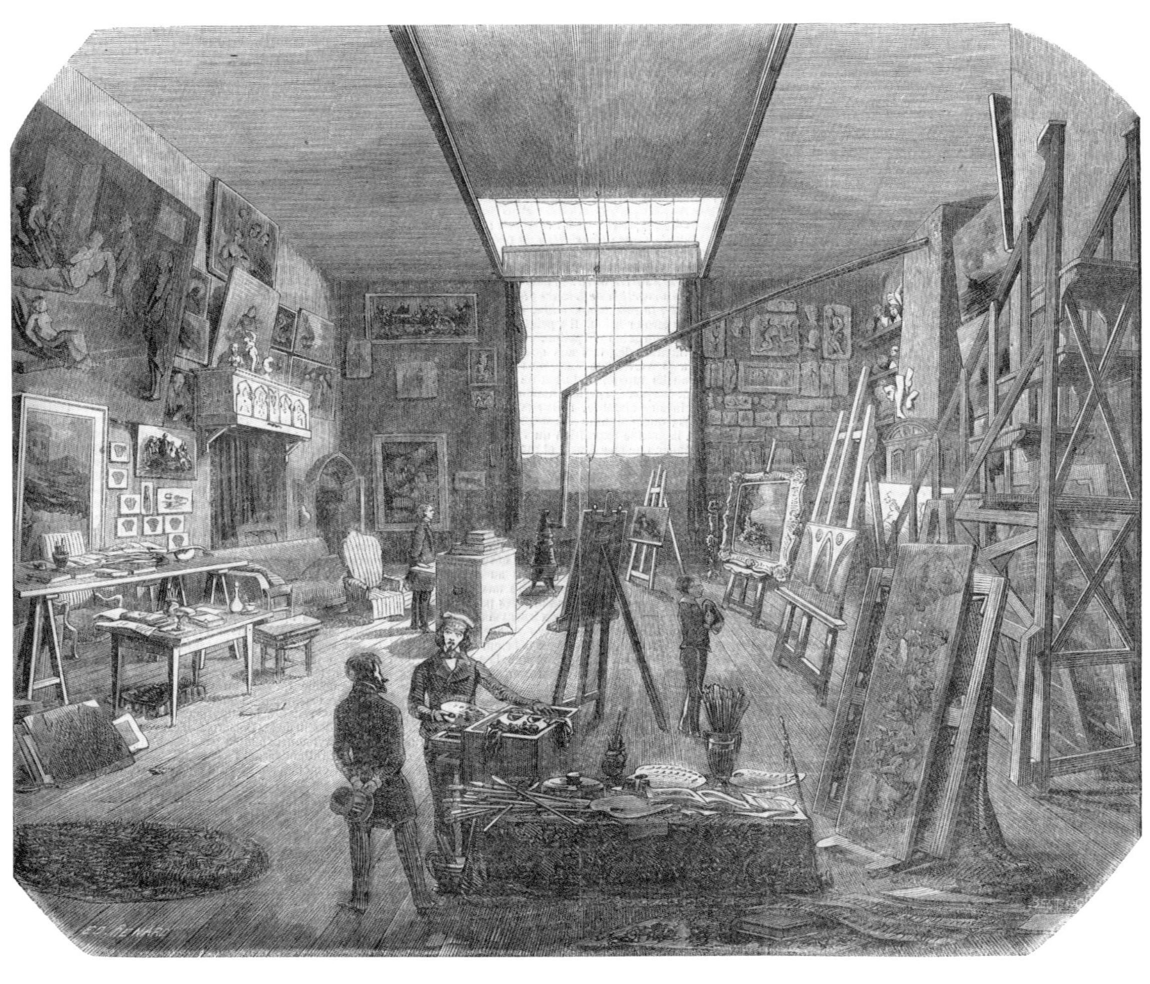

1. Édouard Renard, *The Studio of Eugène Delacroix*, in *L'Illustration*, 1852, engraving, 20.5 × 23.7 cm, Brown University Library, Providence, RI.

Introduction

The Artist's Studio

Theme and Variations

In 1852, Eugène Delacroix's studio at 54 rue Notre-Dame-de-Lorette was featured in *L'Illustration* (fig.1).[1] The spacious, high-ceilinged room with paintings, casts and studies stretching from floor to ceiling and with multiple easels is illuminated by tall, north-facing windows and heated by a potbellied, iron stove. Some paintings, including *Death of Marcus Aurelius* and a sketch for the ceiling of the Galerie d'Apollon at the Louvre, are identifiable. Holding his palette, Delacroix stands beside his open paint box and converses with a well-heeled visitor. The expanse and profusion of artworks and painting paraphernalia suggest an emporium or depot, underscoring Delacroix's prolific output and boundless ambition. Du Pays called this space a 'simple working studio', thus distinguishing it from elaborately furnished show studios like that of Carolus-Duran.[2]

Like many studio depictions, this engraving is an artful construct – both real and fictive – that has been cobbled together from observation and invention and populated with absorbed spectators. On closer inspection, the exaggerated scale, regimentation and tidiness undercut the aura of verisimilitude. Delacroix, who cloistered himself in his studio and detested being disturbed by visitors, is depicted posing awkwardly rather than painting.[3] His image is a composite, loosely based on earlier portraits including *Self-Portrait with Cap* (1832). Delacroix worked in the Notre-Dame-de-Lorette studio (1844–57). Shortly before moving to his purpose-built studio at 6 rue de Furstenberg, he wrote: 'My ambition is enclosed within these walls . . . I cannot leave this humble place where I was sometimes sad and sometimes happy for so many years without being deeply moved'.[4]

Though grounded in material reality, the historiography of the artist's studio, is largely virtual – a chronicle of loss and erasure, of vanished or repurposed spaces that was rarely recorded or extensively documented and must be pieced together from fragmentary visual and textual evidence.[5] However, in the 21st century, when the studio might seem a quaint anachronism, it retains its mystique and powerful associations with the artist's image and creative process, evidenced in the ongoing ritual of studio visits and the popularity of studio museums.[6] The origins of the studio can be traced to the Renaissance *studiolo*, but the modern sense – denoting an artist's private workspace – and French term *atelier* entered the

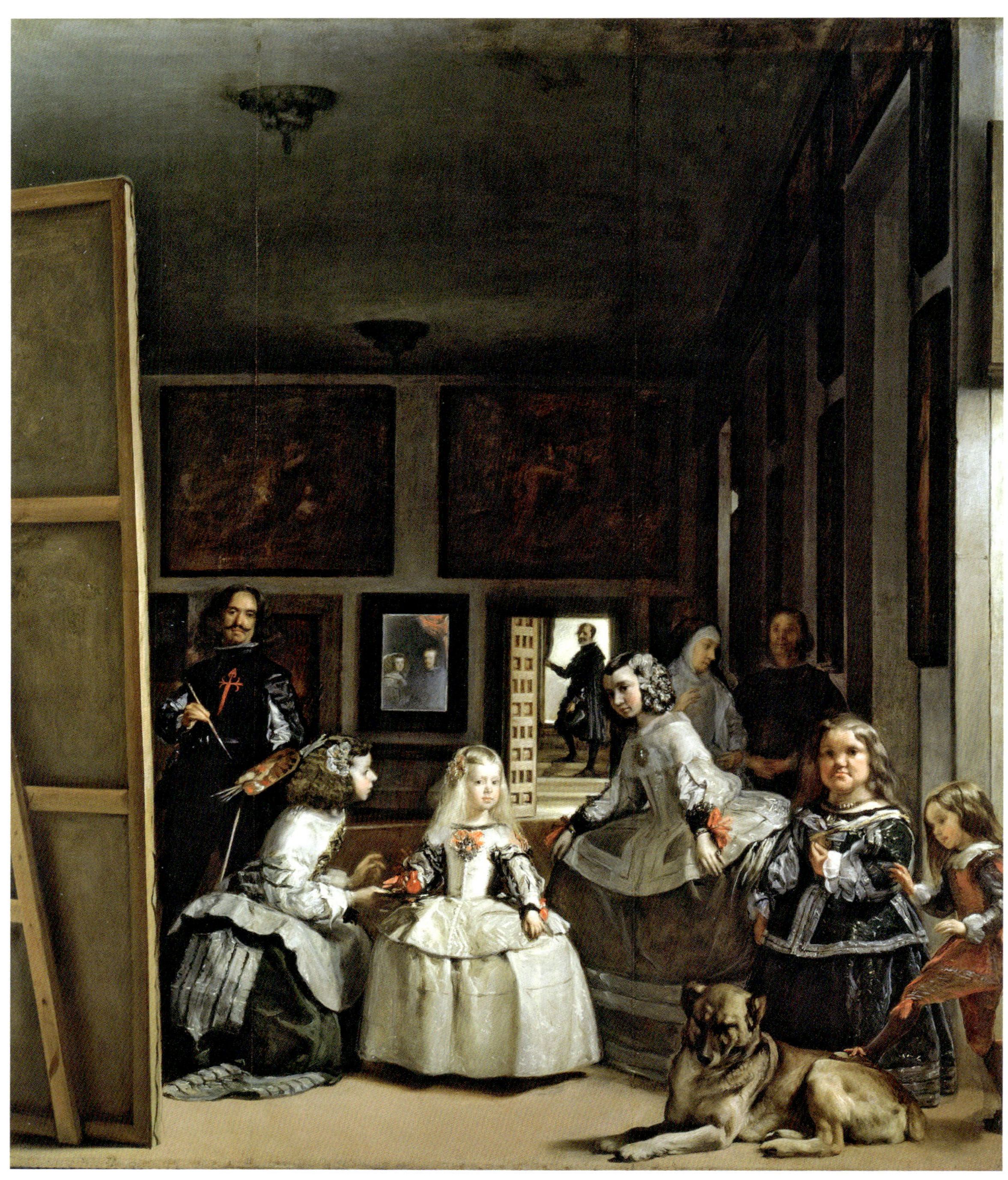

2. Diego Velázquez, *Las Meninas*, 1656, oil on canvas, 320.5 × 281.5 cm, Museo del Prado, Madrid.

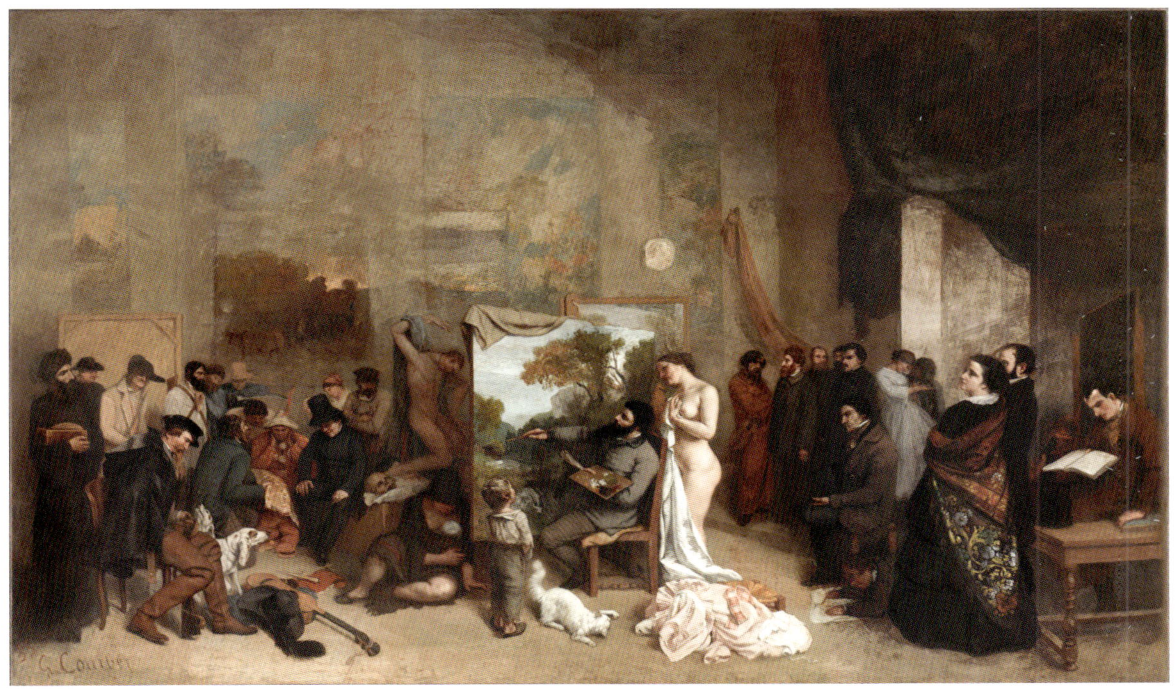

3. Gustave Courbet, *The Painter's Studio*, 1855, oil on canvas, 361 × 598 cm, Musée d'Orsay, Paris.

English lexicon in the 19th century, when the number of artists was growing rapidly and studio depictions were proliferating, especially in France.[7] From the outset, the studio was a workshop for producing art, often communally, a private space for reflection (from the Latin *studium*) and a site for artistic training.[8] Early images of artists at work, such as Jan van der Straet's *Color Olivi* (*c*.1590), which depicts Jan van Eyck's supposed invention of oil paint, were also artistic manifestoes. As interest in individual identity, creative invention and artists' lives grew, images of artists in their studios gained cultural currency.

The solitary painter at the easel preceded the fully developed studio picture.[9] In the 17th century, especially in the Netherlands, varied templates emerged, from Rembrandt's bare bones *Artist in His Studio* (*c*.1628) to ambitious allegorical canvases, such as Jan Vermeer's *Art of Painting* (1666–8). The most complex, multifaceted paradigm is Diego Velázquez's *Las Meninas* (1656, fig.2), which challenged and inspired artists from Manet to Picasso. Gustave Courbet's enormous *Painter's Studio* (1855, fig.3), the most ambitious Realist/allegorical studio depiction of the mid-19th-century, loomed large as an exemplar and catalyst. Artists investigated diverse models for conceptualizing the studio, ranging from descriptive or anecdotal to allegorical and from lightbox to experimental laboratory or phenomenological experience.[10]

Since the Renaissance, the studio has functioned as a physical frame and workspace for art-making and as a conceptual arena and echo chamber of the imagination, reflecting the ambiguous status of artists and far-reaching changes in the profession and studio practices. Debates about the artist's status and the role of art intensified and were rehearsed by critics including

Théophile Thoré, Pierre-Joseph Proudhon and Charles Baudelaire, coinciding with the mapping of bohemia by Henri Mürger and Champfleury. The public's fascination with artists and their milieu was manifested in art and literature, from Honoré Daumier's satirical *Scènes d'atelier* to Honoré de Balzac's *Le Chef-d'oeuvre inconnu*, a cautionary parable about artistic delusion that was published in *L'Artiste* (1831). Beginning in the 1840s, artists' studios were featured in illustrated journals, such as *L'Artiste*, *L'Illustration* and *La Galerie contemporaine*. In 1844, *L'Illustration* initiated a studio visit series, which became a distinctive artistic and literary genre.[11]

Subsuming the professional and metaphorical, the studio was a hybrid, liminal space that blurred distinctions between public and private, professional and domestic, ivory tower and commercial depot, production and display.[12] Though primarily devoted to making art, the studio was an extension of the artist's persona, denoting professional and economic status, aesthetic orientation and taste, and, at times, a refracted self-portrait. *Picturing the Artist's Studio* surveys the studio's multipronged significance as a *lieu de culte*, laboratory of creative struggle and stage for forging artistic identity. Through case studies stretching from Delacroix to Picasso, this book contextualizes and reframes the studio and the shifting image of the artist by focusing on the intersecting socio-cultural and artistic factors that shaped depictions of the studio. I trace how the notion of the studio as a reflexive space, emblematic of artistic identity that originated in the Renaissance, was reinvented and thematized in the late 19th century. My study also sheds light on the studio's multivalent role as creative laboratory, social arena and stage where artistic identity, studio practices and politics of display intersected and played out. For artists from Delacroix to Picasso, the Old Masters became a conduit for defining themselves against the past and a launching pad for experimentation.

Each of the five chapters analyzes key works that serve as springboards for probing artistic identity, strategies of representation and broader socio-cultural issues. The first chapter considers the lure of the Old Masters as an echo chamber and platform for staging identity, focusing on Delacroix's *Michelangelo in His Studio* (1849–50) and Manet's *Spanish Studio Scene* (*c.*1860), which resonate on multiple levels. Delacroix and Manet considered the Old Masters distinguished forerunners and catalysts for innovation, as is evidenced in their interweaving of emulation, invention and engagement with the creative process. For Delacroix, the studio was a precious sanctuary, mentioned repeatedly in his journal. During the 1820s, he made intimate sketches and a painting of his rue Jacob studio.[13] His final, purpose-built, rue de Furstenberg studio is now a museum. Manet's *Spanish Studio Scene* is a complex homage that recasts and ventriloquizes a Velázquez painting, appropriating aspects of his technique.

The second chapter focuses on Corot's intimate depictions of his Paradis-Poissonnière studio, which thematize and commemorate it as a locus of his creativity, a retrospective gallery and a *lieu de mémoire*. More than just a workspace, Corot's studio was integral to his artistic identity and painting method. Widely visited and described by contemporaries, it became a pilgrimage site for independent-minded artists. Although Corot was primarily known as a landscape painter, his studio was essential to his artistic practice. In the enigmatic studio pictures from the final decade of his career, the paintings on display and the poetics of paint assume an authorial function, and the meditative models function as surrogates for the absent artist.

The third chapter examines the evolving functions and permutations of the Impressionist studio during the plein-air painting era, when the studio literally moved outside, altering painting practices and perceptions of the artist. The opening section considers the boat studios of Daubigny and Monet, which narrowed the distance between artist and motif and enabled the artists to experience and represent riverscapes in new ways. I also explore the communal studio as a site of sociability and a repository of individual and collective

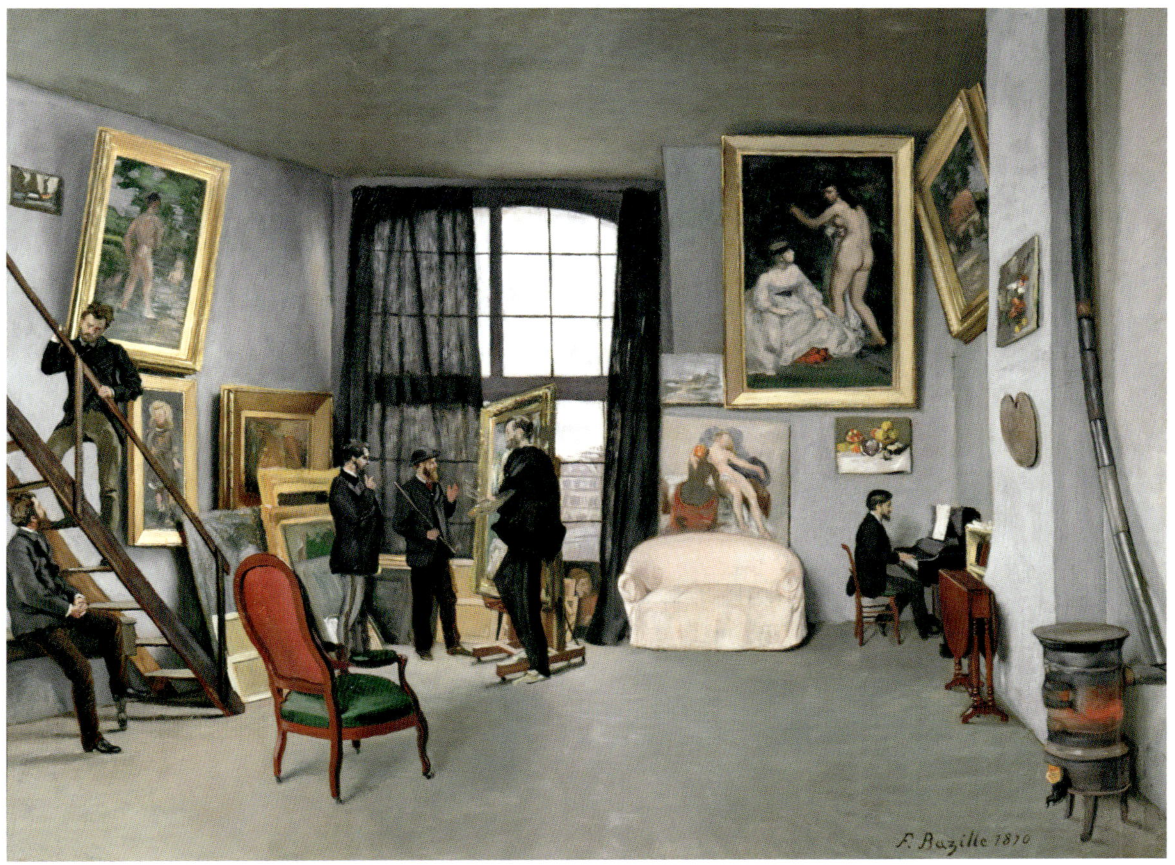

4. Frédéric Bazille, *Studio on the Rue La Condamine*, 1870, oil on canvas, 98 × 128.5 cm, Musée d'Orsay, Paris.

identity that Frédéric Bazille's *Studio on the Rue La Condamine* (1870, fig.4) exemplifies. A casual group portrait *in situ* and an Impressionist manifesto, the painting underscores the artists' camaraderie, shared aesthetic goals and collective painting practice.

The fourth chapter considers the impact of gender and the professional and societal constraints that women faced in obtaining training and pursuing artistic careers, including the lack of a studio. From Berthe Morisot to Marie Laurencin, women artists generally had to make do with improvised workspaces in their homes. I survey the careers of five women artists of different generations and backgrounds, working in a variety of mediums, ranging from aristocratic amateurs to members of the avant-garde. Each woman contended with gender hierarchies and societal conventions that hindered her career and so performed a delicate personal and professional balancing act. The exception is Rosa Bonheur, whose large purpose-built studio at the Château de By is now a museum dedicated to her life and work.

The fifth and final chapter explores the studio as a metaphor for art-making and as a refracted self-portrait in the early 20th century; it juxtaposes the works of Matisse and Picasso, both of whom repeatedly turned to the studio theme and represented the studio as an experiential space and a creative laboratory of the artist's mind. Matisse's self-referential *Pink Studio* (1911) and *Red Studio* (1911), which showcase his works, and his recurring depictions of artist and model attest to the studio's centrality in his creative process. From his early Bateau-Lavoir days, Picasso frequently depicted and photographed his studios. During the 1920s, his preoccupation with the studio and the artist/model theme intensified. Late in life, Picasso engaged *mano a mano* with the Old Masters by creating serial variations on Delacroix's *Women of Algiers* (1834) and Velázquez's *Las Meninas*.

Numerous material, artistic, personal and genealogical strands weave together the chapters: the continuing influence of the Old Masters, especially Velázquez, from Delacroix through Picasso; the studio as a site of metamorphosis and reworking of canvases; the studio's evolving functions and the overlapping of private and public; the studio's role in shaping artistic identity and the image of the artist; the impact of gender and of having (or not having) a studio on artists; and the continuing fascination with the artist's studio as a concrete and an imaginary or allegorical space. Together, this book's thematically linked chapters trace the studio's transformation and reinvention after mid-century and provide a refractive lens for reconsidering the complexities of artistic identity and the changing image of the artist in late 19th-century France. The concluding chapter considers how the studio theme, with its rich historical baggage, was projected forward into the 20th century by Matisse and Picasso.

I

The Echo Chamber

Delacroix, Manet and the Old Masters

> This morning . . . I saw several fragments of figures by Michelangelo that Drolling had drawn. Good God! What a man! What beauty! How singular and marvelous it would be to bring together the styles of Michelangelo and Velázquez! The idea occurred to me upon seeing the drawing.[1]
>
> – Eugène Delacroix, journal, 11 April 1824

PROLOGUE: THE ALLURE OF THE OLD MASTERS

Beginning in the late 18th century, new attitudes toward the past emerged in painting and literature, sparking the popularity of historical paintings devoted to the lives and works of the Old Masters, which figured prominently at the Salon and served as a platform for artistic identification and emulation.[2] Most were produced by minor artists, some of whom, like Pierre-Nolasque Bergeret and Joseph-Nicolas Robert-Fleury, specialized in the genre.[3] The growing interest in artists' lives was also fostered by illustrated journals, including *L'Artiste* and *Le Magasin pittoresque*, founded in the early 1830s, which published biographical articles on the Old Masters as well as popular compendia like C.P. Landon's *Vies et oeuvres des peintres les plus célèbres de toutes les écoles* (published serially, 1803–17). Deathbed scenes, such as François-Guillaume Ménageot's *Death of Leonardo da Vinci in the Arms of François I*, which was a sensation at the 1781 Salon, proved especially popular. Bergeret's *Honors Rendered to Raphael on His Deathbed* (1806) presented an opportunity for rehearsing the elevated status of artists and affirming their posthumous reputation and enduring fame.[4] Actual artworks were often incorporated into depictions of studios to emulate the master's style and to enhance the reality effect. Typically, the Old Masters were aligned with fame and fortune, and idealized relationships between artists and their princely patrons were highlighted, as in Bergeret's *Charles V Picking up Titian's Paintbrush* (1808). Overall, the pictures provided a positive image of the artistic profession; poverty, misfortune and artistic rivalries were banished to counteract widespread negative stereotypes of the artist as a disreputable *rapin* [dauber].[5] The choice of artist, which reflected

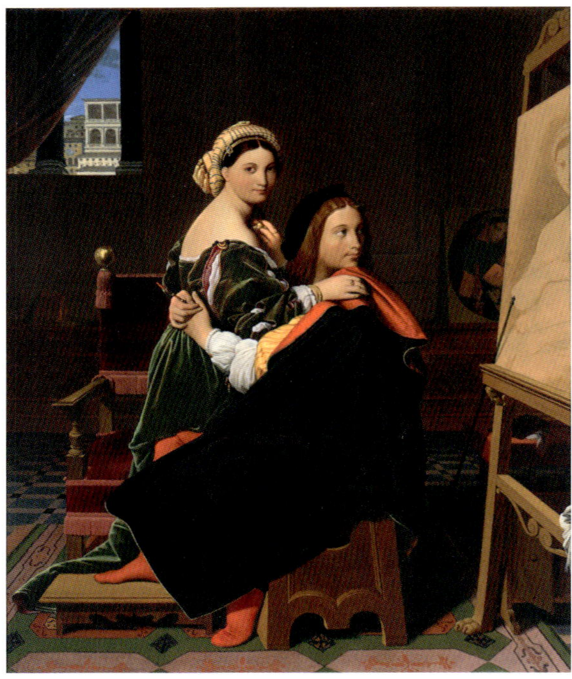

5. Jean-Auguste-Dominique Ingres, *Raphael and the Fornarina*, 1814, oil on canvas, 64.8 × 53.3 cm, Fogg Art Museum, Harvard Art Museums, Cambridge, MA.

the broadening interest in reimagining and reclaiming the past, is also significant for the history of taste.[6] During the first half of the century, Raphael, the most frequently represented Old Master, enjoyed unrivaled esteem. By the 1830s and 1840s, the repertoire of artists had expanded beyond the classical canon to include the Netherlandish school and Spanish masters, with the opening of King Louis-Philippe's Galerie Espagnole at the Louvre in 1838.[7]

Though less numerous initially than deathbed scenes or childhood anecdotes (which emerged in the 1830s), depictions of the artist's studio proliferated as the century progressed. The artist in the studio – the most revealing and reflexive category – offered a positive counter-image to the marginalization and precarious socio-economic state of 19th-century artists. In *Le Magasin pittoresque*, 'Interiors of Italian Studios' and 'The Studio of Today' (1849) offered contrasting images of the decorous Renaissance studio and the bohemian modern studio, which featured fencing, recalling Horace Vernet's famous *L'Atelier* (1821).[8] Early studio depictions include Jean-Baptiste Mallet's intimate *Interior of the Studio of Raphael*, exhibited at the 1814 Salon, which shows Cardinal Bibbiena reading one of his plays to Raphael and his mistress, underscoring Raphael's elevated status and illustrious patronage. Jean-Henri Marlet's *Raphael in His Studio*, exhibited at the 1812 Salon, portrays a distinguished group with Cardinal Bibbiena admiring a painting, possibly the *Transfiguration*, in Raphael's palatial studio. Although both paintings are set in the studio, neither depicts Raphael at work, focusing instead on his distinction and elevated social status. Adolf Henning's undated *Raphael in His Studio in Florence* is indicative of the growing international coterie that turned to the Old Masters as artistic subjects. Surrounded by paintings in an imaginary studio, Raphael, who is clad in black from head to toe, dreamily contemplates a large canvas that is hidden from view. His palette and brushes, artistically arranged on a tabouret, form an elegant still life.

Another popular theme was Raphael in the studio with his beloved mistress/model, La Fornarina, which weaves together love and the art of painting. Between 1813 and 1860, Jean-Auguste-Dominique Ingres made five painted versions of *Raphael and the Fornarina*, as well as a presentation drawing and numerous studies.[9] The Fogg Art Museum version (fig.5), exhibited at the 1814 Salon, depicts the entwined lovers in an elegant studio overlooking the Vatican loggia. Although the amatory relationship between artist and model is foregrounded, Raphael, holds his paintbrush and turns away from the living woman to gaze at her portrait on the easel, underscoring that it is primarily an allegory about the art of painting. Ingres idolized Raphael, frequently quoting from him, incorporating Raphael's works into his paintings and emulating aspects of his style, as he does here by inserting Raphael's *La Fornarina* and the *Madonna della Sedia*. Depictions of artists at work in the studio were relatively rare until mid-century, when the studio assumed heightened thematic significance in conjunction with broader changes in the production, exhibition and marketing of art.

* * *

This chapter examines how Delacroix and Manet looked to the Old Masters as both distinguished forerunners and innovative pathbreakers who sanctioned and spurred on their own unconventional artistic practices. Both artists were independent-minded outliers who engaged with the Old Masters on multiple levels – aesthetically, psychologically and conceptually – throughout their careers. Although they studied the Old Masters intensively and copied them, unlike their more hidebound counterparts, they eschewed colorful anecdotes and sentimental tropes. Rather than looking backward through a retrospective, nostalgic lens, they turned a reflexive, forward-looking gaze on their artistic forebears, especially Michelangelo and Velázquez, and approached them as catalysts for experimentation and invention. During the 1840s, Michelangelo was typically depicted anecdotally either in a classical context, as in Jean-Léon Gérôme's *Michelangelo Showing a Student the Belvedere Torso* (1849) or as a kindly old man, as in Robert-Fleury's *Michelangelo Caring for His Servant*, which was exhibited at the 1841 Salon.[10] Delacroix's moody, psychologically revealing *Michelangelo in His Studio* (1849–50) (fig.6) shatters that mold.[11] Rooted in a longstanding appreciation and study of Michelangelo and his art that is revealed in Delacroix's journal and *Revue de Paris* and *Revue des deux mondes* articles, Delacroix's Michelangelo stands in stark contrast to the anodyne depictions by contemporaries like Robert-Fleury.[12]

Manet's *Spanish Studio Scene* (*Velázquez Painting*) (*c.*1860, fig.7), which was never exhibited and remained in his studio until his death, likewise imaginatively interweaves past and present. Grounded in Manet's deep affinity for the Spanish School and particular interest in Velázquez, the painting is based on *Gathering of Gentlemen*, then attributed to Velázquez, which Manet copied around 1859. *Spanish Studio Scene* is a multilayered reinvention and pastiche that evokes Velázquez's style in its bold handling, sketchiness and casual placement of figures.[13] Manet particularly admired and experimented with these stylistic elements in other works, such as *Music in the Tuileries* (1862). Here, Manet incorporates portraits of himself and his artist friend Albert de Balleroy at the far left, echoing the positioning of the portraits in *Gathering of Gentlemen*, formerly thought to depict Velázquez and Bartolomé Esteban Murillo. The chapter argues that for Delacroix and Manet, the Old Masters served as a lofty standard to measure themselves against and a springboard for identification, emulation and invention – that is, a pivot for oscillating between past and present, tradition and innovation in the contested artistic arena of the 1850s and 1860s.

DELACROIX AND MICHELANGELO

Delacroix referred to the Old Masters in his journal and his paintings and made copies after them, but he showed little interest in portraying them pictorially. His ambitious, full-scale copy of *Charles II of Spain* (1824), then attributed to Velázquez, attests to his early interest in Spanish painting.[14] He bequeathed the copy to Baron Charles Rivet, an old friend, indicating the value that he attached to it. Besides traditional allegorical and religious subjects, Delacroix was drawn to a wide range of historical and literary themes, especially tragic ones, stretching from Shakespeare and Tasso to Byron, Goethe and Scott. Although he was fascinated by artists and the concept of genius, *Michelangelo in His Studio* is his only such depiction except for the small, troubadour-style *Young Raphael Meditating in His Studio* that he exhibited at the 1831 Salon (fig.8).[15] Despite the modest scale and

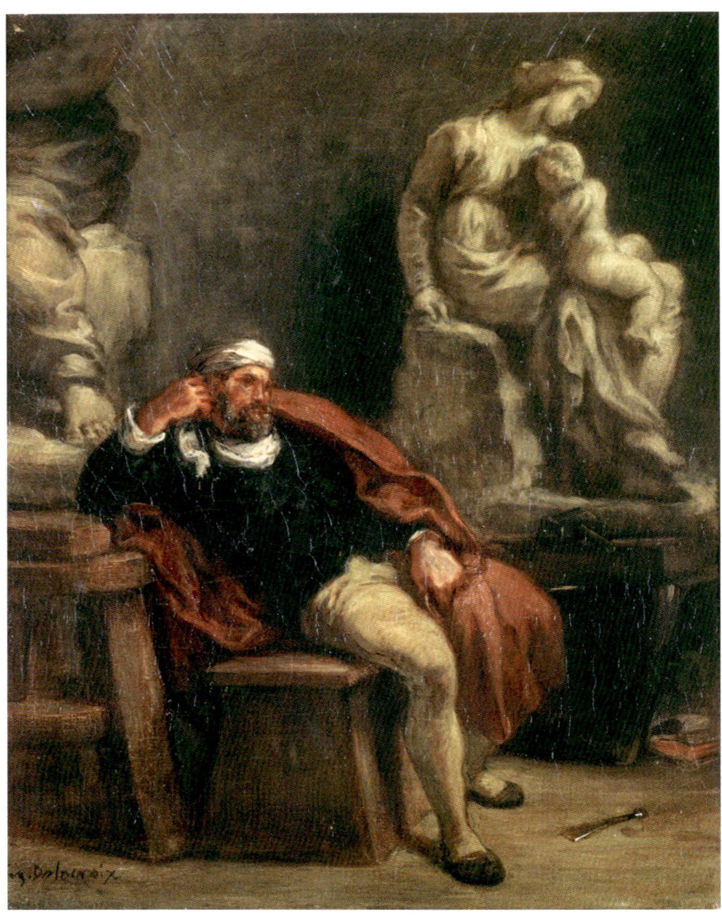

6. Eugène Delacroix, *Michelangelo in His Studio*, 1849–50, oil on canvas, 41 × 33 cm, Musée Fabre, Montpellier.

generic character of the painting, the solitary artist, seated cross-legged on a stepladder in an attitude of pensive contemplation, anticipates aspects of *Michelangelo in His Studio*. The figure of Raphael is modeled on Parmigianino's *Portrait of a Youth* (formerly believed to be a self-portrait of Raphael), which Delacroix had copied early in his career. Besides making copies and mentioning Raphael in his journal, Delacroix published an article on him in the *Revue de Paris* in 1830.[16] The article discusses the unreliability of historical sources, the independence of genius and artistic decadence, which are recurring themes in Delacroix's writings. The article emphasizes Raphael's elevated character, early good fortune and fearlessness in undertaking the Vatican frescoes. Noting that style is his principal merit, Delacroix attributes Raphael's success to his unparalleled talent for imitation and his extraordinary facility in painting. Rather than portraying Raphael at the apex of his glory or in the midst of painting a masterpiece, Delacroix depicts him meditating in his bare studio, like a modern-day Romantic.

Portrait of an Artist in His Studio (*c*.1820), long considered a self-portrait of Théodore Géricault, epitomizes the Romantic topos of artistic alienation. The melancholic young artist, his head resting on one hand, sprawls in a bare studio, with palette, casts and a skull. Representations of solitary brooding

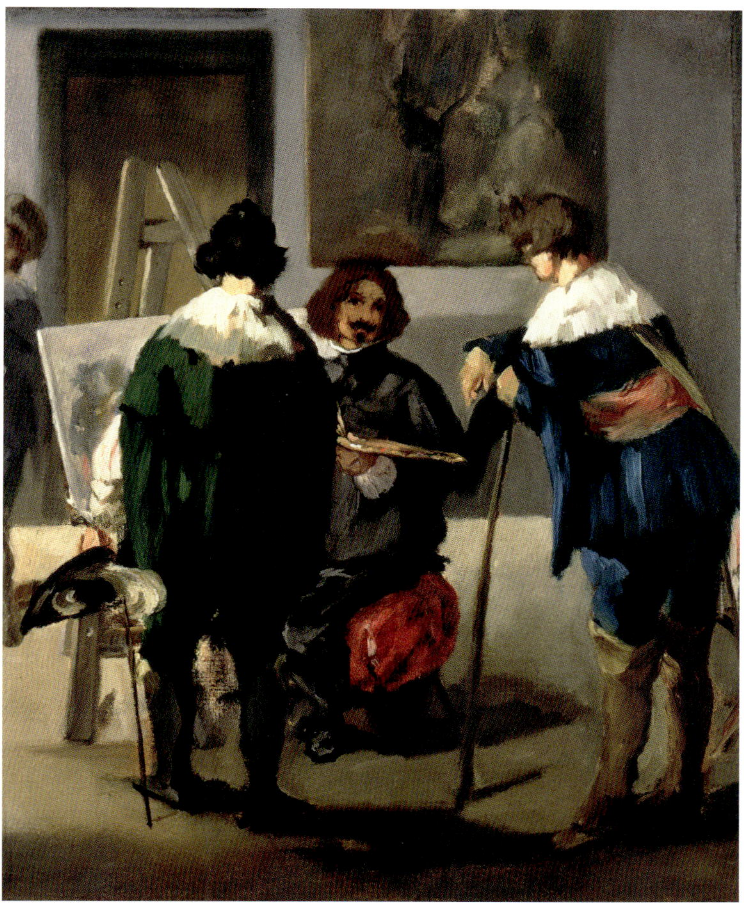

7. Édouard Manet, *Spanish Studio Scene (Velázquez Painting)*, c.1860, oil on canvas, 46 × 38 cm, private collection.

artists remained popular during the 1840s, as works like Robert-Fleury's *Benvenuto Cellini in His Studio*, exhibited at the 1841 Salon, attest. An etching after Robert-Fleury's painting was published in *L'Artiste* in 1841, and Adolphe Mouilleron executed a lithograph of it (fig.9). The petulant gaze, tense, cross-legged pose, echoing the Mannerist sculpture at left, and elaborate decor and theatricality differentiate the print formally and expressively from Delacroix's stark vision of artistic melancholy and frustration – or 'arrested creation' – in his *Michelangelo*.[17] A lost painting of Michelangelo by Robert-Fleury, known only through a print, depicts the dejected artist seated on a piece of sculpture and holding a *modello* of *Night* between his knees.[18] Except for the sculptural backdrop, this image closely resembles Robert-Fleury's generic depiction of Cellini.

Growing public interest in Michelangelo and his art inspired works from Salon paintings and prints to *objets d'art*. Robert-Fleury produced a series of Michelangelo-themed paintings, including *Michelangelo Caring for His Servant* (1841), *Titian and Michelangelo* (1847), *Michelangelo and Julius II* (1858) and *Death of Michelangelo* (1875). A Michelangelo Clock, with a seated bronze figure of the artist by Jean-Jacques Feuchère, was exhibited in Paris in 1849 and at the Crystal Palace in 1851.[19] The cross-legged pose and right arm of

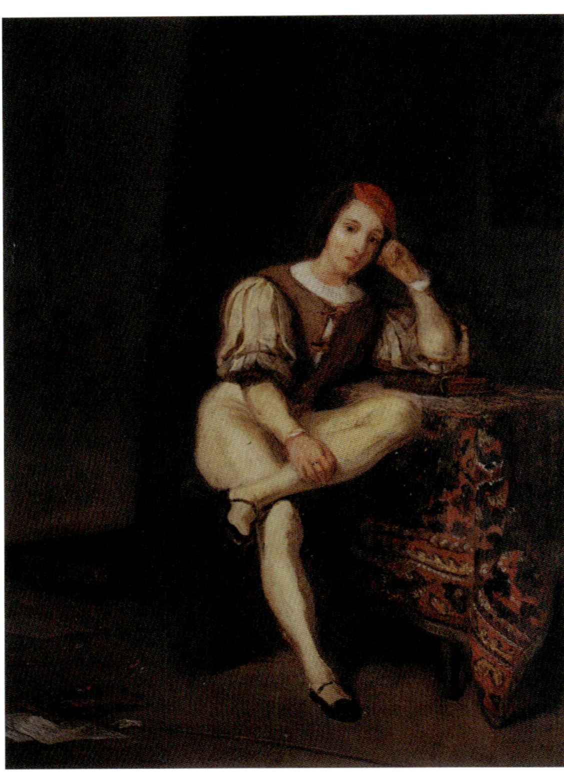

8. Eugène Delacroix, *Young Raphael Meditating in His Studio*, 1831, oil on canvas, 35 × 27 cm, Unknown location.

Michelangelo recall the statue of Lorenzo de' Medici from the Medici Chapel in Florence; and his lowered left arm rests on one of the *Slaves*.[20] Bronze figures modeled after the *ignudi* from the Sistine Chapel ceiling frame the ornate clock face. A drawing portfolio and sculptor's burin and mallet lie at Michelangelo's feet.

Delacroix's admiration for Michelangelo surfaced in his earliest journal entries from September 1822. Having never visited Italy, he knew Michelangelo's work primarily through copies and engravings. The only originals that he could study were the two *Slaves* in the Louvre.[21] He had access to casts of the figures from the Medici Chapel, which had been commissioned for the École des Beaux-Arts in the 1830s, and to Xavier Sigalon's copy of the *Last Judgment*. In *Michelangelo in His Studio*, Delacroix depicted the *Medici Madonna*, which he would have known through a cast (and probably a bronze copy in Adolphe Thiers's cabinet), and a portion of *Moses*.[22] For Stendhal, the *Medici Madonna* exemplified Michelangelo's uncontrolled *terribilità*; Stendhal's admiration may explain its prominent inclusion in the painting.[23] As scholars have noted, *Moses* and the *Medici Madonna*, which appear unfinished, would not have been present in Michelangelo's studio at the same time. *Moses* was executed in Rome (*c.*1513–15), while the *Medici Madonna* was carved in Florence (*c.*1521–32).

The reappraisal of Michelangelo's painting and sculpture that Sir Joshua Reynolds and Henry Fuseli initiated during the late 18th century coincided with the rise of Romanticism and the increasing significance accorded to the sublime.[24] Stendhal, who advocated passionately for Michelangelo's artistic preeminence and sublimity in *Histoire de la peinture en Italie* (1817), was an influential voice.[25] His characterization of Michelangelo as a proto-modern, buffeted by the politics of his time, influenced Delacroix's view of Michelangelo as a solitary, turbulent genius.[26] Stendhal was preoccupied with the notion of *terribilità*, manifested in the extraordinary energy of the infant Christ in the *Medici Madonna* which, for him, evoked Michelangelo's genius and excess.[27] In his *Revue de Paris* articles, Delacroix identified with Michelangelo, ascribing to him personality traits and emotional states that propelled his own creative process. He envisaged Michelangelo as a troubled genius, consumed by his creative passion and subject to bouts of discouragement and anxiety.[28] Delacroix was struck by the psychological crisis that paralyzed Michelangelo in his late twenties, when his creative activity ground to a halt and he could only read or write poetry.[29] According to Théophile Silvestre, Delacroix likened Michelangelo's discouragement and anxiety to his own languor and inability to work after being 'blacklisted' for the *Death of Sardanapalus*.[30] Evocatively, Delacroix imagined

Michelangelo alone in his studio late at night and 'struck with fear at the spectacle of his own creations' – the image he would later paint. He reflexively described Michelangelo as frustrated at his inability to realize the sublimity of his ideas and so turning to poetry for refuge, as Delacroix himself often did. He observed: 'It was the expression of a deep melancholy, or his agitations, his fright, in thinking of future life: the regrets of age, the fear of obscurity and a terrible future'.[31]

Sensing Delacroix's projective mirroring, Silvestre, who penned the first detailed analysis of *Michelangelo in His Studio*, considered it a sort of self-portrait.[32] He recognized the superiority as well as the fatigue, discouragement and melancholy that Delacroix experienced and linked the scarf wrapped around Michelangelo's neck to the one that Delacroix habitually wore in the studio.[33] For Silvestre, Delcroix's *Michelangelo in His Studio* was a pictorial confession that mirrored his journal entries and articles on Michelangelo. In the Galerie Bruyas catalogue, Silvestre noted: 'Michelangelo was always alive and present for Delacroix, who stated: "I am by rights of posterity, the contemporary of the most remote souls"'.[34]

Discussing Michelangelo's style, Delacroix reflexively noted the *bizarreries* and lack of exactitude for which this 'savage genius' had been criticized by mediocre artists, echoing complaints about his own inexactitude and lack of finish.[35] Rather than historical exactitude, in *Michelangelo in His Studio*, Delacroix was preoccupied with evoking the powerful presence of Michelangelo's sculpture and its *non finito* or *inachevé* (lack of finish), as he called it in his journal, which paralleled his own approach to painting.[36] Michelangelo's sculpture looms over the impotent artist, who has abandoned his chisel and is absorbed in melancholy contemplation, as Delacroix described him in his essay. The somber studio is empty except for the despondent artist and the unfinished sculptures surrounding him. Instead of apotheosizing Michelangelo, Delacroix focused on the suffering associated with genius and the artist's agonizing doubts over the value of his work.[37]

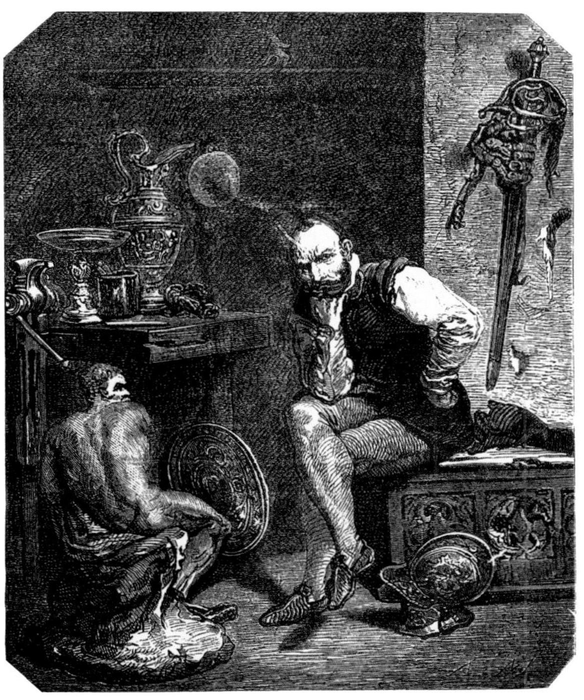

9. Adolphe Mouilleron (after Robert-Fleury), *Benvenuto Cellini in His Studio*, 1841, lithograph, 15.3 × 12.4 cm, private collection.

MICHELANGELO IN HIS STUDIO

Based on Delacroix's journal, we know that he began working on *Michelangelo in His Studio* in September 1849, while staying at Champrosay, and had completed it by May 1850.[38] He made two preparatory studies (*c.*1849–50, figs 10, 11) that offer clues about the composition's evolution and the genesis of Michelangelo's arresting half-sitting, half-reclining pose. More than the sketchy physiognomy, it is the ambiguous pose that conveys the artist's psychological suffering and thwarted creativity. The traditional head-on-hand pose evoking melancholy appears elsewhere in Delacroix's oeuvre, notably in

Tasso in the Madhouse (1839, fig.13). The bearded, reclining figure of Michelangelo also echoes the self-destructive, defeated Assyrian ruler Sardanapalus in *Death of Sardanapalus* (1827), which Delacroix reprised in a reduced version nearly twenty years later. Scholars have interpreted the chillingly detached but controlling figure of Sardanapalus as Delacroix's alter ego. Although various sources, including the Sistine Chapel ceiling, have been proposed, the oblique pose is a recurring trope in Delacroix's Orientalist works beginning in the 1820s. The half-sitting, half-reclining pose of *Woman in Oriental Costume Reclining on a Sofa* (*c*.1849) is strikingly similar to that of Delacroix's Michelangelo, but in reverse.[39] Like his ambiguous pose, Michelangelo's clothing is indeterminate – neither historical nor contemporary.[40] The white scarf wrapped around his head and neck evokes the eccentric head coverings associated with artists, but also suggests exotic Orientalist dress. Equally difficult to categorize are the dark tunic with its white cuffs, the yellowish hue of the hose, echoed in the sculpture and the long reddish cloak.

To conceptualize *Michelangelo in His Studio*, Delacroix began with drawings, which he then revised during the painting process. In the first preparatory study (fig.10), the artist is depicted seated in left profile, his head lowered, holding a tool, perhaps a mallet, in his left hand. In his compositional drawings, Delacroix often struggled to transpose his pictorial ideas, reversing poses and moving figures around in space, as is the case here.[41] The schematically sketched sculptures in the background appear to be *Lorenzo de' Medici* at the left and possibly the *Medici Madonna* at the right. The top inscription: 'Le penseroso [i.e., *Lorenzo de' Medici*] – les marbres gigantesques – la figure de Michelange relativement petite' ('the marbles gigantic – the figure of Michelangelo relatively small'), identifies the statues and elucidates the pictorial concept. The bottom inscription reads, from left to right: 'Pinceaux', 'plans d'architectures/cartons' and, above, 'livre' ('Paintbrushes', 'architectural plans/portfolios', 'book'), cataloguing the scattered objects that encapsulate Michelangelo's multifaceted genius.[42] The compact figure of Michelangelo is dwarfed by the sculptures looming behind him.

In the second study (fig.11), Michelangelo's pose is the same as in the finished painting. There is a small sketch of a reclining figure below. Michelangelo reclines obliquely, his right elbow resting on the sculpture stand. The sculptures are difficult to decipher: the right statue may be the *Medici Madonna*; the standing figure at left is too generic to identify. At upper right, there is a detailed, carefully shaded study of the sculpture stand Michelangelo is leaning against. If the right statue is the *Medici Madonna*, it is shown from a different vantage point in the painting. At the right, Delacroix cryptically wrote: 'non dégrossi[r] le haut seulement' ('not to trim only the top'), which seems to refer to changes in the spatial configuration.[43] Delacroix has tightened the composition, moving the figure of Michelangelo and the statues closer to the picture plane and framing them in a close-up view, as they appear in the painting. The sculptures' scale in relation to the brooding artist is also reduced. The general contours of Michelangelo's costume and cloak are summarily indicated. The chisel is placed in front of the sculpture stand rather than off to the right, as in the finished work.

Although *Michelangelo in His Studio* is unique within Delacroix's oeuvre, it belongs to a subset of intimate easel paintings that fall outside traditional genres and explore subjects that moved him, notably the psychological state of the artist or poet. These small- to medium-format *Gedankenbilder* (thought or idea paintings) include the Tasso paintings and scenes from *Faust* and *Hamlet*.[44] Writing in 1822, Delacroix envisaged painting as a 'mysterious bridge' between the soul of the subject depicted and that of the spectator.[45] From the 1820s, recumbent melancholy figures, from Tasso to Michelangelo, become a recurring motif that, like memory, resurfaces and dissolves historical distance. *Michelangelo in His Studio* was closely associated with Delacroix's artistic psyche, as Silvestre recognized. Delacroix sold the painting to his dealer

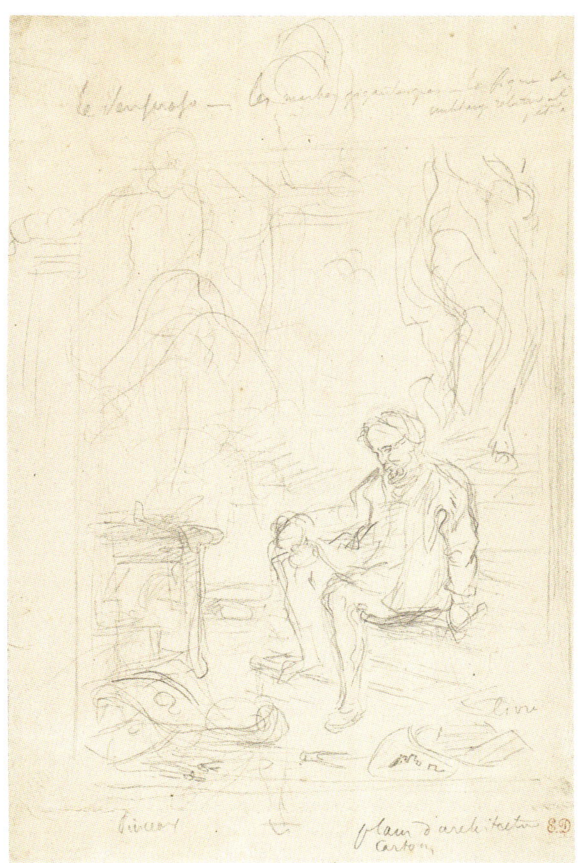

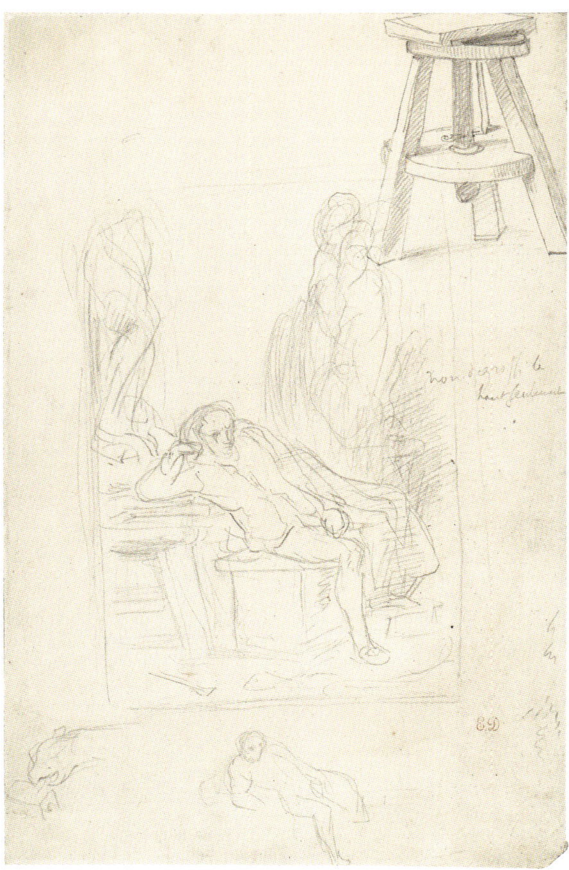

10. (left) Eugène Delacroix, *Study for Michelangelo in His Studio*, c.1849–50, pencil on paper, 38 × 24.3 cm, Fitzwilliam Museum, University of Cambridge, Cambridge.

11. (right) Eugène Delacroix, *Study for Michelangelo in His Studio*, c.1849–50, pencil on paper, 38 × 24.3 cm, Fitzwilliam Museum, University of Cambridge, Cambridge.

known as 'Thomas' in 1853 and possibly had a hand in its acquisition by Alfred Bruyas, whose portrait he was painting.[46] For Delacroix, Bruyas – nervous and pensive – personified Hamlet.[47] *Michelangelo in His Studio* was included in the 1864 Delacroix exhibition and figured prominently in Silvestre's 1876 catalogue of Bruyas's collection. Jules Laurens's lithograph of the painting appeared in *L'École moderne* (1857–60). Delacroix's lifelong identification with Michelangelo supports Silvestre's interpretation of *Michelangelo in His Studio* as a self-portrait and confession, based on visits to Delacroix's studio and conversations in the early 1850s while preparing his *Histoire des artistes vivants*.

A LION IN WINTER

When he began painting *Michelangelo in His Studio* in 1849, Delacroix had nothing left to prove. He had completed a series of daunting, physically demanding

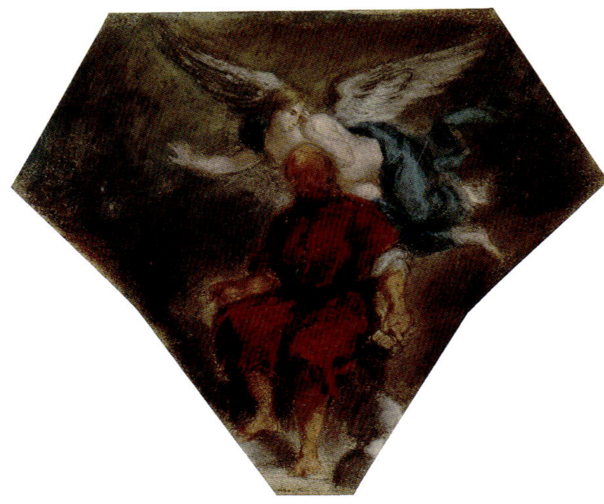

12. Eugène Delacroix, *Michelangelo and His Genius*, n.d., pastel, 24 × 30 cm, Musée Fabre, Montpellier.

decorative murals in prestigious venues, most recently the Deputies' Library at the Palais Bourbon (1841–7), and was working on the Galerie d'Apollon ceiling in the Louvre (1849–51). These official commissions provided the opportunity to emulate and vie directly with the Old Masters, especially Peter Paul Rubens, on a grandiose scale in the public sphere, reinvigorating and deepening his engagement with their art and the technical problems of mural painting. One of the iconographic themes selected for the pendentives in the Deputies' Library was divine inspiration. In *Hesiod and the Muse*, the winged muse hovers above the reclining figure of the Greek poet, proffering a laurel staff symbolizing poetic authority. Initially, the fourth cupola was dedicated to the arts, embodied by figures of Raphael, Michelangelo, Rubens and Nicolas Poussin. As the project evolved, the theme morphed into history and philosophy, and figures of Herodotus, the Chaldeans, Seneca and Socrates were substituted. In preparation Delacroix made an undated study of the *Apotheosis of Michelangelo* (Silvestre's title), or *Michelangelo and His Genius* (fig.12).[48] The pastel portrays Michelangelo wearing a red robe. Bare-headed, his features effaced, he is seated on an invisible throne, a winged spirit hovering behind his head, and a marble bust at his feet. It is virtually identical to the *Socrates and His Genius* pendentive, except that Socrates's robe is blue rather than red.[49] Michelangelo grasps a mallet in his left hand, as Delacroix depicted him in the first study for *Michelangelo in His Studio*. The original program described the subject as Michelangelo holding a model of the cupola of St Peter's in his hand, surrounded by four little geniuses representing painting, sculpture, architecture and poetry.[50] Although the pastel bears little resemblance to *Michelangelo in His Studio*, Delacroix's renewed interest in the theme of divine inspiration for the Deputies' Library was likely a stimulus for his more concrete, deeply personal allegorical depiction of artistic creativity and melancholy.

Other intriguing aspects of *Michelangelo in His Studio* are intertextuality, the complex interplay and slippage between painting and writing, both quintessential for Delacroix, and the *paragone*, or rivalry between painting and sculpture that pitted Leonardo da Vinci against Michelangelo. Delacroix studied sculpture, from ancient to modern, made copies and published articles on Michelangelo and Puget. His conflicted views on sculpture, especially its inherent limitations as a medium and its problematic relationship to painting, surface repeatedly in his journal entries and in more general ruminations on modern beauty.[51] In discussing his concept of 'le beau moderne' ('the modern beautiful'), Delacroix compared the 'essentially modern' arts of painting and music to the 'essentially ancient' art of sculpture and pondered the status of sculpture within art history.[52] Writing in his journal on 9 May 1853, he paradoxically observed that Michelangelo, despite what he himself may have believed, was more painter than sculptor.[53] Although Delacroix rejected the slavish Neoclassical imitation of sculpture in painting, he discussed sculptural modeling – the massing of color, the way a sculptor would build up form from his material – as a template for painting. In late works like *Jacob Wrestling the Angel* (1861), Delacroix sought sculptural equivalences.[54]

Representing Michelangelo surrounded by his sculpture, Delacroix treated the statues like painted figures, focusing on their curves and blurred contours rather than sculptural definition of form and distinct edges. The monumental but human figure of Michelangelo is the most solid element in the shadowy studio.[55] In evoking Michelangelo's struggles and discouragement, Delacroix discussed him primarily as a sculptor. He noted the passion and impetuosity that drove Michelangelo to leave his marbles unfinished, as Delacroix would depict them in *Michelangelo in His Studio*.[56] On 10 August 1850, after viewing Rubens's *Elevation of the Cross* in Antwerp, Delacroix observed that, 'frequenting Michelangelo has exalted and elevated above themselves every successive generation of painters'.[57]

In closing, I would like to suggest that Delacroix's identification with Michelangelo was not just psychologically driven; it was also rooted in his preoccupation with probing the boundaries between painting and sculpture and the affinities and ontological differences between verbal and visual representation. These elements are encapsulated in another meditative subject, *Tasso in the Madhouse*, which Delacroix explored in two paintings and a presentation drawing, focusing on the poet's melancholy and despair when he was incarcerated by his patron, the Duke of Ferrara. In the earlier painting, exhibited at the 1824 Salon, the pensive yet stoic poet is seated upright and appears oblivious to the sinister, mad figures cavorting behind him.[58] The powerfully expressive 1839 canvas depicts the disheveled, psychologically unstable poet, reclining on a *chaise longue* in a bleak interior, with papers scattered across the floor (fig.13). The pose resembles that of Delacroix's Michelangelo, but in reverse. The dominant diagonal linking Michelangelo and the *Medici Madonna*, whose bodies echo and parallel each other, mirrors the sinister spectators staring and reaching through the bars. Here, again, Delacroix was preoccupied with representing a psychological state and tragic suffering rather than a specific narrative or dramatic action.[59] Painted a decade before the *Michelangelo*, *Tasso in the Madhouse* is its literary counterpart. *Michelangelo in His Studio* provides a window into the multivalent significance of the Old Masters for Delacroix – as paragons to emulate, catalysts for innovation and channels for reflecting on the tribulations of artistic creativity.

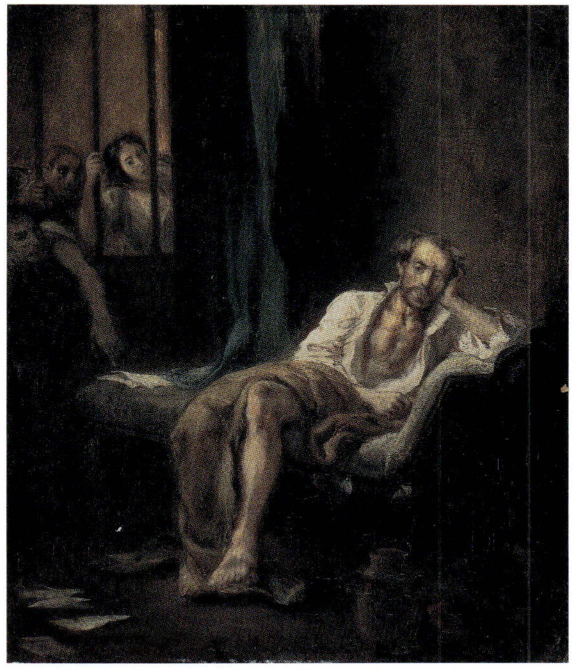

13. Eugène Delacroix, *Tasso in the Madhouse*, 1839, oil on canvas, 60 × 50 cm, Oskar Reinhart Collection, Am Römerholz, Winterthur.

MANET AND VELÁZQUEZ

Born three decades after Delacroix, Édouard Manet represented a younger generation steeped in the realist enterprise and painting of modern life. Although he

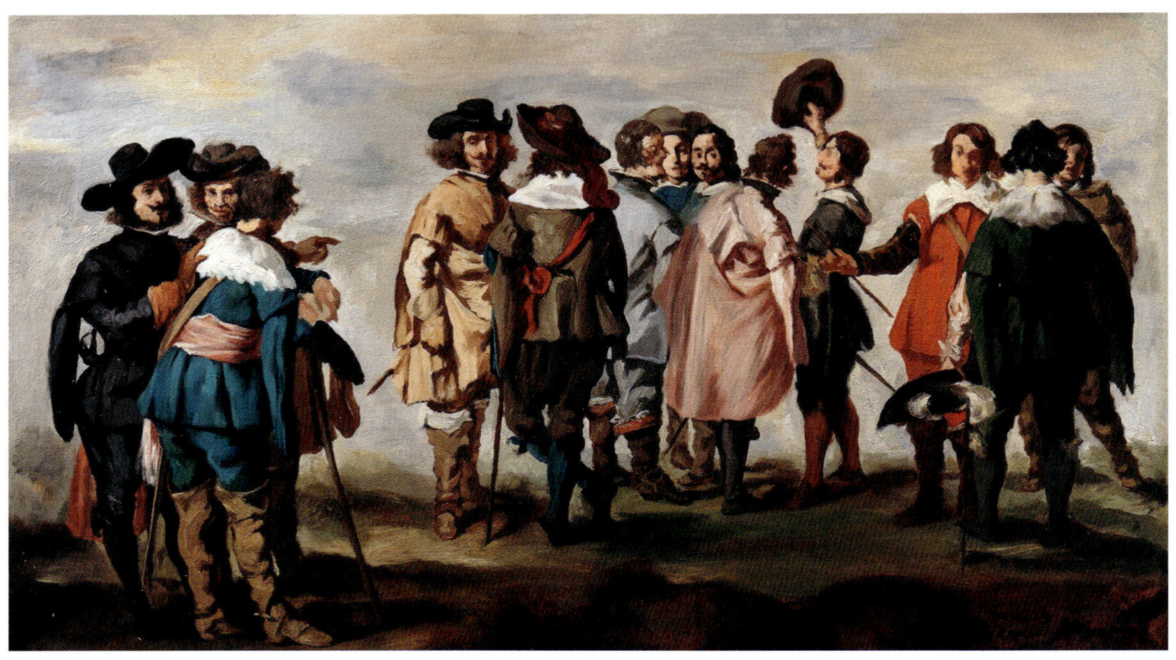

14. Édouard Manet, *The Little Cavaliers, after Gathering of Gentlemen*, *c.*1859–60, oil on canvas, 45.7 × 75.6 cm, Chrysler Museum of Art, Norfolk, VA.

worked outdoors, especially during the 1870s, Manet, like Delacroix, focused primarily on figure painting and habitually worked from the model in his studio. Despite his insistence on painting modern subjects of the sort that Baudelaire promoted in his *Salon of 1846* and 'The Painter of Modern Life', Manet was well versed in and deeply indebted to the Old Masters, and drew on an unusually wide range of artistic influences.[60] While studying in Thomas Couture's studio from 1850 to 1856, Manet traveled to Belgium, Holland, Germany, Italy, Prague and Vienna, visiting museums everywhere and making copies.[61] Because Manet's formative years are sparsely documented and few works completed before 1859 have survived, his interpretations of the Old Masters provide crucial evidence about his development as a painter.[62]

The only living master whom Manet copied was Delacroix. He called on Delacroix at his Notre-Dame-de-Lorette studio (*c.*1851–5) to request permission to copy *Barque of Dante*, which was granted. Manet made two copies: a rapid sketch (*c.*1858–9) and a more literal copy (*c.*1854). Although that was the only direct contact between the two artists, Delacroix was more important artistically for Manet than has generally been realized.[63] Other contemporaries besides Baudelaire forged links between Delacroix and Manet, notably Henri Fantin-Latour, in two large-scale group portraits exhibited at the Salon. In *Homage to Delacroix* (1864), Manet figures prominently among the acolytes honoring Delacroix and his artistic legacy, standing between Delacroix's portrait and Baudelaire. In *A Studio in the Batignolles* (1870), Manet, seated at his easel painting, is the fulcrum – posing for posterity as the leader of the artistic avant-garde.[64]

It would be difficult to overestimate Velázquez's significance for Manet, especially during the early 1860s, when he painted a series of Spanish-themed subjects. *The Spanish Singer* (1860), which received an honorable mention at the 1861 Salon, was his first official success.[65] Although he copied many Old Masters, Manet was especially drawn to Velázquez and the Spanish school. In his memoirs, Antonin Proust recounts Manet's enthusiasm for Velázquez, citing his approval of the cleaner approach (evidenced in *Gathering of Gentlemen*, or *'Little Cavaliers'*), that 'puts you off the brown-sauce school'.[66] In January 1850, Manet registered at the Louvre as a student of Couture, and in June 1851, he requested permission to copy *Portrait of a Monk*, then attributed to Velázquez.[67] For Manet, Velázquez was a venerable model and an antidote to Couture's teachings. In 1859–60, he painted his most consequential copy of *Gathering of Gentlemen*, then attributed to Velázquez (fig.14),which he inscribed lower right, 'Manet d'après Vélasquez' ('Manet after Velázquez').[68] Juliet Wilson-Bareau has suggested that *Gathering of Gentlemen* was a fragment of a larger painting.[69] More than merely a copy, Manet's interpretation of *Gathering* and the other variations he painted after it should be recognized as key works in which he mastered the informal groupings and abrupt tonal contrasts that would become hallmarks of his innovative painting style. In 1867, Manet included his copy and the corresponding etching in his Avenue de l'Alma exhibition. In 1878 he sold the copy to the famous baritone, Jean-Baptiste Faure, a major collector of Manet's work, testifying to Velázquez's importance for Manet.[70]

Manet's copy of *Gathering of Gentlemen*, which enlivens and improves on the 'original' painting, engendered two closely related works, *Spanish Studio Scene (Velázquez Painting)* (*c*.1860, fig.7) and *Spanish Cavaliers* (also called *Souvenir de Velázquez*, or *Boy Carrying a Tray* (*c*.1860, fig.15).[71] In these smaller vignettes, Manet appropriated elements from *Gathering of Gentlemen*, but made significant modifications and additions, extrapolating and rearranging or reversing the figures that he borrowed. In *Spanish Cavaliers*, he placed the figures in a luminous interior with an open doorway at the rear, reminiscent of *Las Meninas*; selectively repositioned and edited the three cavaliers; and added the boy carrying a tray in the right foreground. The cavalier in the pink cape, standing in front of the doorway at far right, is laterally reversed. The frontal figure dressed in orange at the left, originally part of the right grouping, is now juxtaposed with the figure in profile at far left (shown in reverse), holding his hat at his side, rather than waving it in the air. The most intriguing addition is the boy carrying a tray, modeled on Manet's stepson, Léon Leenhoff, with echoes of Velázquez and Murillo. The figure was worked up in a watercolor study that Manet presumably used for making the painting and reproduced as an etching (1862).[72] Manet's seamless juxtaposition of directly observed elements with art historical references – what has been called 'museal' imagery – exemplifies Manet's unorthodox working method – his piecemeal approach to composition and predilection for extrapolating individual figures and reworking them in different contexts, often in different media, as he does here.

In *Spanish Studio Scene*, Manet went further, radically metamorphosing a boisterous outdoor gathering into an intimate studio visit. He appropriated and reconfigured two of the cavaliers that originally appeared on opposite sides in *Gathering of Gentlemen*. The standing figure, leaning on a walking stick at the right, has been reversed, and his costume modified, while the figure at the left, who is viewed from behind, is virtually verbatim. The most significant additions are the invented studio setting and the central figure of Velázquez, holding his palette and brushes and gazing at the viewer – a pose often used in artists' self-portraits. Manet reflexively represented Velázquez, seated at the easel in the act of painting. The left side of *Gathering of Gentlemen*, from which Manet appropriated his figures, appears on the easel, creating a double mise en abyme, conflating Manet's identity with that of Velázquez working in his studio. On the back wall, Manet reproduced in monochrome the bottom half of a full-length Velázquez portrait, which has been identified as *Infante Don Fernando in Hunting Dress*, and may be based on a print.[73] Although the image is sketchy and

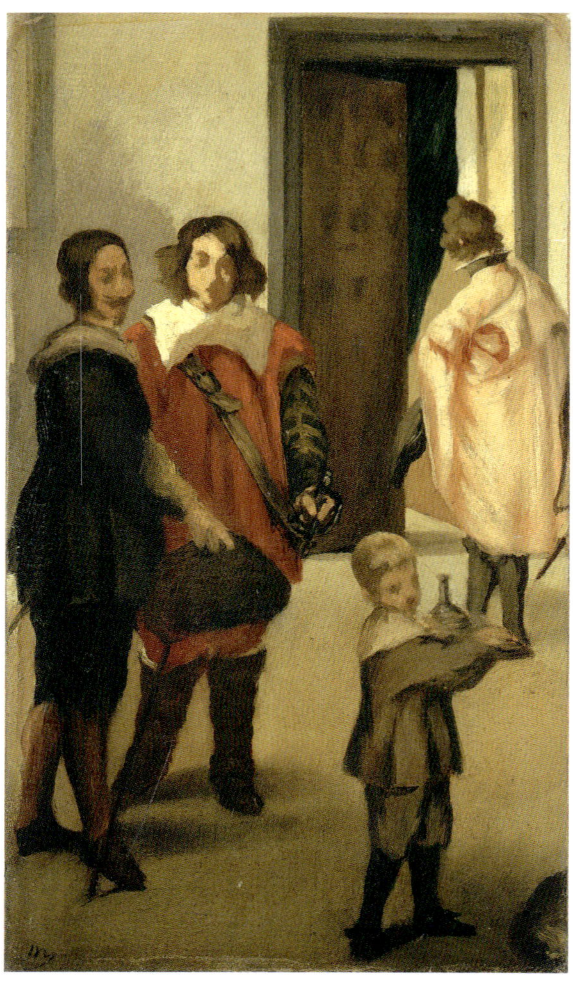

15. Édouard Manet, *Spanish Cavaliers*, c.1860, oil on canvas, 45 × 26 cm, Musée des Beaux-Arts, Lyon.

out of focus, I suspect it is *Philippe IV in Hunting Dress*, then attributed to Velázquez, which Manet copied at the Louvre in the 1850s and later etched.[74]

Peter Rudd has convincingly argued that *Spanish Cavaliers* and *Spanish Studio Scene* were originally part of a larger, more ambitious canvas depicting *Velázquez in His Studio*, in which Manet took the radical step of appropriating and rearranging a Velázquez painting and inventing a new self-referential 'Old Master' composition and homage to *Las Meninas*.[75] In Rudd's hypothetical reconstruction, *Spanish Cavaliers* forms the left portion, there is a missing section in the middle, and *Spanish Studio Scene* forms the right portion. The result is a complex, multi-figured variation on *Gathering of Gentleman*, restaged in a studio interior, in which Velázquez can be read as an allegorical portrait of Manet. This reading is reinforced by the inclusion of Léon Leenhoff, who appeared frequently in Manet's art beginning in the early 1860s. In light of the common source, similar height, close correlation between the paintings and vestigial imagery on the right side of *Spanish Cavaliers* and left side of *Spanish Studio Scene*, Rudd's reconstruction is highly plausible, but remains unproven without technical examination of the canvases. Most striking is Manet's bold recasting and ventriloquizing of an Old Master, while 'borrowing' aspects of his technique, making *Spanish Studio Scene* a reinvention of and meta-commentary on Velázquez's art, as well as a pastiche. Jacques-Émile Blanche, who owned the canvas, called it 'a curious example of an original pastiche by Manet'.[76] Rudd has suggested that Manet's slightly later *Fishing* (*c*.1861–3), which borrows from two famous works by Rubens and includes portraits of Manet and Suzanne Leenhoff in the guise of Rubens and his wife, is a notional pendant that, likewise, illustrates Manet's dualistic relationship with the Old Masters.[77]

When Manet visited Spain in August 1865, he was finally able to study authentic Velázquez paintings at the Prado. He was enraptured by Velázquez, 'who alone makes the journey worthwhile', as he breathlessly wrote Fantin-Latour. Referring to Velázquez as 'the painter of painters', Manet highlighted his portraits, including *Portrait of a Celebrated Actor from the Time of Philip IV* (Pablo de Valladolid), *The Spinners*, *Portrait of Alonso Cano*, *Las Meninas* and the *Philosophers*.[78] He also mentioned a large painting filled with small figures, (like the *Petits Cavaliers* in the Louvre), but superior and free of restoration, and noted the background was by a student of Velázquez. In a letter to Baudelaire after his return, Manet gushed, 'I've really come to know Vélasquez [sic] and I tell you he's the greatest artist there has ever been; I saw 30 or 40 of his canvases in Madrid . . . all masterpieces; he's greater than his reputation'.[79] Until the end of his life, Manet continued to engage with and measure himself against Velázquez, notably in his 1879 *Self-Portrait*. In *A Bar at the Folies-Bergère* (1882), an illusionistic tour de force staged in his last studio, at 77 rue d'Amsterdam, stage and studio, illusion and reality, elide in a complex refractive image of modern life.[80]

MANET'S STUDIOS

From 1850 until his death in 1883, Manet occupied eight different Paris studios. He spent most of his working life in the Batignolles, where he settled in 1861.[81] His studio was like a *chantier* (construction site), with numerous canvases in progress at the same time, which he often reworked or retouched before exhibiting or selling them.[82] Other than the paintings themselves, there is little firsthand evidence of Manet's working methods. Like the artist, his pictures remain elusive and resistant to analysis.[83] Rebelling against academic training and the rigid dictates of Couture's studio, Manet developed a sketchy, radically simplified style and brilliant *alla prima* painting technique. Recent technical analysis has revealed his fastidious preparation, starting with an *ébauche* and tinted washes, which he overlaid with dynamic varied brushstrokes to create a spontaneous-looking painted surface.[84] We know the locations of the studios where Manet painted his groundbreaking works from the 1860s and 1870s: 81 rue Guyot (now 8 rue Médéric) and 4 rue de Saint-Pétersbourg – and the buildings still exist. However, Manet's paintings offer only fragmentary glimpses of his studios and their furnishings.[85]

From 1861 to 1872, Manet rented a studio at 81 rue Guyot, a new building in a developing district with a cafe and laundry on the ground floor, 25 lodgings and two artists' studios. Manet's studio, which occupied the second and third floors, had a double-height ceiling and was 45 m².[86] Contemporary accounts of the Guyot studio are sparse. Émile Zola, who posed there for his 1868 portrait, recalled 'a large dilapidated studio'.[87] Théodore Duret describes posing in 1868 for his Goyaesque portrait in a large room, nearly empty except for stacks of paintings, piled up against the walls – comprising most of Manet's oeuvre – since he had sold almost nothing. Underscoring Manet's isolation and the remote location, Duret observed that only close friends ever stopped by.[88]

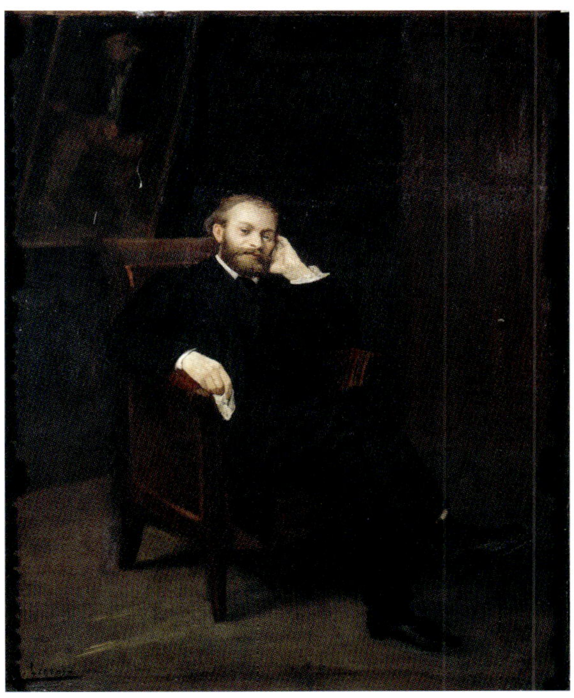

16. Alphonse Legros, *Portrait of Édouard Manet*, 1863, oil on canvas, 61.5 × 50 cm, Musée du Petit Palais, Paris.

Alphonse Legros's intimate *Portrait of Manet* (1863, fig.16) depicts him in his studio with *Spanish Singer*. That is appropriate since Manet's installation in the

Guyot studio was probably due to the honorable mention *Spanish Singer* received at the 1861 Salon. Soberly dressed in a dark suit and black cravat, he sits in an armchair, legs crossed, his head resting on his hand in a characteristic meditative pose.[89] Though more relaxed, his pose subtly echoes that of *Spanish Singer,* hanging on the wall behind. Legros's portrait corroborates Duret's description of the studio as a solitary space, bare except for Manet's canvases. Fantin-Latour's group portrait, *Studio in the Batignolles* (1870), invested Manet's studio with emblematic significance as the locus of the new painting. Although the canvas ostensibly depicts the rue Guyot studio, it actually portrays Fantin's own studio at 8 rue des Beaux-Arts, where the sitters came individually to pose. Fantin's interest in still life is underscored by the inclusion of objects from his studio, including the cast of Minerva, a favorite prop, and a Japanese-style, enameled pot, that evoke his presence, even though he purged his portrait from the final version.[90] A related oil sketch, *Manet in His Studio* (1870), depicts the artist seated at the easel, holding his brush and palette, with Léon Leenhoff at the right, carrying a tray, thus reiterating Manet's admiration for Velázquez by including quotations from *Spanish Studio Scene* and *Spanish Cavaliers.*

Manet's only overt depiction of the Guyot studio, *Eva Gonzalès Painting in Manet's Studio* (fig.17), shows a portion of the wall with a folding screen at far left.[91] Gonzalès, who studied under Manet (1869–70), was his only official pupil. In the Guyot studio, Manet and Gonzalès set up their easels side by side. One day, Manet, seduced by Gonzalès's silhouette, rapidly sketched her at the easel.[92] The small, loosely brushed painting portrays Gonzalès, elegantly attired in a gray dress *à volants* with a black sash, standing at the easel, holding her palette and brushes. Viewed from behind, she is intensely absorbed in painting a large canvas. Gonzalès painted *Le Clarion* or *Enfant de troupe* (*The Trumpeter*), exhibited at the 1870 Salon, under Manet's attentive gaze. Inspired by *The Fifer* (1866), *The Trumpeter* publicly manifested her association with Manet and admiration for his work. At the right, Léon Leenhoff, dressed as a matador, perches on a table and lights a cigarette. Manet's *Lola de Valence* (1862) is partially visible behind him.[93] Velázquez's influence can be discerned in the setting, which echoes *Las Meninas* and recalls Manet's *Spanish Studio Scene,* as well as the luminous gray and brown palette and bravura brushwork.

Concurrently, Manet was painting a life-size portrait of Gonzalès that required numerous sittings (fig.18). Berthe Morisot reported to her sister that Gonzalès posed every day and every night Manet scraped off what he had done and started over, maliciously noting that the portrait was not advancing after 40 sittings.[94] Begun in 1869, the painting was completed by March 1870, in time for the Salon where Gonzalès made her debut with *Trumpeter* and two other works. Gonzalès, wearing a ruffled white muslin dress, with a white peony at her feet, is artfully posed in the dual guise of painter and model. She sits at the easel, with a portfolio behind her chair and a rolled-up sketch bearing Manet's signature at lower right, identifying her as his student. Holding her palette, brushes and mahlstick in her left hand, she delicately applies the finishing touches to the framed flower painting on the easel.[95] Although her body is in profile, she turns her head away from the canvas to gaze at the viewer, blurring the distinction between drawing room and studio, artist and model, as does the indeterminate setting.

Rather than Velázquez, Manet looked to Goya for his elegant portrait of Gonzalès, who was of Spanish descent. She is portrayed in a close-up, profile view, silhouetted against blank walls, on a vibrantly patterned rug, surrounded by attributes of the arts. This larger, more conventional portrait contrasts strikingly with the rapidly brushed, spontaneous sketch of *Eva Gonzalès Painting in Manet's Studio.* Focusing on the studio ambience and what transpires in it rather than on the model, the painting captures her absorption in the act of painting, the poetic play of light and shadow and the illusionist alchemy of paint, conveyed by Manet's rapid

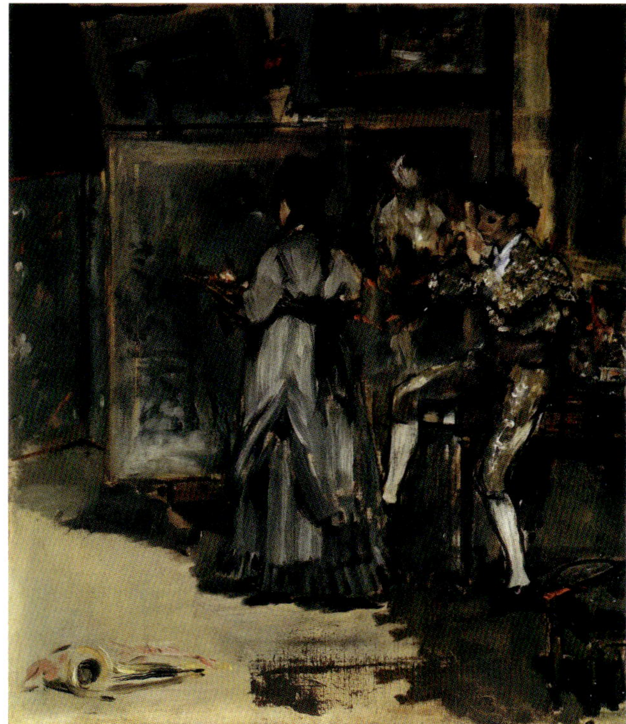

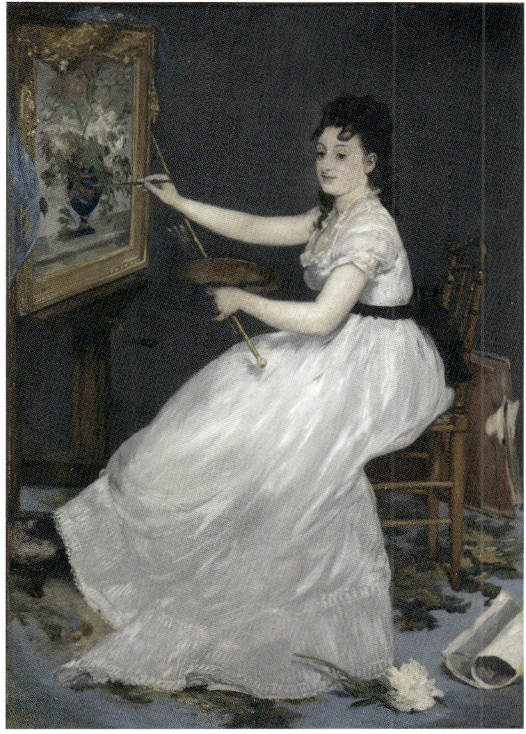

17. (left) Édouard Manet, *Eva Gonzalès Painting in Manet's Studio*, 1870, oil on canvas, 56 × 46 cm, private collection.

18. (right) Édouard Manet, *Portrait of Eva Gonzalès*, 1870, oil on canvas, 191.1 × 133.4 cm, National Gallery, London.

brushstrokes and virtuoso touches, such as the gleaming trumpet at lower left. Although Manet never depicted himself in the studio, his intimate sketch of Gonzalès painting arguably becomes a placeholder for him, just as the Guyot studio alludes to that of Velázquez. Exceptionally, in 1879, Manet portrayed himself as a painter in two self-portraits that also refer to Velázquez.

For Manet, the studio was a flexible palette that could be endlessly transformed and reinvented, fluctuating from neutral backdrop to artful construction or imaginary stage set. The *fonds* (background) and props were crucial in conjuring the artifice of modern life and injecting an animated ambience into his figure paintings, especially portraits.[96] When Zola posed for his portrait in February 1868, the Guyot studio was configured emblematically to evoke a writer's desk; books, a quill pen and a porcelain inkstand were juxtaposed with Zola's recent brochure defending Manet and a grisaille reproduction of his controversial *Olympia*, highlighting Zola's literary career and heroic defense of Manet in 1866 (fig.19).[97] Zola's review of the 1868 Salon recalled long hours spent posing in Manet's studio, surrounded by his powerful, misunderstood canvases, and noted his absorption in his task.[98] Painted as a token of gratitude, the portrait was a manifesto of Manet's artistic influences and modern taste, from the engraving of Velázquez's *Los Borrachos* behind *Olympia* to the Kuniaki woodblock print of a wrestler to the decorative Japanese screen. Even the open book in Zola's lap appears to be a volume from Charles Blanc's *Histoire des peintres*, which Manet kept in his studio and frequently consulted.

Similarly, *Portrait of Zacharie Astruc* (fig.20), painted in the rue Guyot studio in 1866, emphasizes the literary vocation of Astruc, a friend and early champion of Manet. Astruc sits in an armchair beside a table, with an artfully disordered array of papers, books, including a Japanese volume, quill pens and a writing case.[99] Painted shortly after Manet's return from Spain, the portrait portrays Astruc in a close-up frontal view, wearing a black velvet suit and vibrant red sash, his right hand tucked inside his vest. His extended, sketchily rendered left hand echoes the gloved left hand of Titian's *Man with a Glove* in the Louvre.[100] Besides radically cropping the composition, Manet complicates the pictorial space by creating a disjunctive, split-screen effect. Astruc's rigid, tonally contrasted portrait, silhouetted against a dark background, fills the right side. The left side depicts a light-filled interior, at reduced scale, with a young woman, seen from behind, standing at a window. A gilded frame demarcates the composition's two irreconcilable halves. Scholars disagree over whether the luminous interior is a mirror reflection or a painting. Though reminiscent of a Manet painting, the interior is not identifiable with any known work. Not previously noticed is that the draped curtain, rocking chair and stringed instrument on the woman's right are suggestive of an artist's studio. Whether mirror reflection or painting, the incongruous interior creates a disorienting sense of ambiguity and a visual conundrum for the viewer. As Therese Dolan has noted, the divided picture space complicates Manet's tableau on multiple levels. Falling midway between portrait and genre, the canvas embodies Baudelaire's concept of duality and modern beauty, first elaborated in his *Salon of 1846*, which applies equally to portraiture, suspending it between history and fiction.[101]

In January 1872, Paul Durand-Ruel's purchase of 24 paintings stockpiled in the Guyot studio enabled Manet to move to a spacious new studio at 4 rue de Saint-Pétersbourg, where he worked from 1872 to 1878. Although there are no painted depictions, the studio is documented in period photographs and press accounts.[102] The vast former fencing hall on the upper ground floor was illuminated by four large windows at the front. The elegantly decorated studio, with exposed beams, dark oak moldings and an ornate fireplace, had a small salon with a loggia, toilet and changing facilities and a kitchen and pantry, making it suitable for entertaining. On 27 December 1873, in *Le Figaro*, Léon Duchemin (known as Fervacques) described the Saint-Pétersbourg studio and the paintings displayed on the walls.[103] He admired Manet's well-kept studio and its elegant furnishings, including a piano, and emphasized that there was nothing bohemian about it. Gaston La Touche insisted that the immense luminous space was more like an apartment than an artist's studio.[104] Fervacques listed the paintings on the walls including *Déjeuner sur l'herbe*, *Olympia* and *Masked Ball at the Opera*, which he analyzed at length. Other writers praised the tranquility and simplicity of the studio, which had no superfluous furnishings, just dazzling studies on the walls and on easels.[105]

Through contemporary accounts like that of Fervacques and surviving period photographs, we can envision Manet in the rue de Saint-Pétersbourg studio.[106] Typically, he worked mornings until he took a late lunch; on Sundays, he opened his studio to friends and patrons to show them his work. During the 1870s and early 1880s, Manet painted a series of intimate, informal portraits of modern types, primarily women, using backdrops and props from his studio. Friends, including Berthe Morisot, Stéphane Mallarmé, Nina de Callias and Méry Laurent, posed in the rue de Saint-Pétersbourg studio. The same Japanese hanging or wall covering served as a backdrop for portraits of Mallarmé (1876) and de Callias (1873). For some paintings, like *Nana* (1877), Manet constructed elaborate settings with his studio furnishings, deploying a red velvet setee, standing mirror and gilded marquetry table to evoke Nana's lavish dressing room. For *Plum Brandy* (*c.*1877), Manet fabricated a cafe interior. The actress/model Ellen Andrée sits at a marble-topped counter, which he kept in the studio, against a faux background, often identified as the Nouvelle Athènes.[107] In 1876, the Saint-Pétersbourg studio became a public exhibition space and annex to the Salon. When Manet's Salon submissions – *Laundry* and *Portrait of an Artist* (Marcellin Desboutin) – were rejected, he exhibited them in his studio. From 15 April to 1 May, the public flocked to his studio to view and judge the rejected works. Manet and his art were again a contested flashpoint covered extensively in the press.[108]

Manet's last studio, 77 rue d'Amsterdam, where he worked from 1879 until his death, arguably played an even more central role as his health declined and the physical parameters of his daily life narrowed. Vastly different from the rue de Saint-Pétersbourg studio, it was a tall rectangular space at the back of a courtyard with large windows.[109] The teenaged Jacques-Émile Blanche visited the rue d'Amsterdam studio, where Manet painted *Bar at the Folies-Bergère* (1882) and *Jeanne* (1881). He noted Manet's brusque but reflective touch and the care with which he painted, using fine brushes.[110] Underscoring the social dimension of the studio (which replaced the Café de Bade), he recalled Manet jovially serving beer and cocktails to visitors who stopped by at the end of the day, thus blurring the distinction between studio and salon. Blanche described the furnishings, including the buffet and row of liquor bottles depicted in *Bar*, the cheval mirror in *Nana*, a zinc tub and the faded rhododendrons used for the background of *Jeanne*.

Considering Manet's notoriety and prominence as leader of the new school of painting, it is no surprise that other artists including Edgar Degas, Fantin-Latour, Bazille and Legros depicted him. Renowned for his impeccable appearance, stylish allure and gracious manners, he was invariably portrayed as a fashionable *boulevardier*. Fantin-Latour's iconic portrait, exhibited at the 1867 Salon, depicts Manet in a well-cut jacket and top hat with a walking stick, underscoring his bourgeois respectability, following the scandal unleashed by *Olympia* in 1865.[111] In 1867, Manet boldly staged a counter-exhibition of more than fifty paintings in a

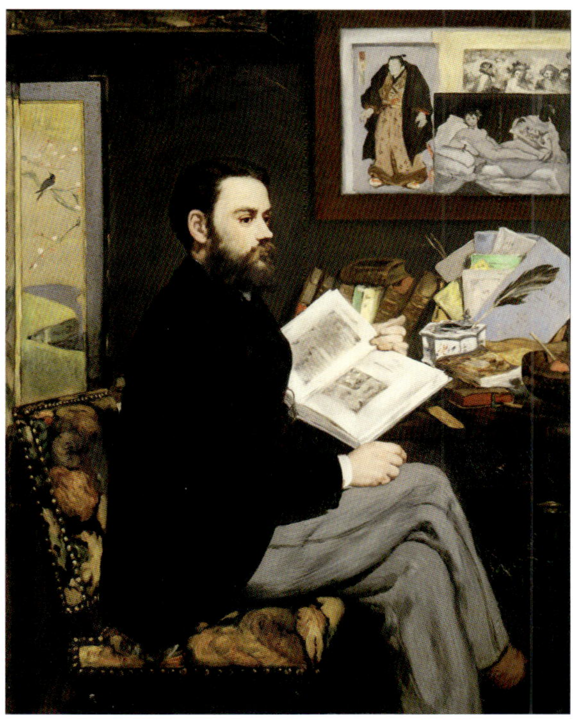

19. Édouard Manet, *Portrait of Émile Zola*, 1868, oil on canvas, 146 × 114 cm, Musée d'Orsay, Paris.

pavilion on the Avenue de l'Alma directly across from the Exposition Universelle; however, his display failed to attract the public.

Unlike Degas and Fantin-Latour, who depicted themselves repeatedly, Manet painted only two self-portraits, both around 1879.[112] Early in his career, he portrayed himself with Suzanne Leenhoff in *Fishing*, a Baroque pastiche, and in a fashionable crowd in *Music in the Tuileries* (1862). By 1879, Manet was gaining the professional success that had long eluded him.[113] The unfinished full-length *Self-Portrait with a Skullcap* depicts him in a yellowish-gray jacket and skullcap, his hands in his pockets. Caps appear often in self-portraits by artists whom Manet admired, including Titian and Filippino Lippi, whose *Self-Portrait* he copied in the

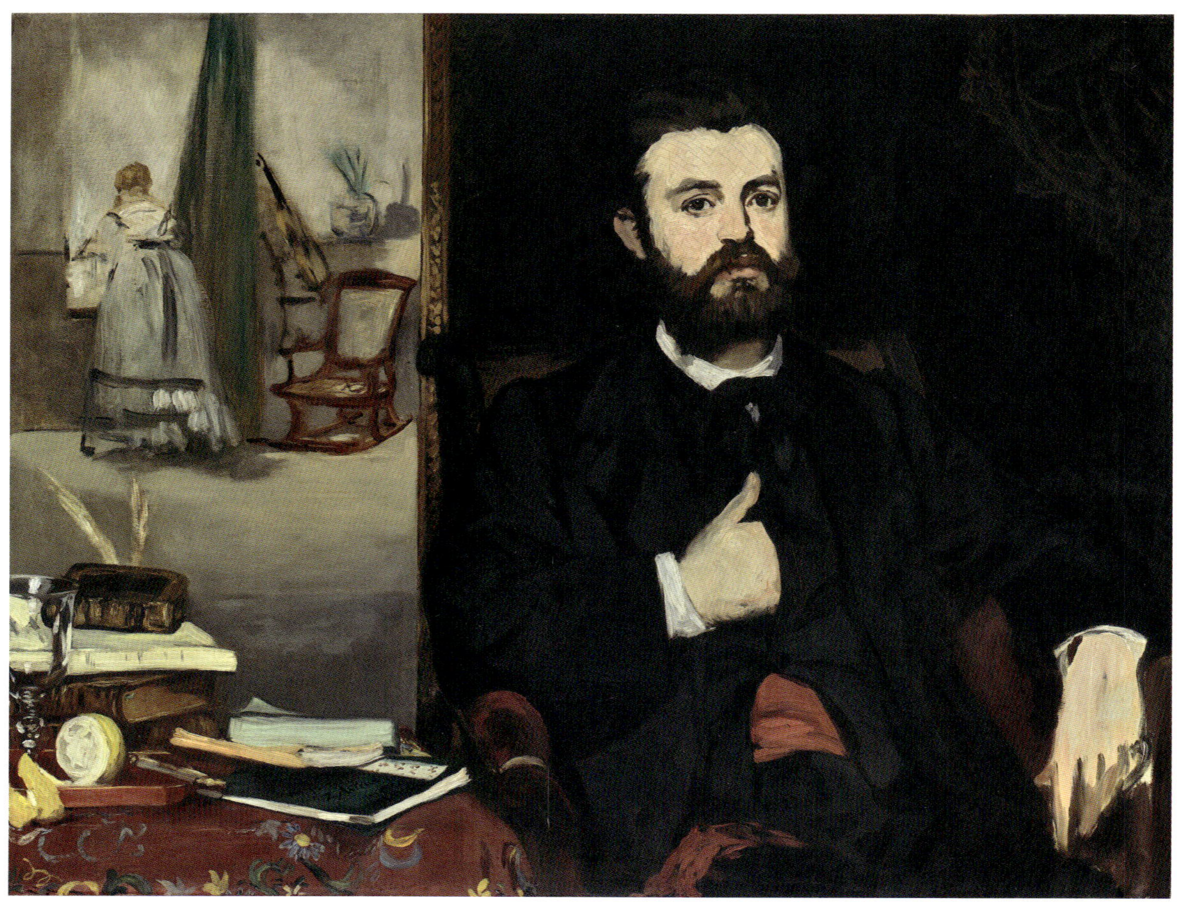

20. Édouard Manet, *Portrait of Zacharie Astruc*, 1866, oil on canvas, 90.5 × 116 cm, Kunsthalle, Bremen.

early 1850s.[114] By recording himself for posterity, wearing a skullcap, Manet was aligning himself with the Old Masters and their enduring posthumous fame.

Manet's sober half-length *Self-Portrait with Palette* is his only self-portrayal as a painter with the tools of his trade (fig.21).[115] His sketchy, rapidly painted portrait recalls Velázquez's celebrated self-portrait in *Las Meninas*. By emulating Velázquez's bravura painting technique, Manet identified himself with and paid tribute to the Spanish master. Bazille and Fantin-Latour had previously portrayed Manet at the easel in group depictions of their own studios. *Self-Portrait with Palette* brings us full circle. Manet alluded to Velázquez's self-portrait but radically cropped and updated it by representing himself in a close-up frontal view, against a dark background, as a fashionably dressed painter of modern life. Echoing Fantin's dashing 1867 portrait, he is pictured as an elegant *flâneur* in a tan jacket, accented with a black bowler hat and a black cravat. However, Manet's vitality has evaporated; his uneasy gaze, half obscured by shadow, appears tentative rather than confident. His blob-like hand, wielding the brush, and the abruptly truncated palette inject a morbid note, turning the self-portrait into a *memento mori*, in which Manet faces down his own mortality in the mirror.

CODA: THE ECHO CHAMBER

Delacroix's and Manet's contested careers present striking parallels – their leveraging of the Old Masters as catalysts for experimentation and innovation and their decades-long struggle for official recognition, evidenced in vitriolic critical responses and rejections from the official Salon. Both artists continued to submit to the Salon but also sought alternative venues, notably Galerie Martinet, which mounted modern exhibitions. The 1860 artists' relief fund benefit held there included 23 Delacroix paintings from different periods. In March 1862, *Death of Saradanapalus*, not seen since 1828, *Large Tigers* (1831), and a sketch of the Galerie d'Apollon at the Louvre were exhibited.[116] In March 1863, Manet showed 14 paintings, including *Lola de Valence* and *Music in the Tuileries* at Galerie Martinet. In 1864 and 1865, he sent works to the Société Nationale des Beaux-Arts exhibitions there.

Suspended between past and present, Delacroix and Manet were museum artists in dialogue with the Old Masters and innovative trailblazers. The seemingly antithetical, yet also intertwined, issues of originality and borrowing from past art surfaced in relation to both artists. Delacroix, who reflected on the difficulty of retaining originality in his journal, was criticized for his indebtedness to past masters and worn-out themes, notably in 1859.[117] Manet's artistic borrowings were also faulted. Arguing that Manet's 'originality' lay more in execution and *métier* than conception, Blanche claimed that all of his works were inspired by ancient or modern paintings.[118] Recognition of Delacroix's and Manet's influence and stature as avatars of modern art only coalesced after their deaths, when major exhibitions honoring them were held in Paris.

The Delacroix exhibition and sale at Hôtel Drouot in February 1864 and the retrospective exhibition held at Galerie Martinet in August 1864 enshrined him as a painter of genius.[119] Noting the crowds, Silvestre decried the public's failure to appreciate Delacroix during his lifetime.[120] In the sale catalogue, Philippe Burty

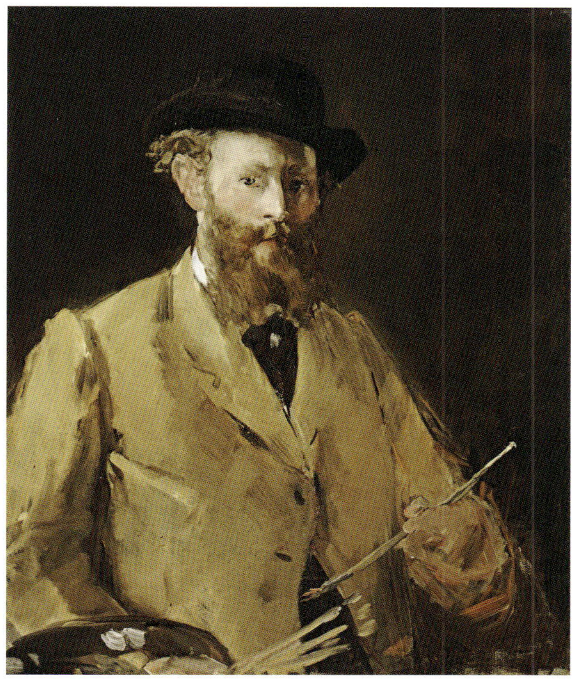

21. Édouard Manet, *Self-Portrait with Palette*, 1879, oil on canvas, 83 × 67 cm, private collection.

characterized Delacroix's life as a succession of struggles, observing that his art was violently attacked until it was featured at the 1855 Exposition Universelle.[121] He commended Delacroix's virtually unknown drawings, watercolors and pastels, noting his attachment to his drawings, which he hoped would counter the complaints about facility and improvisation he had endured, by demonstrating that his art was rooted in persistent study.

The studio sale exceeded estimates, thus affirming Delacroix's posthumous reputation.[122] More than dealers, passionate collectors and artists competed for paintings, sketches and drawings. People who had once fled from Delacroix's work pushed prices for his sketches to unprecedented heights; even copies after the Old Masters fetched high prices.[123] Silvestre emphasized how hard Delacroix had worked, painting from early morning to mid-afternoon without stopping to eat. Striking a more personal note, he observed that Delacroix, like Michelangelo, adored his servants and was adored by them. He recalled Delacroix's devastation when his housekeeper Jenny Le Guillou fell ill, linking Delacroix to the anecdote about Michelangelo caring for his dying servant that Robert-Fleury had depicted.

The stately, red-curtained galleries at the 1864 retrospective, which were filled with 300 of Delacroix's most important works, including *Michelangelo in His Studio*, are recorded in a painting by Édouard Albertini. Théophile Gautier exclaimed, 'Delacroix lives there again in all his glory'.[124] A commemorative life-size bust, commissioned from Albert-Ernest Carrier-Belleuse, was displayed among Delacroix's paintings.[125] The bust presided over the December 1864 banquet where Gautier delivered a toast. Although Delacroix detested posing for portraits and prohibited deathbed photographs, posthumous effigies proliferated, from popular prints to Jules Dalou's allegorical monument to Delacroix's eternal glory (1890) in the Luxembourg Gardens to Fantin-Latour's painted apotheosis, *Homage to Delacroix* (1864), testifying to Delacroix's influence on the next generation.

In the 1884 Manet exhibition catalogue, Zola pointedly noted his sudden 'apotheosis' after his death – the press trumpeting the passing of a great painter, and those who had mocked him now paying homage.[126] He observed that Manet's copies after Titian, Tintoretto and Lippi showed how deeply he, though often accused of ignorance, had engaged with the Old Masters. Organized by family and friends, the retrospective presented a comprehensive, unfiltered survey of Manet's work including the most controversial canvases, that demonstrated Manet's importance as a modern master and innovator. To enhance its prestige as an overdue posthumous triumph, Duret sought permission to hold the exhibition at the École des Beaux-Arts. The request, which the École director refused outright, was green-lighted by Jules Ferry, Minister of Fine Arts, thanks to Antonin Proust's timely intervention and political clout.[127] The 116 paintings and more than 50 watercolors, pastels, drawings and prints, from early copies to late still lifes and portraits, made a powerful case for Manet's place in the lineage of great artists – Ingres, Delacroix and Courbet – and for his influence on French painting.[128]

The memorial exhibition, held from 5–28 January 1884, attracted large crowds and was extensively covered in the press.[129] A sale at Hôtel Drouot, 4–5 February, followed. Due to Manet's notoriety as a renegade, it was uncertain whether his works would find buyers. Although some key works, including *Olympia*, were bought in, Manet's friends and supporters paid what seemed, at the time, extraordinary prices. The exhibition and sale dispelled any remaining doubts about Manet's stature and contributed to the sea change in public opinion. At the 1889 Exposition Universelle, Manet was fêted as one of the leading artists of the century. A public subscription, spearheaded by artists, notably Monet, was launched to purchase *Olympia* for the state. In 1890, after official resistance and considerable maneuvering, the once scandalous canvas entered the Musée du Luxemborg, completing Manet's posthumous triumph.[130]

The next chapter focuses on Corot's studio, which was integral to his identity and painting practice and became a pilgrimage site for artists. In a remarkable series of paintings created late in his career, Corot thematized his studio materially and metaphorically as the locus of his creativity.

2

Absence and Presence

Corot's Studio Revisited

Corot is a true artist. You have to see a painter in his studio to get a real idea of his merit. I viewed again and appreciated completely differently the pictures I had seen at the Museum, which had not particularly impressed me.[1]

–Eugène Delacroix, journal, 14 March 1847

Though trained as a landscape painter, Jean-Baptiste-Camille Corot is a pivotal figure in the reinvention of the studio at mid-century that straddles stylistic and generic categories.[2] Stretching over half a century, Corot's career is emblematic of the evolving functions of the studio and the far-reaching changes that transformed the artistic profession, from working outdoors to the role of exhibitions and the market in shaping artists' careers.[3] The heightened individualism that emerged with Romanticism invested the artist's studio with a metaphoric and metonymic significance as a projection or self-portrait of the artist.[4] More than merely a professional workspace, Corot's studio was central to his artistic identity and painting practice and became a recurring subject in his art. Creative laboratory, exhibition space and archive, the studio was recognized by contemporaries as essential to understanding his method and the meaning of his art. The proliferation of images of Corot painting by friends and acolytes underscores the studio's significance for his painting and his professional identity.[5]

This chapter considers Corot's studio from multiple perspectives: materially as a workspace for producing art and metaphorically or metonymically as frame, retrospective gallery, *lieu de mémoire* and pilgrimage site. At the apex of his career, Corot painted an exceptional group of pictures that shed light on his identification with his studio and its broader artistic and cultural significance. One of the most intriguing aspects of these paintings is the absence of the artist. Examining the studio pictures individually and collectively, I consider how they encapsulate Corot's method and his modernity.

Corot's meticulous depictions of his studio, from varied vantage points, with his pictures displayed on easels and walls, create a complex dialectic of absence and presence, intimacy and distance, that resists easy analysis.[6] Rather than a backdrop for art-making, the

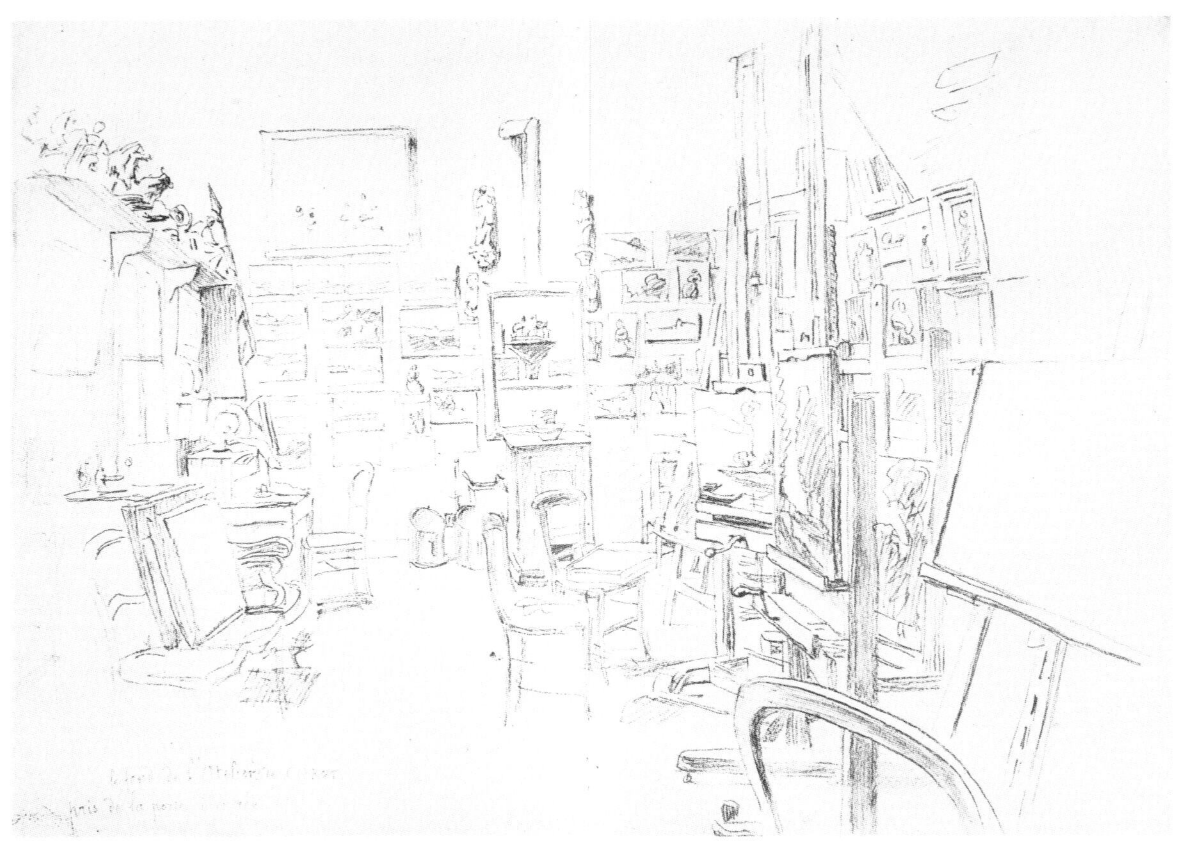

22. Alfred Robaut, *Corot's Studio*, 1875, drawing reproduced in Alfred Robaut, *L'Oeuvre de Corot*, Floury, Paris, 1905, vol.1, pp 316–17, National Gallery of Art, Washington, DC.

studio becomes the subject and functions materially and figuratively on multiple levels – as concrete workspace, imaginary space for reflection and invention, museum and *lieu de mémoire*. Through the inclusion of his works and the poetics of paint, the studio pictures evoke the absent artist, assuming an authorial function. Embedded in that overarching argument are a nexus of collateral questions revolving around creativity, memory, parallels between painting and music, gender and artistic agency, embodied by the contemplative women who animate the studio. Grounded in the quotidian actuality of the studio and metamorphosed in paint, Corot's studio pictures become coextensive projections of the absent artist.

EXCAVATING COROT'S STUDIO

My research on Corot's studio has been haunted by absence and presence. Like most artists, he changed studios periodically. Initially, he rented studios on the Left Bank: 15 quai Voltaire (1835–49) and 10 rue des

Beaux-Arts (1850). In 1851, he moved to the Right Bank, and in 1853, he found the studio at 58 rue de Paradis-Poissonnière (now 56 rue du Faubourg-Poissonnière) that he occupied for the rest of his life and depicted repeatedly during the 1860s and early 1870s.[7] In 1873, Corot set up a second 'private' studio at 19bis rue Fontaine, where he could work undisturbed by interruptions and importune visitors.

Widely visited during his lifetime and unusually well documented, today the Paradis-Poissonnière studio, where Corot worked for over two decades, only exists virtually. The simple stone building with its triple-arched facade is on a nondescript street near the former Conservatory, where Corot attended concerts. The building has a historical plaque but is private and inaccessible. Drawing on archival sources, contemporaneous accounts and visual depictions, I have grappled with the dual challenge of reconstructing Corot's studio materially and metaphorically, as conceptual frame, retrospective gallery and *lieu de mémoire* – how it was represented in art and fixed in memory – during his lifetime and after his death. Alfred Robaut's '*Cartons*' (scrapbook volumes), which contain manuscript notes for the 1905 catalogue raisonné and numerous images, including original artworks, offer the most comprehensive record of Corot's studio.[8]

Excluding studio museums, like that of Delacroix, few artists' studios are so well documented. From contemporary accounts and visual evidence, including Corot's own paintings, we can reconstruct the layout. An 1875 inventory lists the studio's contents. Besides hundreds of paintings, portfolios and sketches, there were: stools, a writing desk, two armchairs covered in grenadine damask, a small desk, paint boxes, six easels and assorted plaster casts.[9] Robaut's meticulous posthumous drawings (figs 22, 23) are the most detailed visual record of the studio; they show the stove, the chair for models and the console holding sculpture, all of which appear in Corot's paintings.[10] His work area consisted of the main studio and a small adjoining antechamber or cabinet, which is depicted in

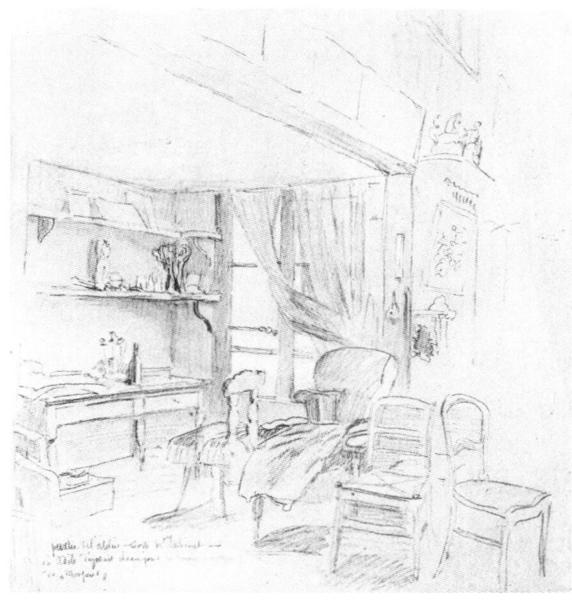

23. Alfred Robaut, *Cabinet Attached to Corot's Studio*, 1875, drawing reproduced in Alfred Robaut, *L'Oeuvre de Corot*, Floury, Paris, 1905, vol.1, p.323, National Gallery of Art, Washington, DC.

two studio pictures. Robaut also made an annotated plan of the studio delineating the main features and furniture placement that helps us envision the space and situate the studio pictures (fig.24).[11] A trained surveyor, Robaut provided a scale, making it possible to calculate the dimensions. The main studio, a slightly irregular square, measured roughly 8 m on each side; the rectangular annex was about 4 m by 2 m. There was a small vestibule with a toilet and two doors, the studio entrance and another door that led to the annex. Robaut marked where Corot habitually set up his easel, facing the back wall and stove – the viewpoint of most of the studio pictures.

Despite their aura of authenticity and exactitude, Robaut's drawings of Corot's studio should be approached with caution because they record its penultimate state after the artist's death and are

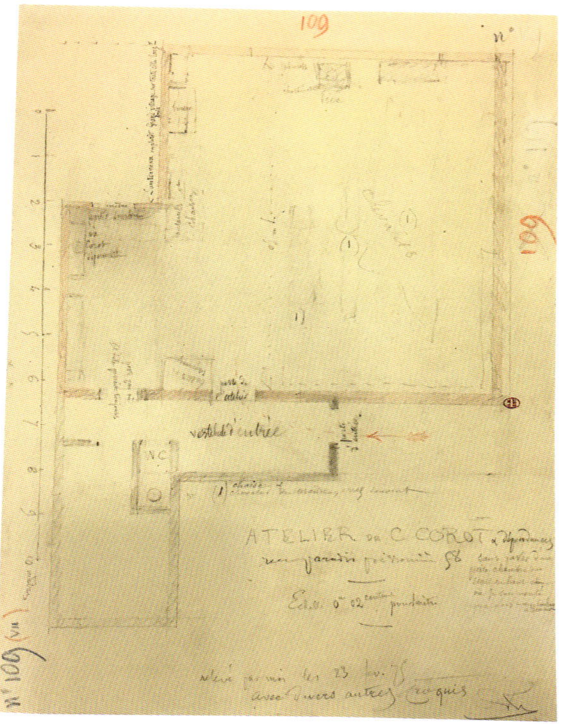

24. Alfred Robaut, *Plan of Corot's Studio*, 1875, pencil on paper, Robaut Cartons, Musée du Louvre, Paris.

coextensive with Robaut's cataloguing project, begun around 1870, which involved recording and photographing hundreds of canvases.[12] That episteme permeates Robaut's tidy, posthumous drawings, which are annotated and carefully staged as if for a photo shoot. Conversely, Corot's studio pictures are fragmentary, subjective depictions of a space in flux – the studio as it was experienced, remembered and reimagined – thus restaging and mirroring the creative process itself.

Corot is indelibly linked to the Paradis-Poissonnière studio, but interest in visiting his studio predates this particular studio. Charles Asselineau's article in *L'Artiste* (1851) is the first published account of Corot's studio. Though based on the rue des Beaux-Arts studio, it tallies closely with accounts of the Paradis-Poissonnière studio, especially its significance as an exhibition space and repository of Corot's oeuvre. Constant Dutilleux discovered Corot at the 1847 Salon, visited his studio in 1848 and became a close friend. Corot's rising reputation and prominence at mid-century and close ties with the Arras School fueled the cult surrounding him and initiated a cycle of paintings and photographs depicting him working in the studio and outdoors. Robaut, who met Corot in 1852, is the most notable of the artist/archivists associated with the Arras School. His exhaustive research formed the core of the 1905 catalogue, which remains the foundation of Corot studies.[13]

Though not illustrated, Asselineau's article gave readers a vivid impression of Corot's studio, grounded in firsthand knowledge. Underscoring the studio's role as gallery and repository of his genius, Asselineau forcefully articulated its broader aesthetic and pedagogical significance:

> The first glimpse of Monsieur Corot's studio tells his life story and reveals the secret of his talent. One's eye wanders over a collection of five hundred painted studies, extending along the walls without the slightest gap . . . relegating canvases from one day to the next toward the friezes, invading the doorways . . . and swallowing portfolios. Often a visitor has called for the remounting of a precious study, long forgotten by its author at the bottom of a carton.[14]

The crowded, picture-filled space was the opposite of a rarefied ivory tower. Boldly asserting that this 'atelier without students' had done more for the progress of art than any academic atelier, Asselineau observed that Corot's 500 works and conversation offered a liberal and spontaneous education to countless artists.[15] He noted that Corot's studio was both ideologically and aesthetically important – signifying opposition to the Academy and the status quo and exemplifying modern, progressive principles in the contested arena of painting at mid-century. Praising Corot's figure paintings, which were virtually unknown, he urged him to exhibit them, rather than reserving them for his studio. For Asselineau, Corot was a *phare* (beacon), to borrow Baudelaire's term – a true painter who for 30 years had devoted himself to his art with a sort of chastity. Asselineau decried Corot's unjustified absence from the Musée du Luxembourg and insisted on his genius, comparing him to Delacroix in the number and superiority of his works.

Following Asselineau's lead, Théophile Silvestre compiled a more detailed study of Corot that became a template for later writers.[16] His reportage, based on interviews and visits to Corot's studio, embraces the concept of 'truth to nature' associated with the Realist school and photography at mid-century. On his first visit to Corot's studio, Silvestre was struck by the artist's cordiality, the bonhomie illuminating his face and his idiosyncratic painting costume – a blue worker's smock and a striped cotton bonnet.[17] However, Silvestre's portrait of Corot is complicated by the melancholy undercurrent beneath his cheerful demeanor, which also inflected his paintings.[18] Like Asselineau, Silvestre highlighted Corot's lengthy struggle to gain recognition, noting how his pictures were exhibited at the Salon in the worst corners where they were barely visible.[19] He also discussed Corot's phenomenal pictorial memory, averring that a rapid study sufficed to make a painting. Underscoring Corot's visceral attachment to his studio and its contents, he recounted the artist's anguished response when urged to purchase fire insurance to protect the 40,000 francs worth of paintings in the studio: 'If such a misfortune arrived, it would kill me.'[20]

Henri Dumesnil vividly described the Paradis-Poissonnière studio and the myriad works covering the walls.[21] Drawing on Corot's recollections and firsthand knowledge, he recounted Corot's artistic struggles and emphasized the studio's role as a communal space for social and artistic exchange and for displaying and validating Corot's work. He highlighted the studio's significance as a retrospective gallery and holding zone in which the studies were subject to revision or alteration and time became elastic.[22] For Dumesnil, Corot's studio was a living archive and *lieu de mémoire*, where the master displayed his works, some famous, others obscure, and delighted in recounting their histories. Dumesnil noted: 'All these little pictures are like detached pages, summarizing the artist's existence and his oeuvre, his attempts, his progress as well as his weaknesses or the hesitation he felt at certain moments between the different paths that opened up before him.'[23] Corot reveled in these precious souvenirs, re-experiencing past impressions through them à la Proust. Even when he was too weak to work, he would go to his studio:

> He loved to be surrounded by his memories, that is to say, his paintings, because there were no luxuries, no tapestries or rare furnishings, no bibelots . . . that middle-sized room, on the fifth floor, was simple, almost severe; the decoration . . . consisted of the studies covering the walls from the parquet to the ceiling.[24]

INSIDE COROT'S STUDIO

Robaut, Corot's cataloguer and friend, compiled the most comprehensive record of his studio and his painting process.[25] He observed that Corot liked to paint on top of old canvases, as X-radiographs confirm. In the studio pictures and figure paintings like *Agostina* (1866), Corot reworked poses, gestures and facial expressions, experimenting directly on the canvas.[26] The most intriguing unfiltered depiction of Corot's studio is a chalk drawing by Robaut of a model in Italian costume (fig.25).[27] Posing in front of a screen, with paintings covering the wall behind her, she pulls back her apron with her right hand and holds a ceramic jug in her left. The sketch depicts the model who posed for *Agostina*, Corot's largest figure painting. In the finished canvas, Corot eliminated the jug, cropped the figure

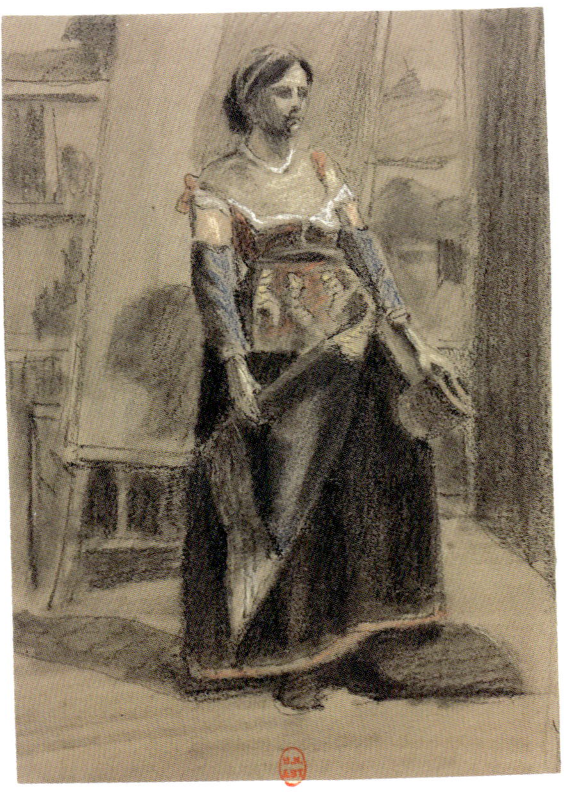

25. Alfred Robaut, *L'Italienne*, n.d., colored chalk on paper, Robaut Cartons, Musée du Louvre, Paris.

to three-quarter length and placed her in an Italianate landscape; her left hand delicately poised on a parapet. This exceptional document takes us inside Corot's studio and reveals how he posed models and reimagined and transformed them during the painting process. In the studio pictures, rather than inserting the model into a landscape, the contemplative women anchor the studio and are subsumed into it.

Corot painted only two self-portraits, later preferring to depict his studio. In both portraits, he presents himself as a painter, with palette and brushes. The first was made before he departed for Italy in 1825, at his father's request.[28] Elegantly dressed in a brown coat and sporting a bright red cravat, Corot stands at the easel, holding a square palette, announcing his artistic vocation. In Rome, he painted small figure studies that anticipate his studio pictures.[29] Nothing is known about the origins of the second *Self-Portrait*, whose date is uncertain (fig.26).[30] Here, Corot is dressed as a painter in a white smock and dark beret, underscoring his professional identity. He is depicted half-length in a close-up, three-quarter view, silhouetted against a luminous background. Painted using a mirror, the image is reversed: Corot holds his brush in his left hand and a large circular palette in his right. To satisfy the Uffizi's request for a self-portrait, Corot donated this image shortly before his death, although he was hesitant to send such an old likeness.[31] Created at the end of his life, the studio pictures arguably become figurative self-portraits, evoking the absent artist.

Beyond the works themselves, there is little concrete evidence about Corot's studio pictures. Though they are traditionally dated between 1865 and 1870, their order of execution is conjectural, and only one is dated. Whether they even constitute a series in the usual sense of the term is debatable since their chronology is uncertain and there is no clear progression.[32] Although scholars have proposed various explanations, we do not know why Corot depicted his studio or made multiple versions with slight variations. Confinement to his studio, due to poor health or inclement weather, is not a sufficient explanation, nor is his growing interest in figure painting and desire to extend his repertoire, though they likely played a role. The influence of Dutch painting is also often invoked, but Corot's seamless blending of art and music, realistic studio setting, pensive model and landscape painting has few, if any, historical precedents.[33] The studio pictures deviate from the standard iconography of the artist at work by subtly undercutting hierarchies of gender and the gaze and blurring the distinction between artist and model.

The contemplative women at the center of Corot's studio paintings are the most perplexing conundrum. Are the women ordinary models, rarefied muses or surrogates for the absent artist? Corot painted classical muses, such as Poetry and Tragedy, but they are iconographically distinct.[34] It is widely recognized that the studio pictures selectively record the appearance of Corot's studio.[35] More speculative is the extent to which they also function metaphorically. Were they intended to be multilayered allegories about painting, or music or both? Or are they psychological self-portraits of the artist?[36] The range of interpretations that the paintings have elicited reflects Corot's unconventional, open-ended approach to the studio theme. What enriches them and makes them modern is the way in which they envisage the studio as both concrete workspace and inner chamber of the artist's mind, thematizing the dualities of the creative process. Besides signifying his attachment to his studio, the paintings are a projection of the artist that elucidates his creative process and propensity for reprising and reworking compositions and making variants.

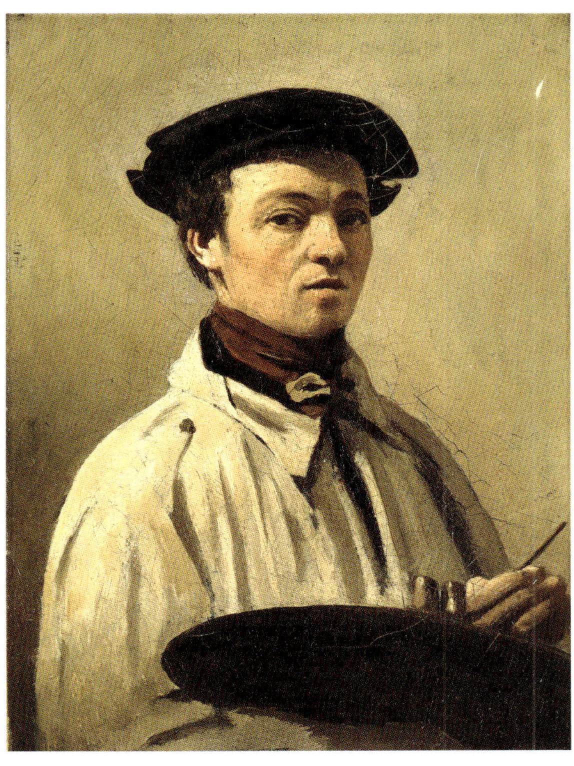

26. Jean-Baptiste-Camille Corot, *Self-Portrait*, c.1835–40, oil on canvas, 33 × 25 cm, Uffizi Gallery, Florence.

COROT'S STUDIO: THEME AND VARIATIONS

A young woman meditates in front of an easel, displaying a framed or unframed landscape, with pictures and studio paraphernalia behind her. She usually holds or plays a mandolin, invoking music, a leitmotiv in Corot's late figure studies. Viewed from different vantage points or angles, these paintings are microcosms of Corot's studio. The majority depict the back wall and the stove, seen from the entrance; others depict the small, adjoining cabinet. Showcasing landscapes from different periods, the paintings highlight the intertextuality of the picture within the picture, underscoring the studio's archival function as a retrospective repository of Corot's oeuvre; however, they are not strictly documentary. The paucity of paintings and artistic liberties, such as omitting the stovepipes or rearranging objects, indicate that the pictures are subjective reinventions. None were exhibited publicly during Corot's lifetime. Only the Washington canvas (fig.27), which Corot displayed in the sitting room, remained in his possession, testifying to the importance he attached to it.[37] The earliest mention of the studio pictures is by Dumesnil, who describes, a '*Woman in an Interior* . . . dressed in a red blouse and a yellow skirt; at her left is a tapestry chair that was in the studio' (fig.31). Dumesnil also praised the color and the harmonious effect.[38]

The six studio paintings that Robaut grouped in his catalogue constitute a distinctive subset (figs 27–32). Researching them, I came to realize that the studio permeated Corot's work more extensively than has been recognized in the literature. Beyond these six examples, the studio corpus should be expanded to include the recently discovered Karlsruhe painting (not illustrated),

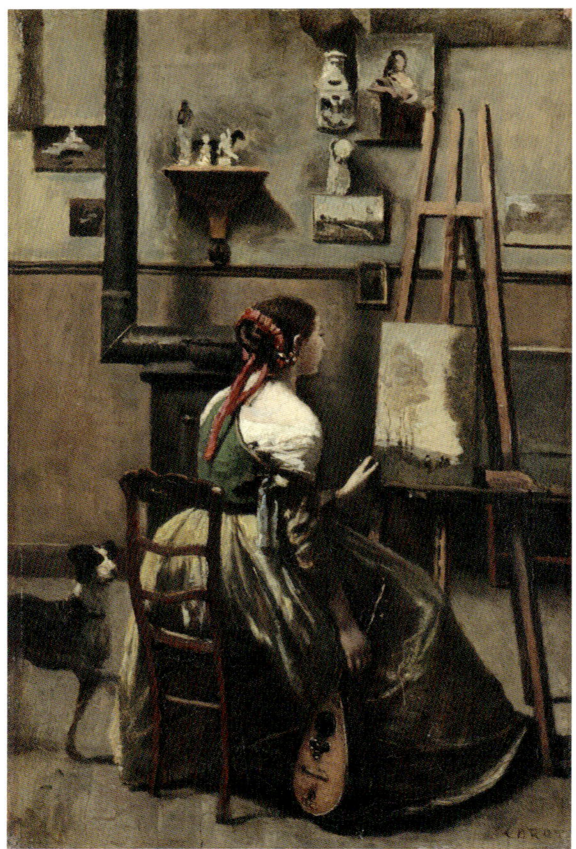

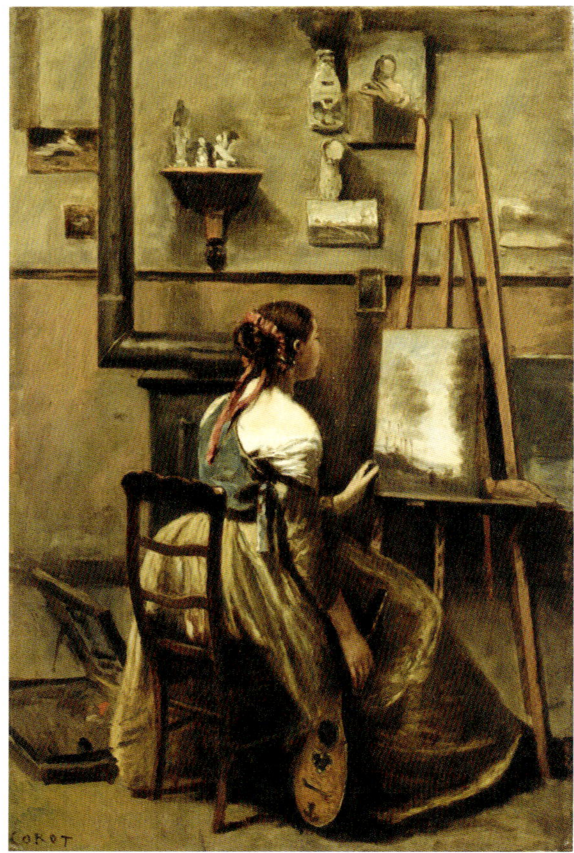

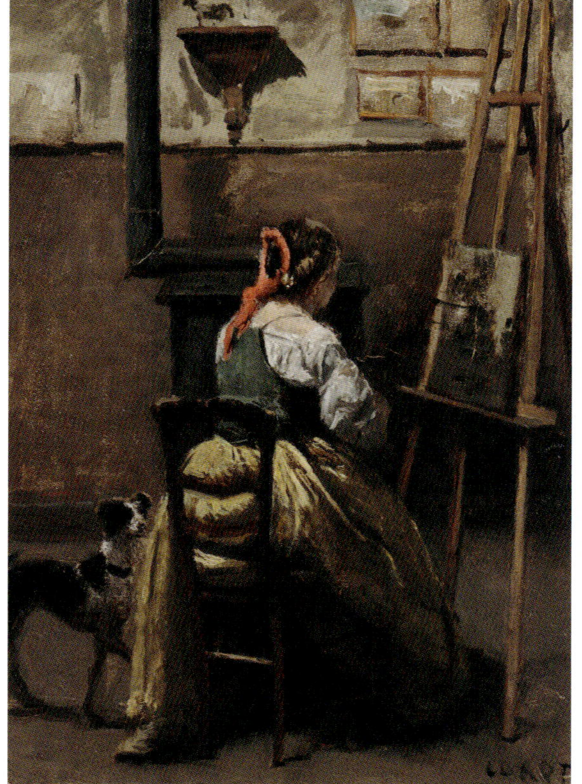

27. (top left) Jean-Baptiste-Camille Corot, *Corot's Studio*, c.1868, oil on wood, 61.8 × 40 cm, National Gallery of Art, Washington, DC.

28. (top right) Jean-Baptiste-Camille Corot, *Corot's Studio*, c.1865–8, oil on canvas, 63 × 42 cm, Musée du Louvre, Paris.

29 (left) Jean-Baptiste-Camille Corot, *Corot's Studio*, 1865–8, oil on wood panel, 40.6 × 33 cm, The Baltimore Museum of Art, Baltimore, MD.

Woman Reading in the Studio (fig.33), *Young Woman Playing a Mandolin in the Studio* (fig.34), *Young Girl Holding a Palette* (fig.36) and *Lady in Blue* (fig.37).[39] Surveying this expanded corpus of more than a dozen paintings, mostly executed *c.*1865–70, we can better comprehend the expressive range and inventiveness of Corot's studio variations and reassess their significance within his oeuvre.

Though similar in theme, the studio pictures fall into two distinct subgroups. The first group comprises the smaller, sketchier Baltimore and Karlsruhe paintings and the larger versions in Washington, DC and at the Louvre. The same model, seen from behind in lost profile, wearing an Italian peasant costume, gazes at an unframed landscape on the easel. In the Louvre and Washington versions (figs 27, 28), she grasps a mandolin in her right hand and touches the painting with her left, invoking the senses of sight, touch and hearing. The Baltimore painting (fig.29) is considered a study for the Washington and Louvre versions, which are virtually identical, except that a paint box has replaced the whippet (fig.28). It is unclear whether the Karlsruhe or Baltimore variant initiated the series since neither can be precisely dated.[40]

These four closely related works raise intriguing questions about duplication and replication, the rationale for Corot's repetition and effects of scale. The Baltimore and Karlsruhe versions are approximately half-scale; the model looks stockier and less refined than in the more polished Washington and Louvre versions. In the latter versions, Corot used a more vertical format that shows more of the studio but keeps the model's relationship to the stove and back wall the same. The Baltimore and Karlsruhe paintings depict a smaller, sketchier landscape on the easel, rather than the larger, classical landscape in the Washington and Louvre *Studios*.[41] In addition, they are are freehand variants, with subtle differences, while the Washington and Louvre paintings are exact replicas, except for the paint box. Corot kept the Washington *Studio* and could have copied it, but the exactitude of replication suggests that he used tracing to transfer the composition. Although neither is dated, Corot presumably painted the Louvre *Studio* after the Washington one that he owned.

In the Washington and Louvre *Studios*, some of the paintings on the back wall can be identified, including *Blonde Gascon* (*c.*1850) at the upper right, a favorite of Corot's.[42] The paintings, which include landscapes from different periods and a figure study, constitute a mini-retrospective, documenting Corot's career. The addition of the portable paint box in the Louvre version transforms the dynamics, placing the model between the landscape on the easel and plein-air painting accoutrements. There is no obvious rationale for the whippet that enlivens the Baltimore and Washington versions. The Washington *Studio* is painted on an elaborately pieced together panel, constructed with scarf joints. Though it is unclear why Corot used this unconventional support, it highlights the hands-on materiality of painting that his studio embodied.

The second, less homogeneous group of studio pictures differs in terms of viewpoint and the costume and attitude of the model. Portrayed in three-quarter profile, the woman's gaze rotates away from the landscape on the easel toward the spectator (figs 30–32). Exceptionally, in *Young Woman Playing a Mandolin* (fig.34), the model is flipped around and viewed almost frontally, and the painting on the easel is placed diagonally, making it visible only to her. There is a shadowy doorway behind her; at the left, a framed landscape is obscured by the easel.[43] The awkward overlapping of the painting on the easel (seen from the back) and the painting on the wall behind visually conflates and blocks them from view, creating a mise en abyme in which the paintings are illegible. This is the only painting in which the woman at the easel plays the mandolin, underscoring the correspondence between touch and sight, music and painting, and embodying all of them. Her Italianate costume is accented with a red toque, a head covering traditionally associated with painters, including Corot. Turned toward the spectator rather than facing away, her attitude reverses that of the models in the Baltimore and Karlsruhe paintings, whose ambivalent pose suggests they could be playing an invisible mandolin.

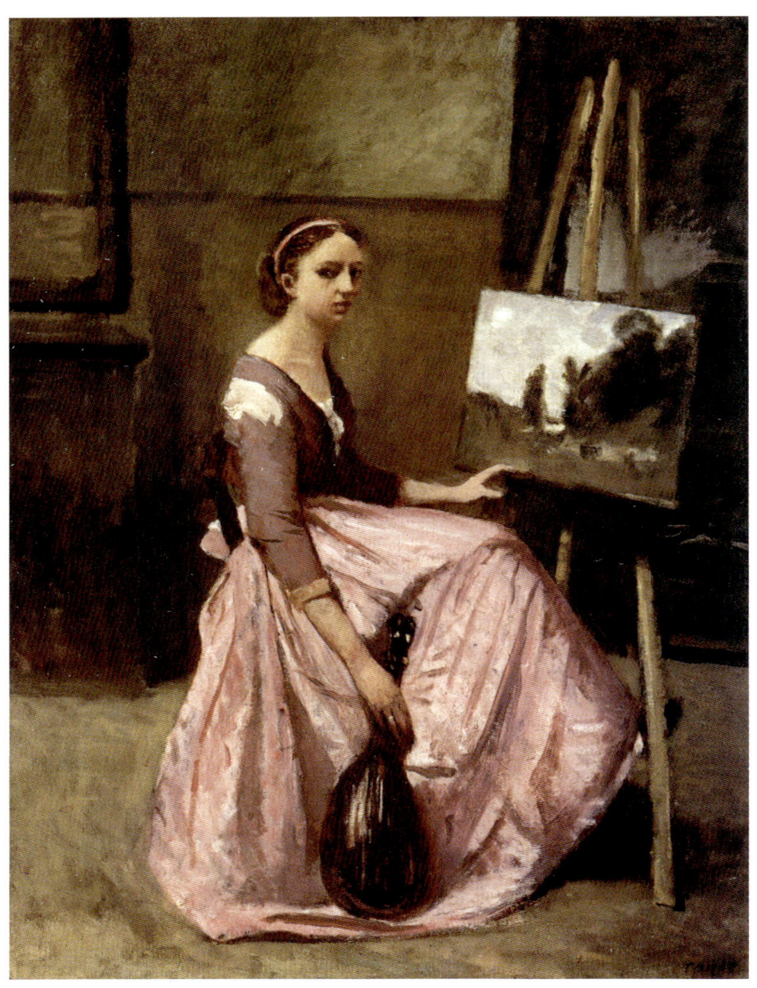

30. (left) Jean-Baptiste-Camille Corot, *Corot's Studio*, c.1865–6, oil on canvas, 64 × 48.4 cm, private collection.

31. (below left) Jean-Baptiste-Camille Corot, *Corot's Studio*, c.1865–6, oil on canvas, 56 × 46 cm, Musée d'Orsay, Paris.

32. (below right) Jean-Baptiste-Camille Corot, *Corot's Studio*, c.1868–70, oil on canvas, 62.9 × 48 cm, Musée des Beaux-Arts, Lyon.

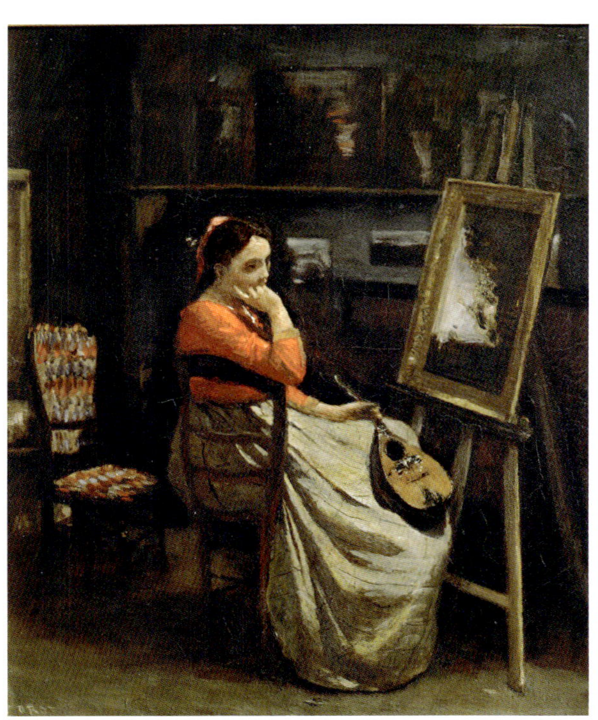

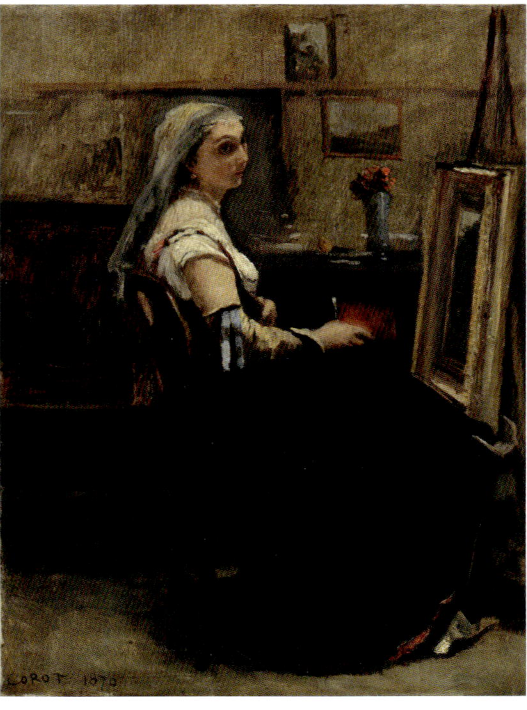

Her posture and gestures reappear in *Young Girl Holding a Palette*, except that she holds paintbrushes.

Corot's Studio (fig.30) is emblematic of the difficulties in establishing the sequence of the studio pictures and the way the series doubles back on itself. Scholars have placed it at the beginning and the end of the series, with dates ranging from *c.*1860 to 1872.[44] The young woman grasps a mandolin in her right hand and touches the landscape with her left hand, as in the Washington and Louvre *Studios*, but looks away from the easel toward the spectator. The landscape on the easel, identified as *Plain on the Bank of a River* (R1762), is illuminated and unusually detailed. In his draft catalogue entry, Robaut described the simple background, with two blank canvases and a brushy area of color behind the easel, which is reminiscent of a landscape, echoing the painting on the easel. He especially admired the vivid effect of the model's pink skirt, noting, 'Although this painting is not fully finished, it creates a sensation'.[45]

The painting also exemplifies the convoluted, retrospective genesis of the studio pictures. Noting the significance of memory and variations, Germain Bazin observed that it reprises in reverse an early Italian study, *Seated Woman Holding a Mandolin* (R94).[46] During the 1860s, Corot sketched meditative women holding or playing the mandolin from different angles in varied poses that echo the attitudes in the studio paintings. Drawing on his prodigious pictorial memory, he often reprised and subtly reworked earlier studies. The studio pictures can best be understood as thematic variations in which Corot, like a virtuoso musician, experimented with different poses and gestures. Moreau-Nélaton observed that Corot, like the musicians whom he adored, improvised on the canvas, creating works that were both real and imaginary.[47] Across rapid, theatrical sketches and more worked up figure studies, Corot explored a range of emotional states, notably reverie and melancholy, that amplified the expressive gamut of the studio series.

Rather than following a linear trajectory, the studio pictures oscillate and intermingle; like variations on a musical theme, changing incrementally while retaining the main melody line. This musical analogy is apt since most of the paintings feature a mandolin, and Corot's lifelong love of music is well-established.[48] Robaut linked Corot's painted variations to his musicality, observing that he sang musical themes from memory after concerts. Underscoring the reciprocity of music and painting, Robaut noted, 'He analyzed a symphony as a picture'.[49] For Corot, music was an iconographic source, as well as a compositional model and expressive ideal, especially in his late works. The studio pictures, which straddle generic categories, explore correspondences between art and music, color and tone, sight and touch on multiple levels.[50]

Two of Corot's studio pictures depict the small cabinet adjoining the main studio. In the Musée d'Orsay *Studio* (fig.31), the model poses pensively, with a mandolin across her lap and her cheek resting on her right hand in the traditional attitude of melancholy. X-radiographs show that Corot adjusted the position of her right arm and painted over an earlier composition.[51] The focus on reverie suggests the act of listening, linking the contemplation of a painting to listening to music.[52] The landscape on the easel, which recalls *Orpheus Saluting the Dawn*, likewise alludes to music; the other paintings are not identifiable.[53] Although the Lyon *Studio* (fig.32) depicts the same corner of the cabinet, the dominant tonalities and ambience differ – the setting, though more luminous, is sparer and includes a vase of flowers. The landscape on the easel, viewed obliquely, is only partially visible; none of the paintings on the back wall are identifiable. Corot focuses on the pensive model, depicted in three-quarter profile, who gazes past the easel, absently grasping an open book (rather than a mandolin) in her right hand. Critics have been struck by the air of reverie and melancholy permeating the Lyon painting, which was completed during the Franco-Prussian War when Corot took refuge in his studio.[54] Robaut hailed it as one of Corot's most beautiful figures that equaled Velázquez in the richness of tones in a limited gamut.[55]

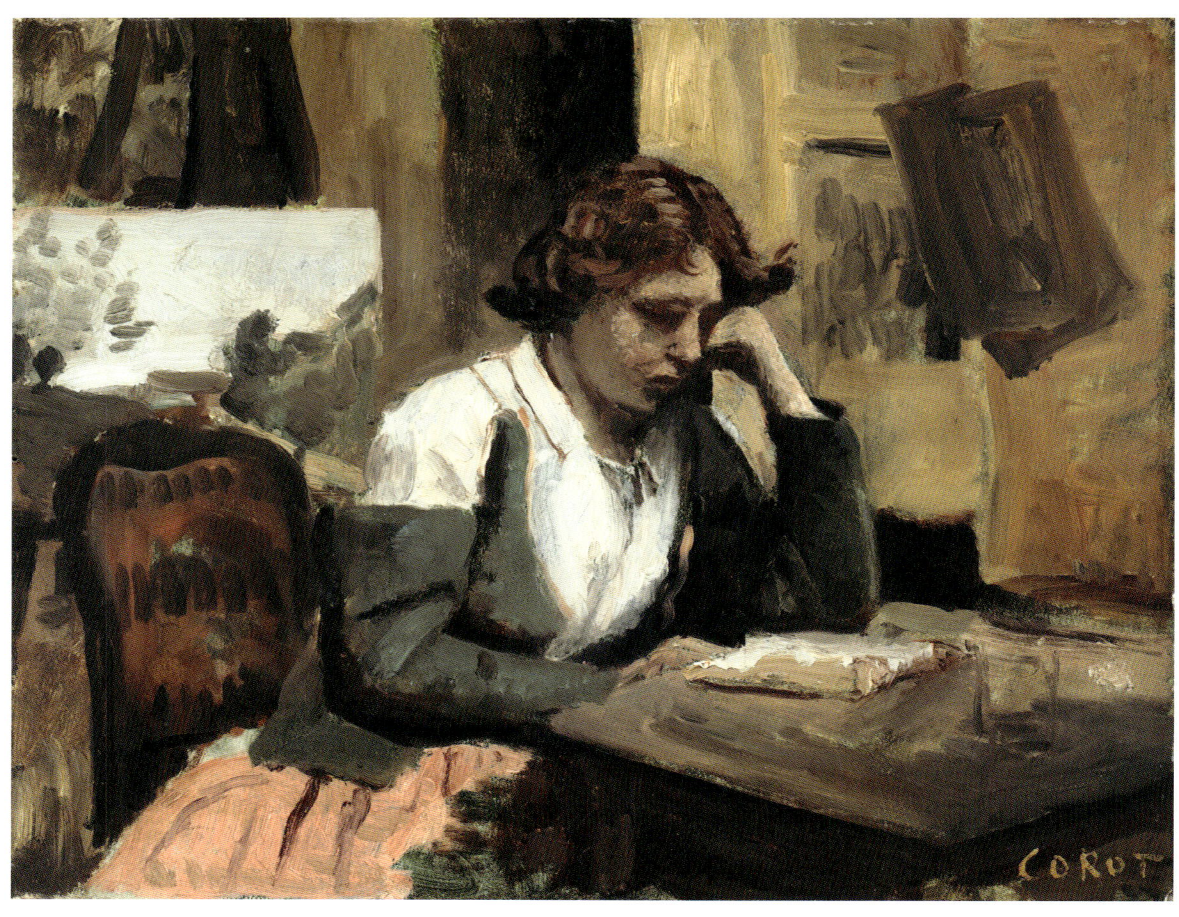

33. Jean-Baptiste-Camille Corot, *Woman Reading in the Studio*, c.1868, oil on paperboard on wood, 32.5 × 41.3 cm, National Gallery of Art, Washington, DC.

The Lyon *Studio* echoes other depictions of readers, including *Girl Reading* (c.1845–50, R393) and *Woman Reading in the Studio* (fig.33). Here, the pensive model, her cheek resting on her left hand, is seated at a table in the same tapestry-covered chair that appears in the Musée d'Orsay *Studio*; a landscape is visible behind her. Although the landscape format, rough impasto and unusual support (paperboard mounted on a mahogany panel) differentiate it from Corot's other studio pictures, *Woman Reading in the Studio* should nevertheless be included in the studio corpus, as Lorenz Eitner has proposed.[56] Though dressed in an Italian peasant costume, the young woman is not posing and seems oblivious to her surroundings. Depicted in a close-up, three-quarter view, she is absorbed in the book in front of her. Unlike the other models who dreamily contemplate the painting before them, she turns her back on the landscape displayed on the easel behind her. In his draft catalogue entry, Robaut called the painting an *Étude* (Study) and noted that Corot had reproduced the landscape in the left corner precisely as it appeared on the studio wall.[57] The rigorous composition and loose, spontaneous paint application inject a modern sensibility.

Corot's Studio, the title that most of the studio pictures are known by today, is both straightforward and elusive. Highlighting their self-referentiality, it also connotes their seriality by emphasizing their collective identity as thematic variations. In the 1905 catalogue, this common title is followed by descriptive qualifiers. Robaut identified the Louvre version as a variant of the Washington painting and the Baltimore painting as a variant of the other two.[58] In his draft notices, the titles were less consistent. The most striking instance is the Baltimore painting, which he titled *Femme peintre au chevalet* (*Woman Painter at Her Easel*), suggesting this is how it was referred to in Corot's circle, and positing an alternative reading of the young woman. The description reads: 'One of those women painters or amateurs seated before an easel, seen from behind'.[59] In the Baltimore painting, the model could be either painting or playing the mandolin since her hands are hidden. Robaut's draft title raises the issue of female agency and connects the Baltimore *Studio* to *Young Girl Holding a Palette*, which unequivocally depicts a female painter.

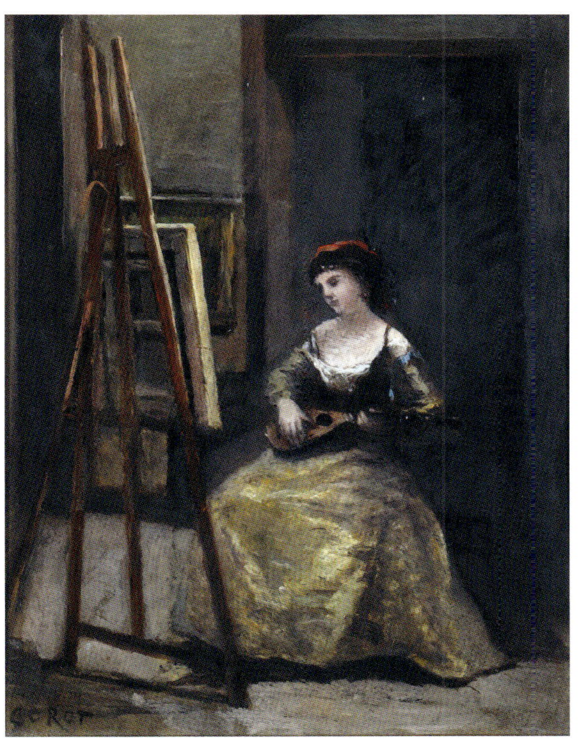

34. Jean-Baptiste-Camille Corot, *Young Woman Playing a Mandolin in the Studio*, c.1870, oil on canvas, 44 × 34.3 cm, private collection.

Corot's two cryptic depictions of women painters elucidate the studio pictures and their protagonists. *Painter at Her Easel* (fig.35), a carefully finished pencil and gouache drawing, portrays an unidentified female copyist at the Louvre, perched on a high stool, working at her easel. Modestly dressed in a white ruffled dress and triangular shawl, she is circumspectly viewed from the rear. Face obscured, she is absorbed in the act of painting. Though seated on a stool rather than a chair, the female painter, like the model in the Baltimore *Studio*, is seen from behind in lost profile, but she holds a mahlstick and wields a paintbrush. The drawing is from a sketchbook of figure studies and copies dating to the 1820s, linking this unknown female artist to Corot's formative years when he made copies at the Louvre.[60]

The close-up, half-length *Young Girl Holding a Palette* (*c*.1860–65, fig.36) could be construed as an allegory of painting.[61] On closer inspection, the portrait-like specificity and directness and intensity of her gaze ground her in actuality rather than allegory. Viewed almost frontally, she sits at the easel, holding palette and brushes, in a pose often found in self-portraits made using a mirror. The elegantly dressed young artist, adorned with a necklace and pearl earrings, is coiffed with a red toque. In the Uffizi *Self-Portrait* and mid-century photographs, Corot is similarly posed, holding his palette and brushes, and wearing a dark toque. *Painter at Her Easel* and *Young Girl Holding a Palette* function as counterweights, challenging traditional gender hierarchies and the demarcation between artist and model, and adding another layer of referentiality to the studio pictures. Complementing Robaut's intriguing identification of the Baltimore picture as a female painter, *Painter at Her Easel* and *Young Girl Holding a Palette* suggest an alternative studio scenario in which artist and model are fluid categories that mirror each other.

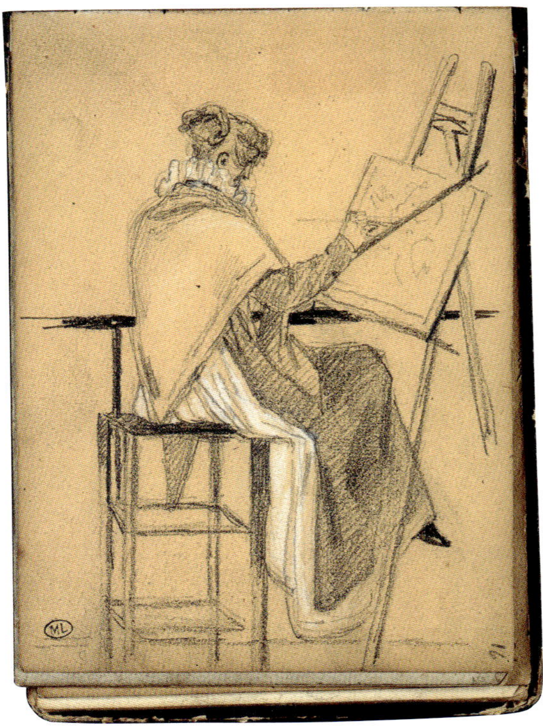

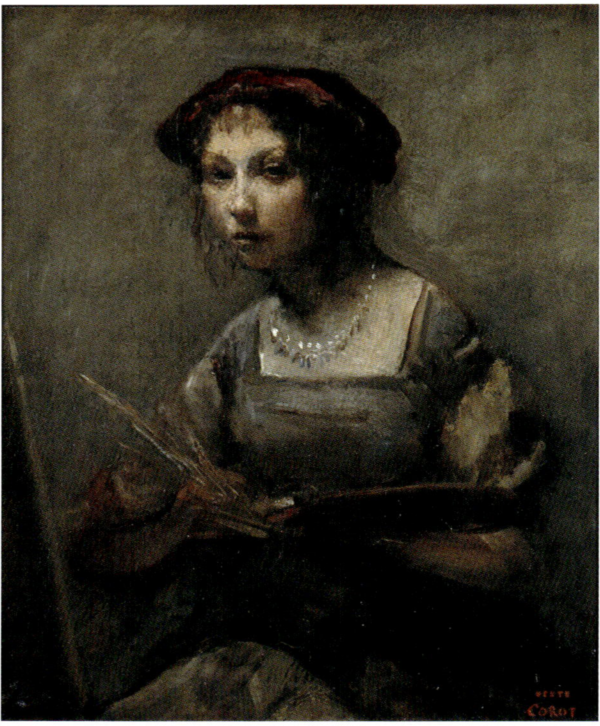

35. (left) Jean-Baptiste-Camille Corot, *Painter at Her Easel*, c.1823–5, charcoal on beige paper, unknown dimensions, Musée du Louvre, Paris.

36. (right) Jean-Baptiste-Camille Corot, *Young Girl Holding a Palette*, c.1860–65, oil on canvas, 32.5 × 27 cm, Nationalmuseum, Stockholm.

The Lady in Blue (1874, fig.37), the coda to the studio series, signals a new direction. The fashionably dressed young woman, who brandishes a fan, stands rather than sits, and leans against a cushion, resting on books or albums, in Corot's studio. Although the cushion was probably placed on a table, the silhouette suggests a piano, invoking music and blurring the distinction between drawing room and studio.[62] X-radiographs reveal that Corot modified the young woman's meditative pose, especially the position of her hand, painted over the gloves she originally wore and adjusted the placement of the pictures on the back wall.[63] Her fashionable Second Empire dress departs from the Italian costumes that he generally favored. An afternoon dress, it would normally have had long sleeves; the sleeveless bodice here is anomalous. The model for *Lady in Blue*, though pensive, is clearly contemporary and dominates the composition, relegating the studio to the background.[64] The stove was painted out; only the two small landscapes on the wall behind the model evoke the studio and the absent artist. The brilliant color of her fan provides a sort of punctum, like the paint box in the Louvre *Studio*. Both a summation and a new departure, *Lady in Blue* points forward to Degas and beyond.

MEMORIALIZING COROT'S STUDIO

As Corot aged, his associates became preoccupied with documenting his oeuvre, securing his artistic legacy and preserving his memory. His close ties with the Arras School, whose members congregated in Dutilleux's studio, inaugurated a cycle of depictions of Corot working in the studio, which were probably an impetus for the studio pictures. Adalbert Cuvelier's carefully staged still-life photograph (1852, fig.38) powerfully evokes Corot's influence and virtual presence in Dutilleux's studio, from his landscape, *Soir Classique*, painted in Arras in 1851, prominently displayed on the easel, to his painter's smock suspended from it. A photograph at lower left and a male *académie* at upper right testify to the range of art emanating from the studio. Both grounded in actuality and metaphorical, Cuvelier's photograph thematizes the camaraderie and collaborative ethos of Dutilleux's (and Corot's) studio by highlighting emulation and the parity of painting and photography and juxtaposing the different modes of reproduction practiced by Dutilleux and his circle.[65] In 1853, Cuvelier introduced Corot to the *cliché-verre* technique, a hybrid process that combined photography and etching, which he enthusiastically took up.[66]

Dutilleux ran a printing establishment in Arras. After he met Corot in 1847, they became lifelong friends. From 1851 to 1860, Corot visited annually, usually in the spring. In 1860, Dutilleux moved to Paris to be closer to Corot, who was deeply affected by his death. Corot also forged close ties with Dutilleux's artist sons-in-law: Charles Desavary, a painter, lithographer and photographer who took over the print shop, and Alfred Robaut, an experienced archivist who was ideally suited for documenting Corot's life and art. In 1871, Robaut moved to Paris to prepare his catalogue of Corot's oeuvre. He frequented Corot's studio and was authorized to photograph and make sketches of his works.[67] Desavary worked alongside Corot, copied his paintings and photographed hundreds of them for Robaut's catalogue.[68]

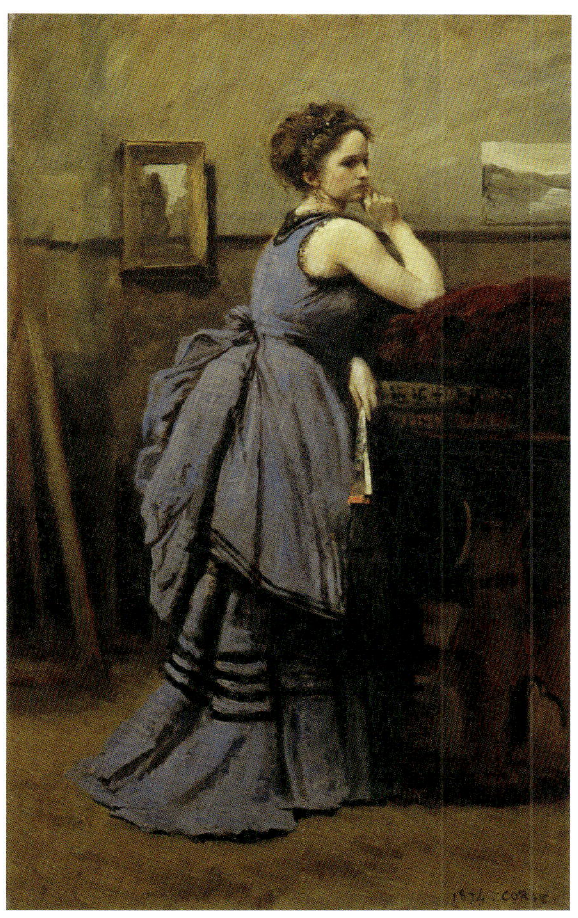

37. Jean-Baptiste-Camille Corot, *The Lady in Blue*, 1874, oil on canvas, 80 × 50.5 cm, Musée du Louvre, Paris.

Beginning in the 1850s, Robaut and Desavary depicted Corot painting in Dutilleux's studio, the nucleus of the Arras School – an informal group of artists, influenced by Corot – who practiced plein-air painting and worked communally in the studio, which, like Corot's, was filled with paintings and sculpture.[69] In 1856, Robaut discreetly portrayed Corot from the rear, working in Dutilleux's studio, initiating the series of studio depictions (fig.39).[70] Wearing a blue smock,

Corot sits at the easel and sketches, with his paint box beside him and a wide-brimmed hat at his feet. Only the top corner of the landscape that he is painting is visible; the pictures on the wall are not identifiable. A draped mannequin and a partially nude female statuette, both viewed from the rear, seemingly turn their backs. Although the workspace is more cluttered and Corot is shown from behind, the close-up format and studio setting anticipate Corot's studio pictures.

In April 1871, Corot fled north to escape the Commune. Desavary made three paintings of Corot working in Dutilleux's studio. *Corot Painting* depicts the artist seated at the easel, painting *Shepherds of Arcadia* (1871–2), which Desavary owned.[71] Corot is seen from behind in a close-up, three-quarter view; he faces left – the reverse of the model's pose in the Washington and Louvre *Studios*. Bareheaded and wearing a white smock, his open paint box beside him, he smokes his beloved pipe while he works. As in Robaut's depiction, Corot is a monumental, almost anonymous presence; his face averted, he is absorbed in the act of painting. In early April, Desavary painted two larger canvases of Corot in profile, seated at the easel in Dutilleux's studio, his paint box beside him, and a stuffed dove at his feet.[72] His straw hat is suspended above the easel; his pipe rests on a nearby chair. Wearing a blue smock and striped cap, Corot focuses intently on the canvas that he is painting, *Shepherds of Arcadia*, which is depicted obliquely. Dutilleux's replica of *Bathers of Bellinzona*, made under Corot's tutelage, is behind him, underscoring the collaborative ethos evidenced by the circulation and replication of Corot's canvases. *Ville-d'Avray, Road Leading to a Villa* (1858), a wedding gift to Desavary which he copied, hangs above Corot's head.

Robaut studied Corot's studio *in situ* and gathered anecdotes about him, for example, his 1851 visit to Courbet's studio in Saintes, during which the Realist master remarked, 'The only real painters today are you and me'.[73] The *pièce de résistance* is Robaut's elegiac description of the studio that conveys verbally the exacting detail of his drawings. He evokes Corot at the end of his life, working in his studio, wearing his habitual striped cotton bonnet, blue smock and clogs, and the 'marvels of this sanctuary' – Corot's studies – spanning decades, from his first trip to Rome to a drawing used for a painting in 1874:[74]

> Here is the studio . . . of the Great Corot . . . where this goodly man spent six hours or more every day . . . where we will no longer see him or hear his beloved voice! . . . but in our thoughts, in our hearts, they will live on . . . Even when this sanctuary, still filled with his precious works, is denuded . . . when there will not remain a single picture . . . when all the portfolios stuffed with drawings and sketchbooks have disappeared . . . we will re-experience in our minds this generous and dear friend, this 'bon Papa Corot'![75]

No one was more instrumental than Robaut in shaping Corot's legacy and fostering the studio cult. Immediately after his death on 22 February 1875, Robaut began to produce articles commemorating Corot and his studio. On 27 February, *Le Monde illustré* published engravings of *Corot in His Painting Costume* after Desavary (top) and of *Corot's Studio, rue Paradis-Poissonnière* after Robaut (bottom) (fig.40), together with a description of his studio.[76] Robaut's print synthesizes views of the main studio and annex, providing a complete interior cross-section that includes the high windows. The text conjures Corot's studio as experienced and remembered; Robaut describes where Corot set up his easel and how he worked, moving from one easel to another, the painting table with his indispensable tools and the stream of visitors he benevolently received. The image of Corot that accompanies Robaut's text is a composite based on the lost version of Desavary's 1871 painting. In this meta-image, time and location blur – images and recollections of the master at work in his studio (and Dutilleux's) metamorphose into a collective memorial commemorating Corot in the studio, surrounded by the works of a lifetime.

On 6 March 1875, *L'Illustration* published a full-page composite image of Corot dressed in his painting

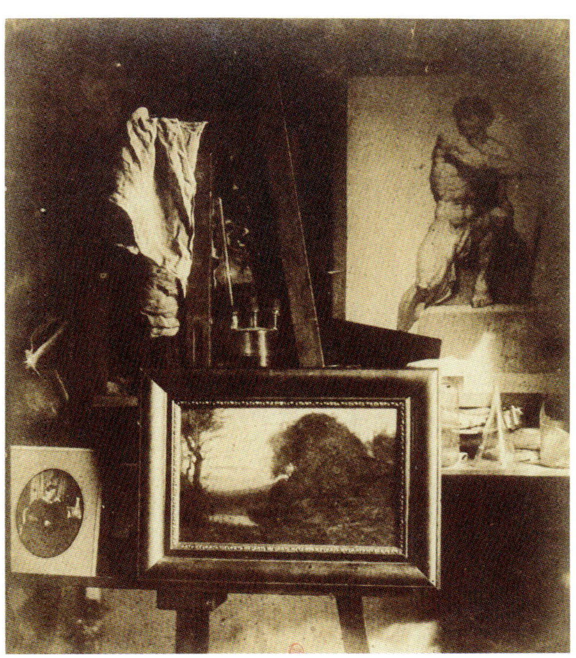

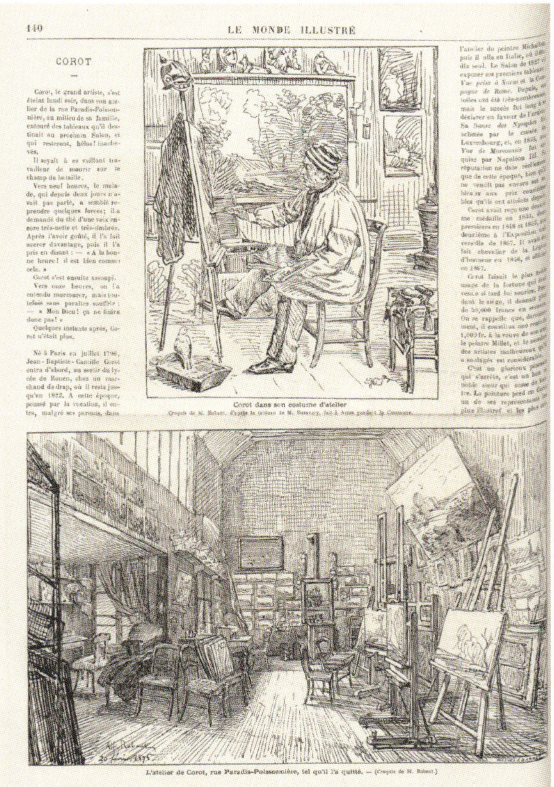

140 LE MONDE ILLUSTRÉ

COROT

—

Corot, le grand artiste, s'est éteint lundi soir, dans son atelier de la rue Paradis-Poissonnière, au milieu de sa famille, entouré des tableaux qu'il destinait au prochain Salon, et qui resteront, hélas! inachevés.

Il seyait à ce vaillant travailleur de mourir sur le champ de bataille.

Vers neuf heures, le malade, qui depuis deux jours n'avait pas parlé, a semblé reprendre quelques forces; il a demandé du thé d'une voix encore très-nette et très-timbrée. Après l'avoir goûté, il l'a fait sucrer davantage, puis il l'a pris en disant : — « A la bonne heure! il est bien comme cela. »

Corot s'est ensuite assoupi.

Vers onze heures, on l'a entendu murmurer, mais toutefois sans paraître souffrir : — « Mon Dieu! ça ne finira donc pas! »

Quelques instants après, Corot n'était plus.

Né à Paris en juillet 1796, Jean-Baptiste-Camille Corot entra d'abord, au sortir du lycée de Rouen, chez un marchand de drap, où il resta jusqu'en 1822. A cette époque, poussé par la vocation, il entra, malgré ses parents, dans

Corot dans son costume d'atelier

L'atelier de Corot, rue Paradis-Poissonnière, tel qu'il l'a quitté. — (Croquis de M. Robaut.)

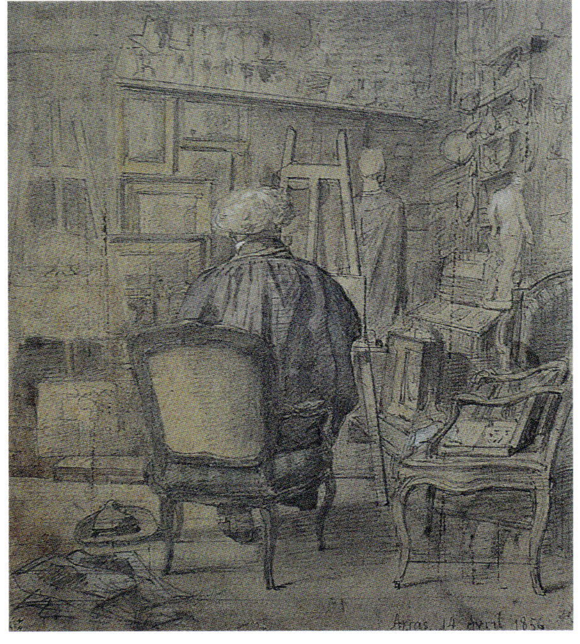

38. (top left) Adalbert Cuvelier, *Corot's Soir Classique in Constantin Dutilleux's Studio*, 1852, photograph, 17 × 14.3 cm, Bibliothèque nationale de France, Paris.

40. (top right) Alfred Robaut, *Corot in His Painting Costume* (top), *Corot's Studio, Rue Paradis-Poissonnière* (bottom), in *Le Monde illustré*, 27 February 1875, p.140, Bibliothèque nationale de France, Paris.

39. (left) Alfred Robaut, *Corot in Constantin Dutilleux's Studio*, 1856, black chalk and watercolor on paper, 27 × 22.7 cm, Musée des Beaux-Arts, Arras.

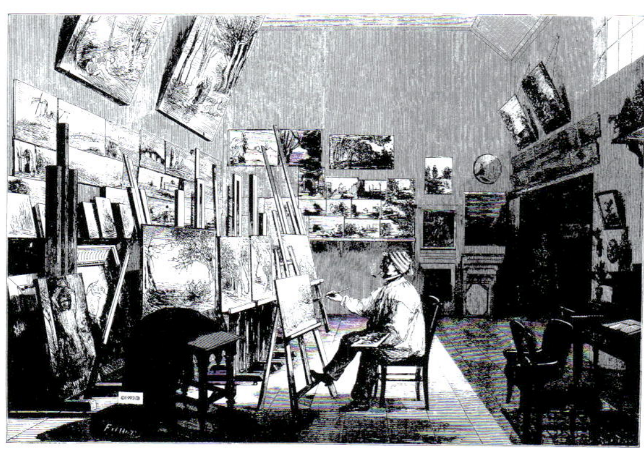

41. Michel Charles Fichot (after Alfred Robaut), *L'Atelier de Corot*, in *L'Illustration*, no.1671, 6 March 1875, p.157, Bibliothèque nationale de France, Paris.

costume, seated at the easel in the Paradis-Poissonnière studio (fig.41). Engraved by Michel Charles Fichot, the print amalgamates Bénédict Masson's study and Robaut's reworked drawing of Corot's empty studio, encapsulating appropriation, collaboration and the studio cult.[77] Robaut shifted the viewpoint, amplified the number of paintings and inserted Corot's housekeeper, Adèle, bringing his daily soup. The studio overflows with paintings, including *St Sebastian* and *Venus Playing with Cupid* at the left, *St Sebastian in a Landscape* and *Dante and Virgil* at the top and countless landscape studies, creating a museum without walls. Corot, seated at his easel painting a landscape, is the fulcrum, echoing Courbet's *Painter's Studio*. With this composite image, Robaut enshrined Corot's studio as an archive and a *lieu de mémoire*.[78]

Robaut pursued his multipronged campaign to secure Corot's posthumous legacy through the catalogue that he was compiling and articles in *La Galerie contemporaine*, *Journal des arts* and *L'Art français*. In an undated drawing, he invented a more elaborate studio scenario that shows Corot painting at the easel and conversing with painter Demeur-Charton.[79] Wearing a smock, Corot is bareheaded and pipeless. Here Robaut stands behind Corot, holding up the canvas of an amateur, seeking the master's opinion. Robaut has literally inserted himself into the studio, creating a didactic, staged tableau that highlights his own documentary role and Corot's benevolence and charity. A print after the drawing was shown at an exhibition benefitting the *crèche* (nursery) of the 19th arrondissement.[80]

Robaut's drawings of the empty studio, in which Corot's presence is almost palpable, are more resonant than his staged scenarios. His meticulous notes and drawings and the recollections and depictions of contemporaries attest to the cult surrounding Corot's studio. Encapsulating his art, it was a living museum, retrospective gallery and pilgrimage site for artists, who sometimes took one of Corot's studies as a talisman. Corot's studio provides an illuminating entry point and frame for assessing the complex matrix of aesthetic, socio-cultural and metaphorical meanings associated with the artist's studio at mid-century, and underscores its significance as a multilayered site of artistic and social exchange and *lieu de mémoire*.

CODA: DECODING COROT'S IMAGE

Corot was depicted in numerous paintings, drawings and photographs, mostly during the final decades of his career.[81] The majority are photographs, taken by more than 15 different photographers, which were reproduced and circulated. Examining these images, several patterns can be discerned. Many originated from artists close to Corot, especially members of the Arras School, attesting to the collaborative dimension of his practice and the synchrony of painting and photography in Dutilleux's studio.[82] There are two contrasting images of Corot: the austere, soberly dressed bourgeois in a dark suit and stiff collar of formal portraits and official photographs and the jovial, pipe-smoking comrade in idiosyncratic painting garb. The more informal image evoked by Silvestre and Dumesnil, which humanized and embellished the Corot legend, is foregrounded in the studio depictions and impromptu images like

Robaut's sketch of Corot standing on a table while painting a decorative panel (1873).[83]

There are also distinctions according to medium. Although Corot was photographed painting outdoors, no photographs of him in his Paradis-Poissonnière studio survive.[84] Henri Lavaud made two photographic portraits of Corot as a painter (*c.*1865–70).[85] One depicts him half-length, almost frontally, with palette and brushes, and wearing a toque, as in the Uffizi *Self-Portrait.* More nattily dressed than in other studio depictions, he sports a patterned cravat and vest under his smock. The neutral background and lack of easel suggest that it was taken in the photographer's studio. A variant depicts Corot in the same outfit, with palette and brushes, but seated in three-quarter view, in front of a landscape painting. Despite the half-length format, it recalls Corot's studio pictures and *Young Girl Holding a Palette.* Victor Laisné's photograph (*c.*1852–3) portrays Corot elegantly dressed in a dark suit and high cravat, in standard three-quarter view. Most photographs and painted portraits, including Léon Belly's sober, half-length (1858) and Louis-Alexandre Bouché's bust-length portrait (*c.*1860), follow this template.

In 1874, Bénédict Masson painted two portraits of Corot in his Paris studio. His imposing life-size portrait breaks the mold.[86] Depicted frontally, the aged artist sits in an ornately carved chair and rests his hands on his knees, echoing Ingres's iconic *Monsieur Bertin* (1832). Painted from life, he is impeccably dressed in a black suit and black cravat; the Legion of Honor glows on his lapel. The palette and brushes at the left and the picture visible behind him indicate the studio setting. Though mentioned by Robaut, Masson's life-size portrait is not listed in the 1905 catalogue and nothing is known about the circumstances of its creation or early history. Masson also painted a small study of Corot from life, seated at the easel in his Paradis-Poissonnière studio, as the inscription and studies behind him confirm (fig.42).[87] He is dressed as a painter in a blue smock, clogs and a simple red head covering, rather than the striped bonnet depicted in Desavary's paintings and Bonaventure Laurens's profile drawing (*c.*1855). The

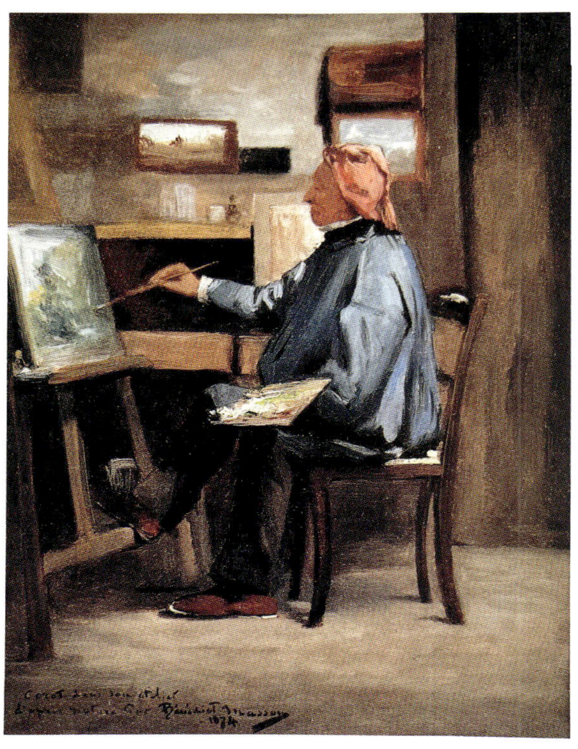

42. Bénédict Masson, *Corot in His Studio*, 1874, oil on canvas, 33 x 25.5 cm, private collection.

head covering is reminiscent of portraits of Dante, as is the severe classical profile, linking Corot with the immortal poet and the Italian *campagna* he discovered in the 1820s and never forgot. His pipe, which would have marred the classical aura, was banished. Masson's timeless image inspired Robaut's composite depiction of Corot painting in his studio – filled with his paintings – preserving it virtually in perpetuity as *musée imaginaire* and commemorative monument.

The next chapter considers how the studio evolved during the Impressionist era, from Daubigny's and Monet's boat studios, where the distance between artist and motif narrowed, to Bazille's *Studio on the Rue La Condamine,* which became a collaborative space for camaraderie and social exchange.

3

The Virtual Studio

Daubigny, Monet and Bazille

> We are taking, as you see, short day trips . . . above all wanting to make *pochades* along the way. You should see the great pandemonium of *pochades* being executed on board the *Botin*.[1]
>
> – Charles-François Daubigny, 1857

> My studio! But I have never *had* a studio, and personally, I don't understand why anyone would shut themselves up in a room.[2]
>
> – Claude Monet, 1880

This chapter examines the evolving functions and permutations of the Impressionist studio, which have been largely overlooked.[3] Rather than a fixed locale, the studio was becoming a malleable frame or set of conditions that was transportable and subject to mutation. Svetlana Alpers has argued that the development of landscape painting put pressure on the artist's studio and its relationship to the 'real' world outside, which intensified during the 19th century and redefined the parameters of the profession.[4] With plein-air painting, the studio moved outside, altering painting practices and perceptions of the artist.[5] From the 1840s, images of artists working outdoors proliferated, reflecting evolving artistic practices and technical innovations, such as standard-size, prepared canvases, portable easels and metal paint tubes. Associated with independence, rejection of academic conventions and shifting attitudes toward *fini* (finish), plein-air painting became a cornerstone of modern artistic identity.

At Argenteuil, Monet and his fellow Impressionists set up their easels side by side and painted pictures of one another. This collaborative approach underscored their camaraderie and shared aesthetic goals. In 1873, Pierre-Auguste Renoir portrayed Monet working outdoors at a lightweight folding easel in his garden, with his portable paint box and metal paint tubes on the grass by his feet.[6] In *Monet Painting in His Garden at Argenteuil* (fig.43), the artist stands confidently at the easel, holding his palette and brushes, absorbed in the motif he is painting. Highlighting his direct encounter with nature, self-sufficiency and intense concentration, Renoir portrays Monet as the quintessential Impressionist painter immersed in nature.[7] While Renoir painted his portrait, Monet, who disliked posing, was painting his garden from a slightly different viewpoint.[8] In *The Artist's Garden in Argenteuil* (1873), Monet edited out the surrounding houses to accentuate the idyllic natural setting and the dahlias.[9] During the summer of 1874, Manet worked beside

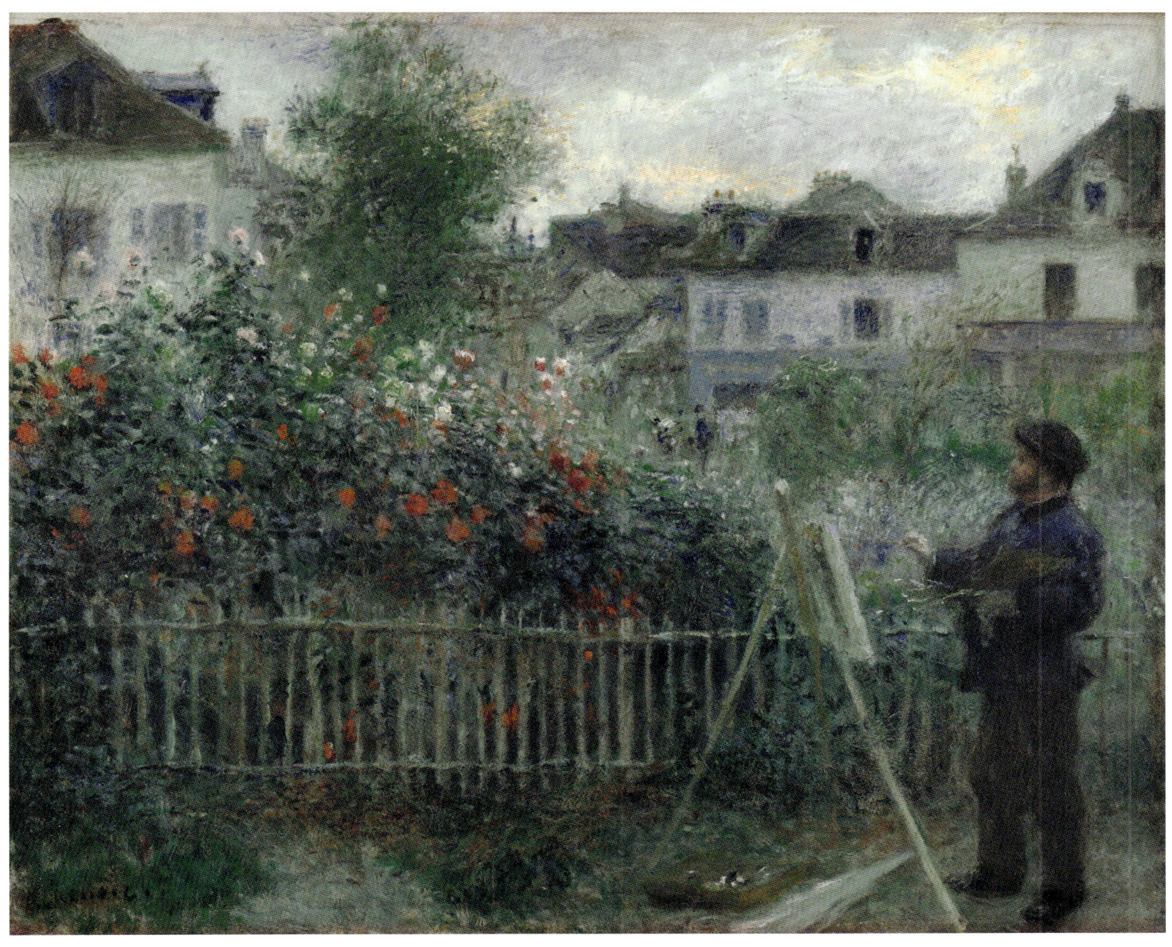

43. Pierre-Auguste Renoir, *Claude Monet Painting in His Garden at Argenteuil*, 1873, oil on canvas, 46.7 × 59.7 cm, Wadsworth Atheneum Museum of Art, Hartford, CT.

Monet at Argenteuil. While Manet was painting *Monet Family in Their Garden at Argenteuil*, Monet portrayed Manet working at his easel under a canopy of trees, creating an image that was in dialogue with Renoir's portrait of Monet painting. Renoir concurrently painted Monet's wife and son, further testifying to the appeal of communal plein-air painting and the collaborative nature of Impressionism. Monet's lifelong fascination with gardens would reach its apogee with his floating water lily garden at Giverny.

Although the Impressionists embraced painting outdoors directly from the motif, the myth of unmediated spontaneity and obsolescence of the studio that Monet propagated has been thoroughly debunked. In an 1880 interview with journalist Émile Taboureux, Monet, gesturing toward the Seine, exclaimed, 'This is my studio', and denied ever having had a conventional studio.[10] In reality, the studio remained essential to the painting practice of the Impressionists, including Monet, who maintained his Paris studio while living at

Argenteuil. Although he habitually worked outdoors, even during the Argenteuil years, he typically reworked his canvases over multiple working sessions and completed them in the studio.[11] As recent scholarship and a growing body of technical evidence have shown, Monet's technique was a complex, multilayered process that entailed much reworking.[12] After moving to Giverny in 1883, he had three indoor studios, two of which were purpose-built and large enough to accommodate his monumental water lily canvases. Throughout his career, Monet positioned himself as a leading proponent of plein-air painting and promoted the myth of the lone artist, heroically confronting and rapidly transcribing unmediated nature.[13]

The opening section of this chapter considers Daubigny's and Monet's boat studios which exemplify the mutability of the studio as a newly portable workspace. Narrowing the distance between artist and motif, floating studios enabled them to experience the natural setting more directly by inserting themselves into the waterscape they were painting. In 1857, Daubigny converted a former ferry boat into a studio. Baptized *Le Botin* ('Little Box'), it transformed his approach to landscape painting and became a central component of his creative process and artistic identity.[14] Soon after moving to Argenteuil in December 1871, Monet bought an old fishing boat and added a small cabin to create a similar studio, which he used to explore scenic sites in the vicinity and depicted repeatedly during the 1870s. Coinciding with the development of tourism and growing popularity of river scenery and recreational boating, Daubigny's and Monet's floating studios provided mobility and furthered their agenda of painting unspoiled natural sites.[15] The Impressionists' preoccupation with natural light, high-value colors and modern subjects, which transformed their painting practice, also impacted their indoor studios. Rejecting the penumbra and false lighting of traditional studios, they preferred brighter, light-filled spaces with large windows, such as Frédéric Bazille's rue La Condamine studio, and favored full-face lighting.[16]

The concluding section considers the communal or shared studio as a site of masculine sociability and a repository of individual and collective identity, which overturned the Romantic prototype of the alienated artist working in isolation. Although the Impressionists rarely painted commissioned portraits, they often painted one another, individually or collectively, including informal depictions in the studio or working outdoors, as well as self-portraits.[17] Their preference for spontaneous-looking subjects in modern settings, including group portraits, paralleled their informal social gatherings at the Café Guerbois and La Nouvelle Athènes or in their studios.[18] Bazille's *Studio on the Rue La Condamine* (fig.4), which documents the studio that he shared with Renoir, thematizes camaraderie and collaboration and is emblematic of evolving ideas about artistic identity and the studio. Bazille's casual studio picture is more complex and multilayered than it initially appears. Personal testament, collective portrait and Impressionist manifesto, it was also a virtual gallery that anticipated Henri Matisse's reductivist *Red Studio* (fig.79) with its wall of paintings.

LE BOTIN: PERIPATETIC STUDIO AND OBSERVATIONAL INSTRUMENT

Although the 17th-century landscapist Jan van Goyen purportedly painted from a boat, Charles-François Daubigny initiated the modern *bateau-atelier* (boat studio) – a new, portable studio type – that influenced the Impressionists, especially Monet.[19] Daubigny was the first artist to record excursions on his own boat, created specifically for plein-air painting. His floating studio inspired photographer Idelfonse Rousset to outfit a boat studio and photograph idyllic river scenes during the 1860s.[20] Over two decades, Daubigny navigated the rivers of northern France, painting, fishing and living on his floating studio, enabling him to observe passing river scenery and to experience nature and changing atmospheric

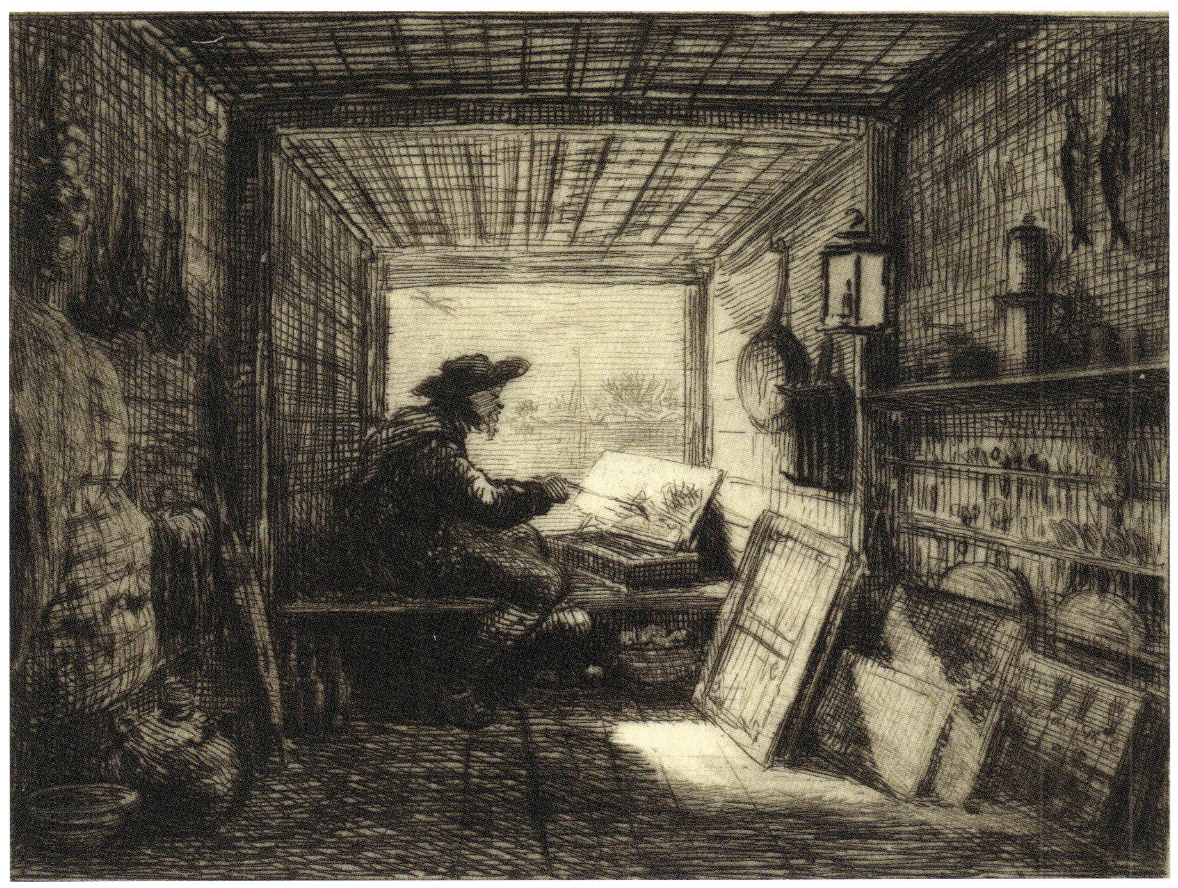

44. Charles-François Daubigny, *The Boat Studio*, 1862, etching, 13 × 17.7 cm, Metropolitan Museum of Art, New York.

and meteorological effects in real time.[21] Daubigny's letter of 28 October 1857 to sculptor Adolphe-Victor Geoffroy-Dechaume, recounting his first excursions aboard the *Botin*, making *pochades* en route, includes lively sketches.[22] Simultaneously serving as transport, observational platform, workspace and living quarters, the *Botin* immersed Daubigny in the scenic riverways of rural France. He took extended trips with his sons and friends along the Seine and Oise, recording his adventures on the *Botin* in anecdotal sketches, 16 of which were published in *Voyage en bateau* (Boat Trip, 1862).[23] Initially printed in a small edition for family and friends, the volume was reissued in 1876.[24] The *Botin* was a badge of artistic independence and self-sufficiency – a manifesto of Daubigby's painting method, an observational device for framing the passing riverscape and a peripatetic floating studio that permitted him to transcribe his sensations directly.[25]

Daubigny's boat studio was 8.5 m long and 1.8 m wide; the cabin was about 1.8 by 2.2 m. The flat-bottomed vessel, which was equipped with mast, sail and oars, could be rowed, sailed, or, if necessary, towed.[26] It provided a low, immersive vantage point that brought the water closer and heightened the sense of immediacy and actuality in Daubigny's paintings. In canvases like *Banks of the Oise* and *Riverbank and*

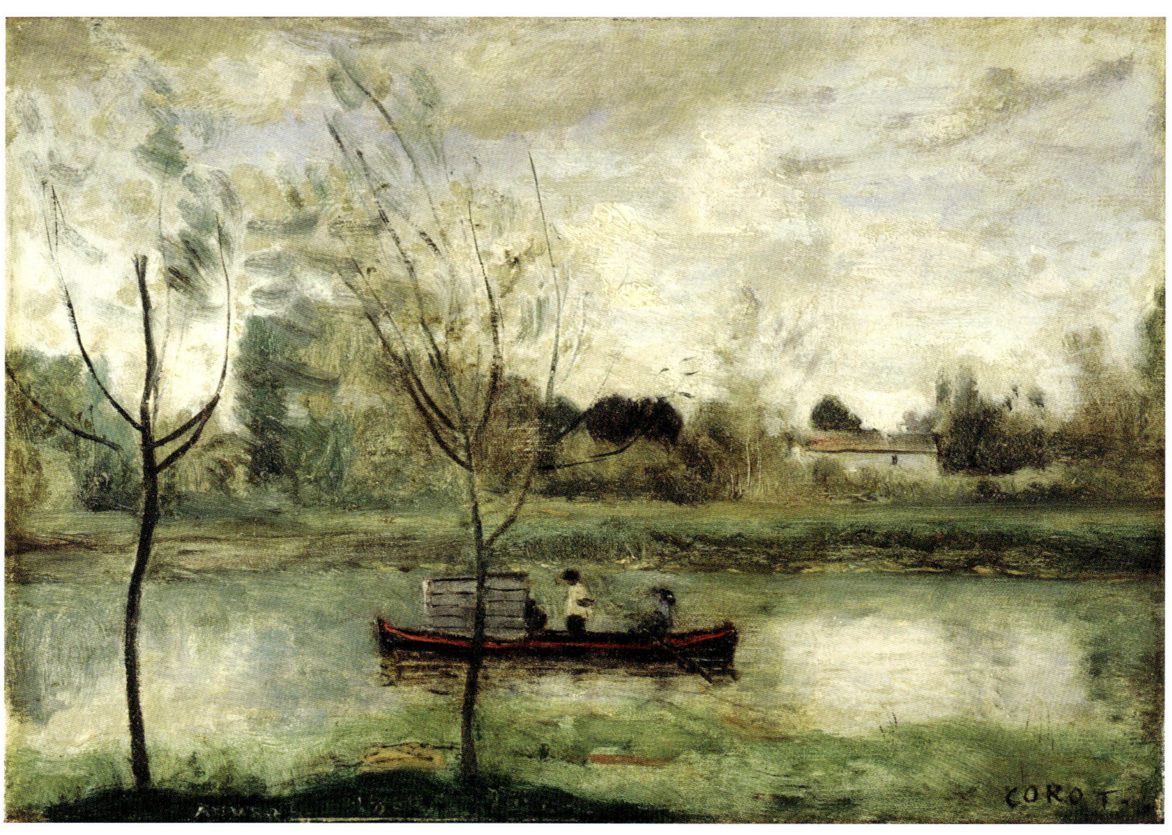

45. Jean-Baptiste-Camille Corot, *Daubigny Working on His Botin near Auvers-sur-Oise*, 1860, oil on canvas, 24.3 × 34 cm, Princeton University Art Museum, Princeton, NJ.

Herd Drinking, both painted in 1859, the spectator experiences the scene from the middle of the river, as if inside Daubigny's boat. In *Le Paysagiste aux champs* (1876), Frédéric Henriet extolled Daubigny's unique approach to landscape painting. He described how the *Botin*, whose multi-colored stripes made it instantly recognizable, floated past limpid riverscapes and picturesque villages and islands that Daubigny's canvases faithfully recorded.[27]

Boat Studio (fig.44) is Daubigny's most detailed depiction of the *Botin*. The viewer looks through the compact cabin to the riverscape that the artist is painting. Seated in profile, Daubigny uses his paint box as an ad hoc easel to support his canvas.[28] The open-ended cabin doubles as a floating platform and optical device, framing the river scene and enhancing its authenticity and verisimilitude. The word 'Réalisme' ('realism'), inscribed on the back of the painting at far right, attests to Daubigny's insistence on direct observation of nature.[29] The side walls display pots and pans, a lantern and stacks of paintings and bedding, indicating the *Botin*'s practical and aesthetic function. Bearded and wearing a broad-brimmed hat, Daubigny is silhouetted against a luminous, window-like opening, in a shadowy interior that recalls 17th-century Dutch studio interiors. More specifically, *Boat Studio* pays homage to Rembrandt's down-to-earth *Self-Portrait Etching at a Window* (1648). Seated at a table likewise illumined by a window, Rembrandt holds an etching needle or pen in his right hand and gazes up from his work. In the second state of the print, Rembrandt etched his name at the top of the window, underscoring the significance of light.

Daubigny and Corot met around 1849 and became lifelong friends.[30] In 1860 Corot painted *Daubigny Working on his Botin near Auvers* (fig.45), the year Daubigny purchased property there. Produced as a token of friendship, the picture figured in an exchange of portraits between the artists. Corot depicted Daubigny working in front of the cabin; his son, Karl, holding a palette, observes, while his other son, rows. Daubigny painted a small undated portrait of *Corot at his Easel*, working outdoors, smoking his pipe.[31] Besides anecdotal sketches for *Voyage en bateau*, Daubigny made several studies of the *Botin* (*c.*1857), in profile, reflected in the river, and moored on the riverbank, surrounded by trees. Around the same time, he executed a small painting titled *Botin on the Oise*.[32] He kept the *Botin* moored near his house in Auvers and launched it every season. The original *Botin* was retired from service in 1867 and replaced by a larger, better equipped vessel in 1868. Daubigny made a large painting of the second *Botin* in profile view, with the sails unfurled, likely soon after its launch. The replacement boat had two small windows on each side of the cabin, larger sails and more elaborate rigging, differentiating it from the original *Botin*. Daubigny sits on the deck painting, facing the cabin, creating a pendant to *Boat Studio*.

Besides contributing to Daubigny's artistic success, the *Botin* was emblematic of his authenticity as a painter of river scenes, signifying his reliance on immediate sensations from nature. As the protagonist in *Voyage en bateau*, the boat was both a character and a narrative vehicle. The album evokes the simple joys and happenstance rhythms of life on the river through a series of humorous vignettes. At Alfred Cadart's behest, Daubigny selected and transferred his original sketches to etching plates, using tracing paper so that the prints would retain the original orientation of the drawings.[33] *Boat Studio* was the central image – a calling card and manifesto that encapsulated Daubigny's working method. It illustrated how Daubigny used the *Botin* to gather raw visual data from direct observation, which he transcribed into sketches that could be used for making paintings.

In Auvers-sur-Oise, Daubigny constructed a spacious 7.9 × 6.1 m studio, surrounded by other rooms, that drew admirers and acolytes.[34] Designed by Achille Oudinot, the studio was decorated with paintings by Daubigny, his son Karl and artist friends, including Honoré Daumier, Oudinot and Corot, who designed the large landscape panels adorning the studio walls. Because of Corot's and Daubigny's presence, Auvers-sur-Oise became a popular artists' colony that attracted the next generation of landscape painters.[35] In 1863, Berthe Morisot and her sister, Edma, who were vacationing nearby, visited Daubigny, who inspired them to try painting from a boat. During 1872, Camille Pissarro, Paul Cézanne and Armand Guillaumin came to Auvers to paint. Dr Paul Gachet, an amateur painter, printmaker and collector, settled there in the same year, and his house became a gathering place for artists. Vincent van Gogh, who revered Daubigny as 'one of "the great forerunners"', arrived in Auvers in May 1890.

Literally following in Daubigny's footsteps, van Gogh painted panoramic views of the wheatfields surrounding Auvers and used the same 'double-square' format favored by Daubigny. In July, van Gogh visited Daubigny's widow and painted two views of the house and garden in homage to a painter who had inspired him over the years and had served as a touchstone.[36] Léonide Bourges's posthumous tribute, *Daubigny, souvenirs et croquis* (1894) enriched and burnished his legend with its 33 etchings. Among these were illustrations of the studio and a commemorative group portrait of Daubigny painting outdoors, with parasol and portable easel, on Île de Vaux, a favorite site. His son and daughter, sculptor Jean-Louis Chenillon and Bourges herself are pictured working companionably on the *Botin*, which was moored nearby.[37] Over the past decade scholars have increasingly recognized Daubigny's pioneering contributions to landscape painting and the development of Impressionism.

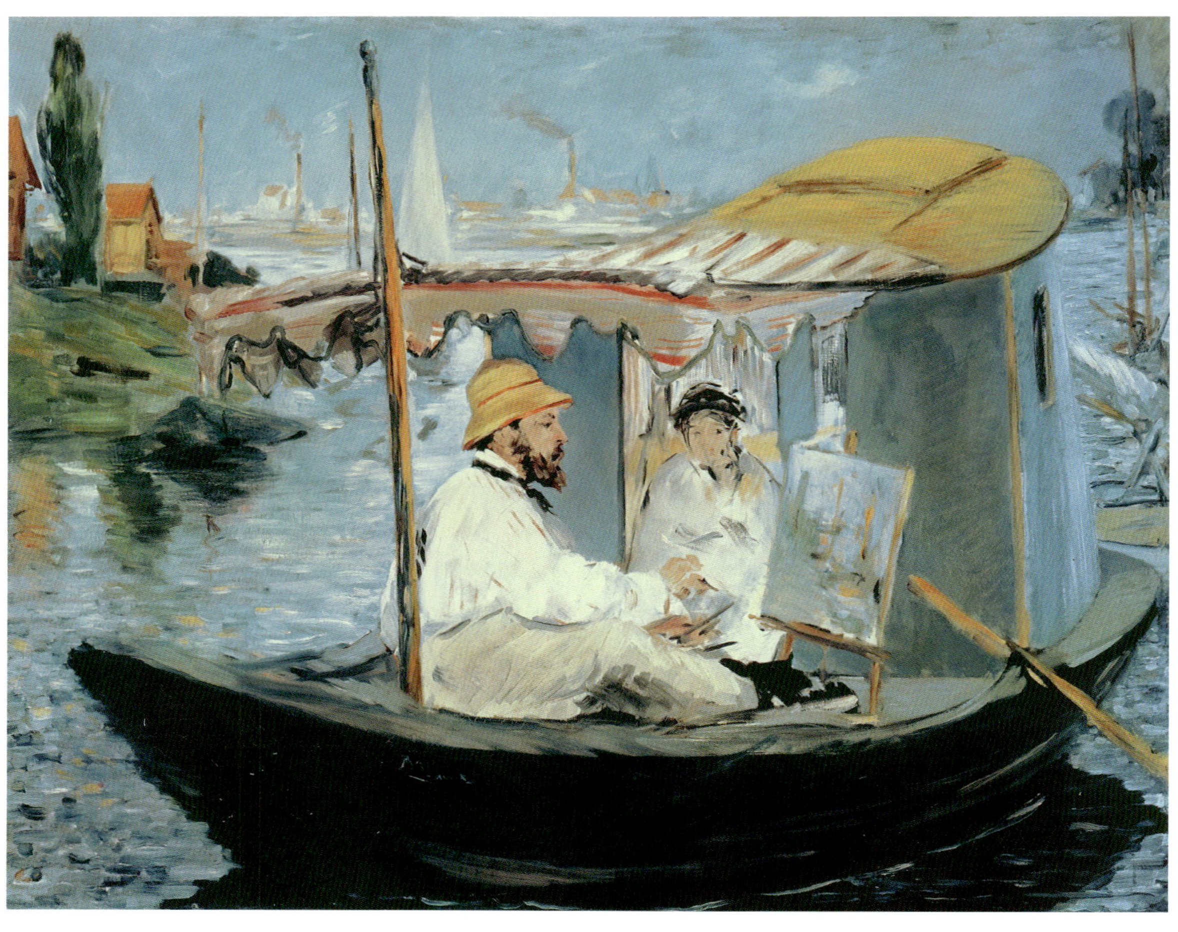

46. Édouard Manet, *Monet Painting in His Boat Studio*, 1874, oil on canvas, 82.5 × 105 cm, Neue Pinakothek, Munich.

MONET'S FLOATING STUDIOS: FROM ARGENTEUIL TO GIVERNY

At the 1859 Salon, Monet was impressed by Daubigny's groundbreaking canvases, including *Banks of the Oise*. Daubigny's preoccupation with recording nature and changing atmospheric effects using a rapid, sketchy technique and a panoramic format anticipated Impressionism and had a lasting impact on Monet's choice of subject matter and approach to painting.[38] As a member of the Salon jury, Daubigny defended the Impressionists and campaigned to admit Monet and his colleagues to the 1868 Salon. When Monet's painting was rejected by the jury in 1870, Daubigny resigned in protest. In temporary exile in London during the Franco-Prussian War, Daubigny introduced Monet to Durand-Ruel, who purchased 63 of Monet's paintings (1872–3) and became the leading Impressionist dealer.[39] Soon after settling in Argenteuil, a popular recreational boating center, in December 1871, Monet followed Daubigny's example and constructed a floating studio of his own. During the mid-1870s Argenteuil became the epicenter of Impressionism; Renoir, Alfred Sisley, Manet and, later, Gustave Caillebotte came there to paint.[40]

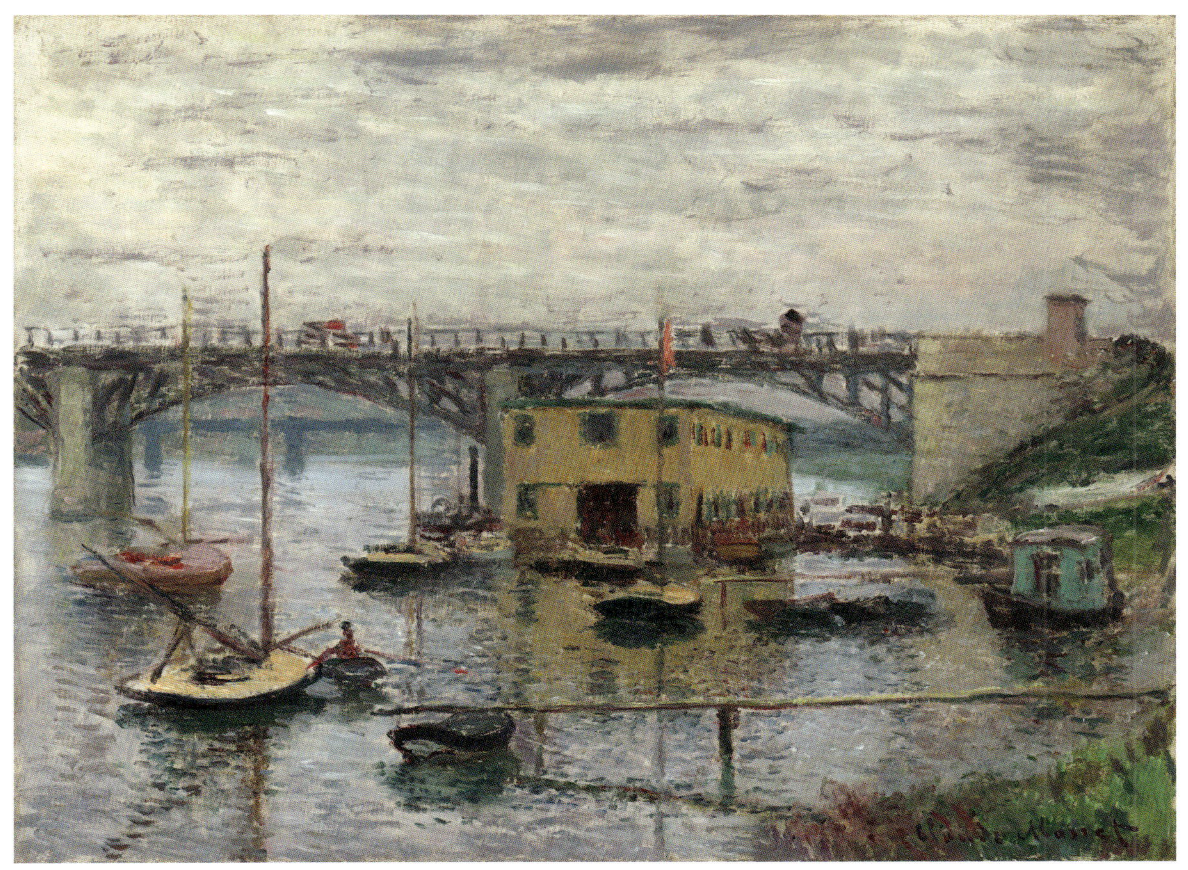

47. Claude Monet, *Bridge at Argenteuil on a Gray Day*, c.1876, oil on canvas, 61 × 80.3 cm, National Gallery of Art, Washington, DC.

Monet's boat studio resembled the *Botin*, although the cabin looks more cramped in Manet's 1874 *Monet Painting in his Boat Studio* (fig.46). Monet described it as 'a cabin made out of planks where I had just enough room to set up my easel'.[41] The boat and cabin appear more substantial in Monet's oblique, foreshortened view from the same year (fig.48). In 1874, Henriet published a detailed article on Daubigny in *Gazette des Beaux-Arts* that included reproductions of *Boat Studio* and *Steamboats* from *Voyage en bateau*.[42] Although Daubigny's and Monet's floating studios were similar in design, the two artists used their boats differently. While Daubigny made longer trips and was away for days or even weeks, Monet took shorter, day excursions. He kept his floating studio moored downriver from the boat rental area and used it to explore unspoiled sites nearby, especially along the branch of the Seine between Île Marante and Colombes. With his boat, he could easily navigate from site to site and compose novel, spontaneous-looking juxtapositions of boats and bridges from unexpected viewpoints. Occasionally, Monet surreptitiously introduced his boat studio into general views of Argenteuil and, later, Vétheuil, making it part of the river setting.[43] In *Bridge at Argenteuil on a Gray Day* (c.1876, fig.47), he seamlessly integrated his boat, moored at the right, into a bustling, commercial

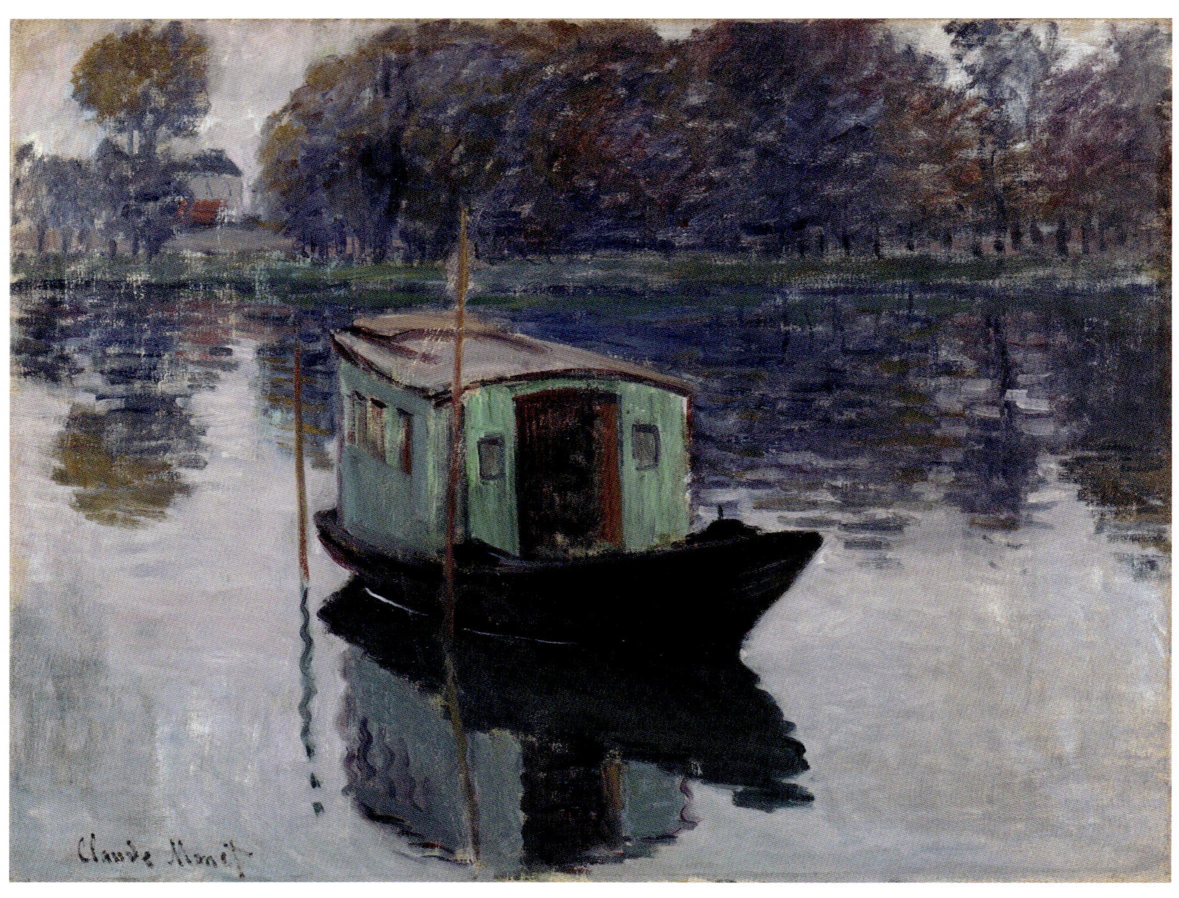

48. Claude Monet, *The Boat Studio*, 1874, oil on canvas, 50.2 × 65.5 cm, Kröller-Müller Museum, Otterlo.

riverscape.[44] In this paean to modernity, Monet highlights industrial progress through the factory smokestacks and infrastructure and the geometry of the bridge, which together form the backdrop for the boathouse and bobbing sailboats in the foreground. By pinpointing the precise location and viewpoint he was working from, Monet inserted himself virtually into the picture, underscoring his artistic agency. The modest, itinerant boat, powered by oars, stands out from the slick pleasure craft, signifying Monet's authenticity and rugged individualism.[45]

From 1874 to 1876, Monet painted his floating studio five times from different vantage points in pristine natural settings; these five paintings constitute a mini-series.[46] The existence of multiple versions, one of which remained in Monet's possession at Giverny, suggests that the boat studio was closely associated with his Impressionist identity and his approach to painting water subjects. The fact that Monet invited guests onboard his boat and was depicted painting on it by other artists, including Manet and John Singer Sargent, is a further indication of its significance for him. The early provenance of his boat studio pictures demonstrates their appeal to Monet's coterie and leading collectors. One belonged to Zola, a friend and early defender of the Impressionists; two others were purchased around 1876 by Georges de Bellio and Victor Chocquet, early patrons of Impressionism.[47]

Although none of Monet's *Boat Studios* is dated and the order in which they were painted remains unclear, they fall into two distinct groups. My discussion focuses on the two versions that are most closely connected to Daubigny's *Botin* (figs 48, 49). Both canvases present the boat studio isolated, surrounded only by water and trees. In *Boat Studio* (fig.48), which is thought to be the earliest, the motionless boat, moored with two poles, is reflected in the mirror-like surface of the river, evoking solitude and contemplation. The basin downriver from the Argenteuil Bridge and the fashionable promenade in the background are deserted; the color of the foliage suggests autumn. The unusually somber palette, which recalls that of Daubigny, invests the painting with an aura of melancholy.[48] The sketchy figure in the cabin, presumably Monet, is subsumed into the boat studio, blurring the distinction between the artist and the subject that he is observing. The foreshortened boat is painted as if viewed from an imaginary point in space outside the canvas. Monet's virtuoso portrayal of his floating studio showcases his mastery of reflections and light effects, demonstrating how it dovetailed with his Impressionist agenda.

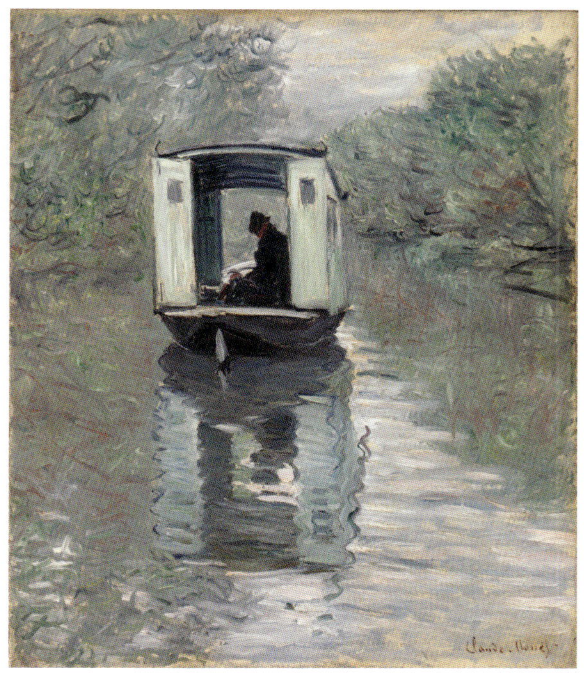

49. Claude Monet, *The Boat Studio*, 1876, oil on canvas, 72.7 × 60 cm, Barnes Foundation, Philadelphia.

Boat Studio (fig.49), executed two years later, presents the most striking analogies with Daubigny's *Botin* etching. Using the same perpendicular viewpoint, Monet depicts himself seated on the floor at the back of the boat, in profile, looking down; he is tightly framed by the cabin's open doorway, which serves as an optical frame. Other than the scenic riverscape, the primary focus of the composition is Monet's absorption in his work, underscoring the solitary, reflexive nature of the creative process. His intense concentration and pose subtly echo Daubigny's in *Boat Studio*. Silhouetted against the greenish water and trees, Monet becomes an extension of the surrounding nature that he is transcribing. In this daringly reductivist canvas, his image is sketchily reflected in the water below, punctuated with loose swirls and squiggles of paint. As in the earlier canvas, Monet's palette is less luminous and more muted than usual. Although Monet often anchored his boat to work, he sometimes painted as he drifted down the river, as was perhaps the case here.

In the other three paintings that comprise the second group, the river and vibrant foliage dominate the composition. Distanced and viewed from above, the toy-like boat studio is almost swallowed up in the vibrant natural setting. In contrast to the previous examples discussed, the viewer is at a remove and no longer has the sensation of being afloat in the middle of the river. All three paintings include figures other than the artist and depict the boat in motion – actively rowed, rather than stationary. In two of the canvases, there are two figures on the boat; in the third, a figure, viewed from behind, observes the tiny boat from the riverbank above. In these paintings, as in the later Vétheuil canvases, the boat studio has devolved from protagonist to picturesque staffage. All five paintings depict the floating studio adrift and immersed in nature, with no other vessels in sight, underscoring the idyllic rural calm and isolation and Monet's direct engagement with nature.

Manet's *Monet Painting in His Boat Studio* (fig.46), offers a different image of the artist and Argenteuil. Smartly dressed in light-colored boating attire and a straw hat, Monet works at a small portable easel, with his wife/muse, Camille, seated across from him in the open doorway. Depicted close-up and in profile, Monet wields his brush,with his palette and brushes propped between his knees. The canvas that he is painting, *Sailboats on the Seine at Petit Gennevilliers* (1874), is identifiable and still exists.[49] Juxtaposing Manet's painting of Monet and Monet's riverscape, it is evident that Manet and Monet were painting the same view of Argenteuil. In both paintings, factory smokestacks form the backdrop for the idyllic boating scene. Manet's depiction of Monet's boat studio forms a pair with Monet's *Sailboats on the Seine* and pays homage to Monet's innovative approach and sketchy technique, which Manet emulates and seeks to replicate in the painting within the painting. Manet's intimate representation of bourgeois leisure, in which sailboats are interspersed with smokestacks on the horizon, highlights fashionable recreation and the touristic attractions and conviviality of Argenteuil. Monet's depictions of his boat studio project a contrasting, ruggedly independent image of a plein-air painter – isolated and engulfed by nature that is at odds with Manet's shallower, more cosmopolitan depictions of boating as a slice of modern life.[50]

After he left Argenteuil, Monet continued to use his boat studio. He rented a house in Vétheuil from 1878 to 1881 and settled in Giverny in 1883. When Émile Taboureux visited him at Vétheuil in 1880, there were two boats moored at his dock, one for rowing exercise, the other for working. Monet showed Taboureux his rustic residence (which the critic compared to a 'Botin') and took him out on the boat studio. Noting Monet's robust physique and nautical prowess, Taboureux called him a 'true freshwater sailor'.[51] On a visit to Giverny in the 1880s, John Singer Sargent painted *Monet on his Boat Studio* (*c.*1887) in a close-up, cropped view, framed by the boat's doorway, with another artist working alongside. In 1891, Monet wrote to Caillebotte and asked to borrow his boat for a series of canvases depicting poplars on the River Epte that he was currently painting.[52]

Monet's final water series, *Mornings on the Seine* (1896–7), demonstrates Daubigny's enduring influence. The site, where the Epte empties into the Seine, was a few minutes by boat from Giverny.[53] In *La Revue illustrée* (1898), Maurice Guillemot poetically evoked the artist setting up his easel at 3:30 am on a summer morning in order to capture the subtle light and ephemeral effects of mist.[54] He described Monet's technique and reported seeing 14 paintings in progress on the boat. By the 1890s, Monet had a different boat studio, which he characterized as 'quite a large sort of barge-cabin; one could sleep there'.[55] The flat-bottomed, floating studio was equipped with grooves to hold several canvases so that Monet could work on multiple canvases at once and easily revise them, fulfilling the same purpose as the grooved painting boxes that Monet used for late series such as *Rouen Cathedral* (1892–3), which he worked on for two years and reworked extensively in his studio.

During his late years at Giverny, Monet's indoor studios played an increasingly vital role. Although he continued to work outdoors, the relationship between plein-air painting and the studio evolved, and he systematized his serial spproach. To supplement the small studio/sitting room in his house, in 1897 he constructed a two-story pavilion, which had a darkroom on the ground floor and a large, high-ceilinged studio with skylight on the top floor, overlooking the garden.[56] The new 'second studio' provided a commodious space for working on oversized canvases and for revising paintings, begun the previous spring or summer, during the winter months. In 1915, to accommodate ever larger canvases, Monet constructed a third studio, which resembled a barn. The 'grand atelier', measuring 24.1 by 11.9 m and 14.9 m high, and equipped with large skylights and rolling easels, easily accommodated 1.8 by 3.7 m canvases.[57] The industrial-scale studio was a controlled, virtual universe where Monet could adjust the overhead lighting with fabric panels and move around and modify his paintings at will. This carefully regulated environment was crucial for painting his '*Grandes Décorations*' – continuous, panoramic views of the water lily pond that he donated to the state in 1920 at age 80.[58] Monet increasingly opened his studio to visitors and posed for photographs, holding an oversized palette, standing in front of the immense water lily panels, as elder statesman of Impressionism.[59] In 1922, the American opera singer Marguerite Namara visited and gave a recital with the *Nymphéas* (now in the Musée de l'Orangerie in Paris) as a backdrop.[60]

Working on a monumental scale and contending with reduced vision from cataracts changed Monet's working method; he started painting more broadly, using a massive palette and long-handled brushes. For the rest of his career, he focused on painting vast, increasingly dematerialized depictions of the water lily pond at Giverny, which became a virtual studio – a controlled 'natural' environment – where, like a modern-day alchemist, he could experiment endlessly with the chemistry of color and light. His late canvases transform the waterscape into a diaphanous, floating world where sky, water and reflections converge. In 'Splendors' (1907), Marcel Proust described Giverny as a 'color-garden', composed of colors and tones more than of flowers; comparing it to a 'living sketch', or an artfully arranged palette. Recognizing Monet's garden as 'a real transposition of art', in which nature is reborn through the eyes of a great painter, Proust associated Giverny with his own transformative creative process.[61]

FORGING ARTISTIC IDENTITY: BAZILLE'S REFLEXIVE STUDIOS

This section considers the praxis of the studio and its evolving role as a dialogic social space and frame for artistic collaboration and exchange through the lens of Bazille's studio pictures. Though a proponent of plein-air painting, Bazille manifested a cult-like devotion to his studios, which were integral to his artistic identity. That is evident from numerous references in his letters and the corpus of paintings and drawings thematizing the practice of painting and the studio's hybrid functions as workspace, artistic and social nexus and gallery. Focusing on *Studio on the Rue La Condamine* (fig.4), I analyze the studio's multivalent significance as a collective social space for art-making and manifestation of the personal ties and collaborative spirit that animated the Batignolles group during the 1860s. Despite his abbreviated career, Bazille was a pivotal figure and linchpin, who sustained his colleagues, especially Monet, financially and otherwise.[62] Bazille was tied personally and artistically to Monet and Renoir, with whom he shared studios in the 1860s. The collaboration of these artists both in the studio and outdoors anticipated the communal plein-air painting sessions at Argenteuil in the 1870s. More than just a visual record, Bazille's depiction of his rue La Condamine studio is about praxis – how the studio functioned as an arena for camaraderie and collective creativity – and evoking its artistic and social ambience pictorially. The walls display recent paintings by Bazille and his colleagues, who populate the light-filled interior, foreshadowing the casual, *in situ* portraits that preoccupied the Impressionists throughout the 1870s.

The picture's meaning, which is more complex and cryptic than it appears, extends beyond the studio's social dimension.[63] Artistic collaboration is literally embedded in the multilayered canvas, which updates the studio picture and charts the independent artistic trajectory of Bazille and his colleagues. X-radiographs reveal that the scene was painted directly over a study

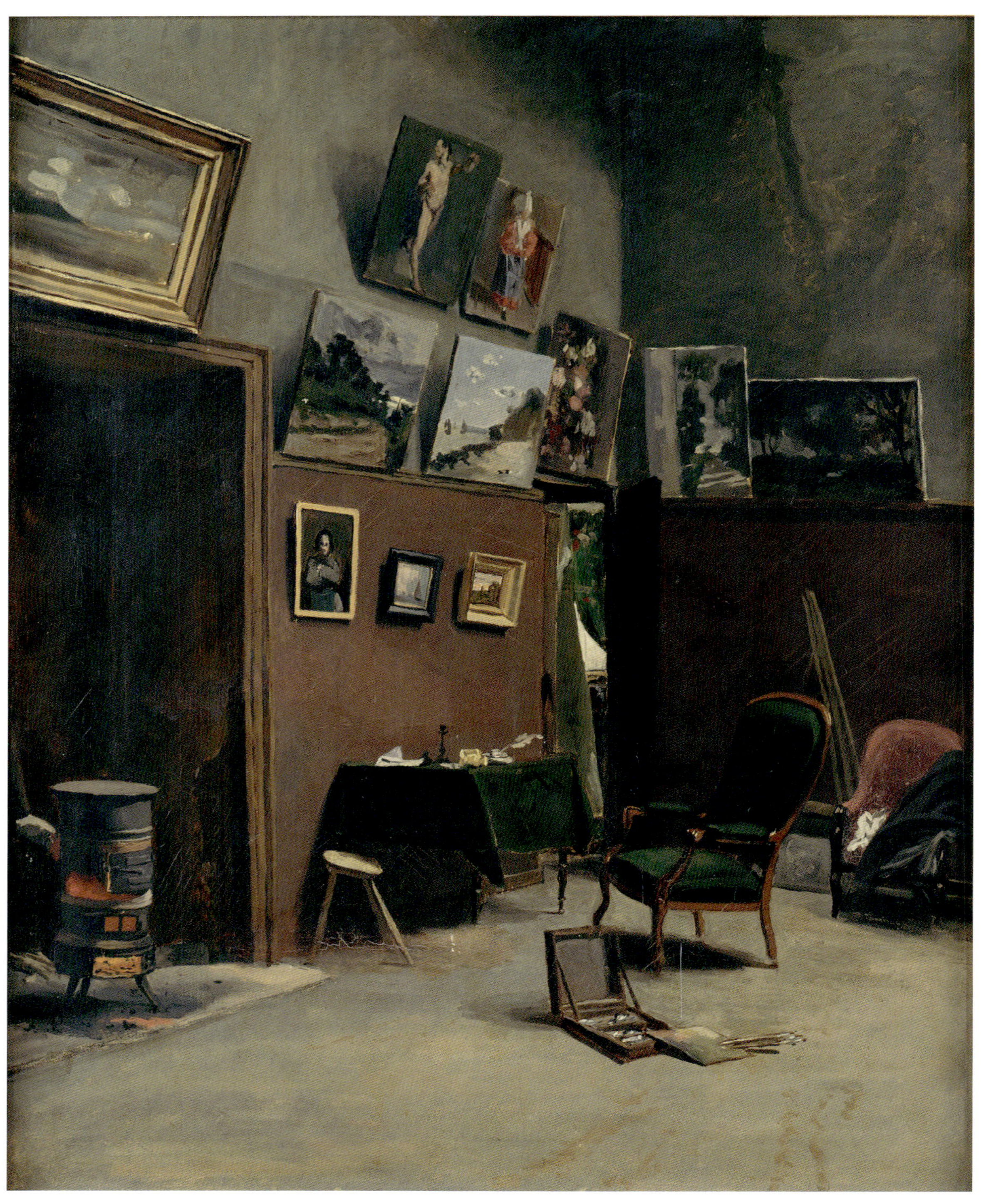

50. Frédéric Bazille, *Studio on the Rue de Furstenberg*, 1865, oil on canvas, 81.2 × 65 cm, Musée Fabre, Montpellier.

of Renoir's *Diana, the Huntress* (1867), of uncertain authorship.[64] That indeterminacy underscores the artists' communal practice and sharing of materials and models. Rather than a formal public artistic manifesto like Fantin-Latour's *Studio in the Batignolles*, *Studio on the Rue La Condamine* offers a casual, behind-the-scenes view of the studio as a fluid interactive space. Although Bazille, who stands at the easel, dominates the composition, his portrait was an extempore addition by Manet, who reportedly quipped, 'Your studio without you, it's not possible.'[65] The difference in paint handling in Bazille's portrait confirms Manet's spontaneous intervention. In the concluding section, Whistler's enigmatic *Artist in His Studio* (1865–6, fig.56) will be introduced as a counterpoint on multiple levels to Bazille's *Studio on the Rue La Condamine*.

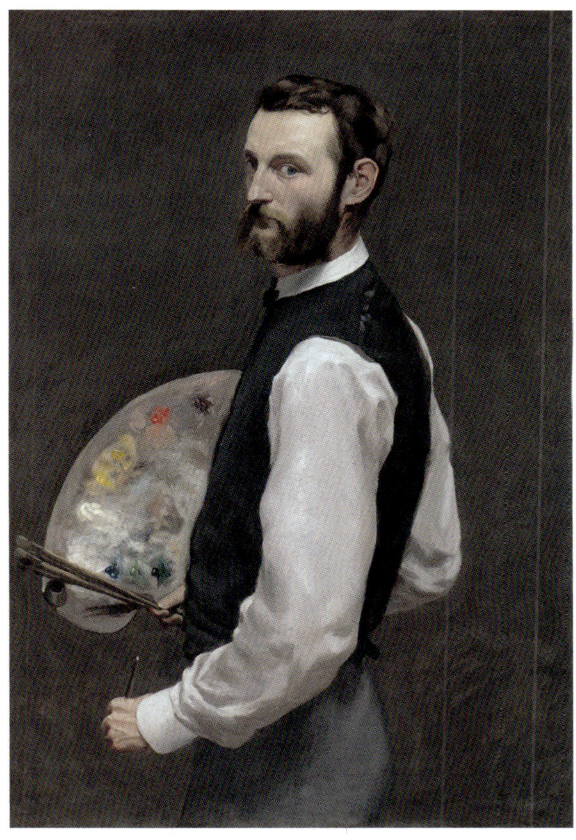

51. Frédéric Bazille, *Self-Portrait with Palette*, c.1865, oil on canvas, 108.9 × 71.1 cm, Art Institute of Chicago, Chicago.

STUDIO PORTRAITS AND INTERIORS

Before examining *Studio on the Rue La Condamine*, it is helpful to situate it relative to Bazille's other studio pictures, *Self-Portrait with Palette* (fig.51) and depictions of Manet and Renoir at the easel. Bazille also painted informal portraits of Monet, Renoir and Edmond Maître, all of whom appear in this painting. From January 1864 to November 1870, Bazille occupied six different studios, mostly on the Left Bank near the École des Beaux-Arts. The three studios that he commemorated in paint were those shared with Monet and Renoir (1865–70), which held personal significance for him and were crucial to his artistic development. After meeting at Charles Gleyre's liberal teaching studio in 1863, Bazille, Monet and Renoir became close friends and began painting outdoors together. In January 1865, Bazille and Monet moved to a studio at 6 rue de Furstenberg, the building where Delacroix spent his final years, which added to its allure. When Bazille first encountered Delacroix's paintings at Alfred Bruyas's gallery, he was dazzled by *Femmes d'Alger*.[66] Delacroix's brilliant color and lighting were a revelation and a formative influence. Bazille's view of the empty rue de Furstenberg studio, with its glowing pot-bellied stove at the left (fig.50), pays homage to Delacroix's intimate *Corner of the Studio* (c.1825–30).

The austere Furstenberg studio Bazille and Monet shared is devoid of decor, except for the paintings displayed on the walls, including landscapes by Monet and Gilbert de Sévérac's portrait of him. Although no works are definitively attributed to Bazille, he painted flower pieces like the one shown over the doorway. The male *académie* and costume study in

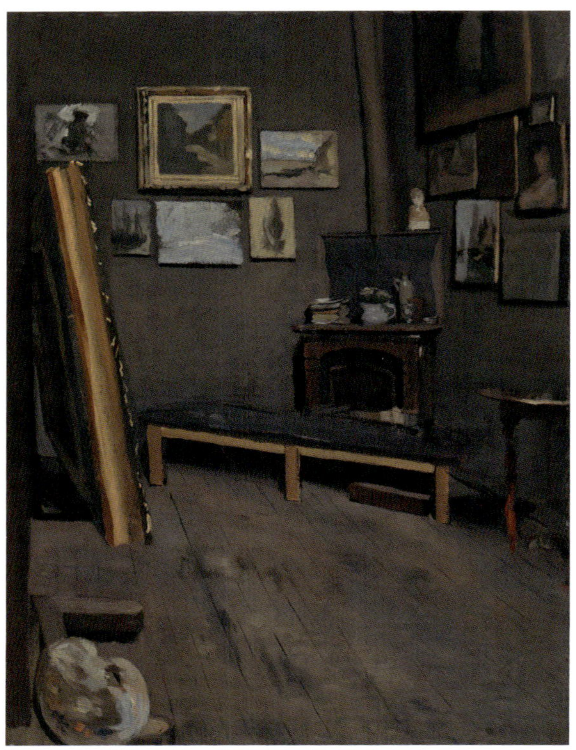

52. Frédéric Bazille, *Studio on the Rue Visconti*, 1867, oil on canvas, 64.8 × 48.3 cm, Virginia Museum of Fine Arts, Richmond, VA.

the top row indicate Bazille's predilection for figure painting, including male and female nudes. The palette and brushes resting on the portable paint box in the foreground evoke the absent artist and the painting profession. The prominently placed green armchair nearby, which Bazille referred to as his 'only luxury', reappears, viewed from behind, in the *Studio on the Rue La Condamine*.[67] The dark red walls recall Delacroix's Furstenberg studio. The functional workspace, highlighting the practice of painting, signals Bazille's serious pursuit of art. The pictures on display encompass different approaches, from academic to avant-garde, and a variety of genres, including life drawing, portraiture, still life and plein-air landscapes, testifying to Bazille's wide-ranging interests.

Bazille's arresting *Self-Portrait with Palette* (fig.51), which was probably painted in the Furstenberg studio, boldly asserts his artistic vocation and technical prowess.[68] By portraying himself in the act of painting, he was implicitly measuring himself against past masters and claiming his place in the genealogy of modern painting. Bazille is depicted, nearly three-quarter length, in close-up profile, his head in three-quarter view, silhouetted against the dark background. His tense expression and strained posture, as he gazes over his shoulder, register the difficulty of capturing his image, reflected in reverse in the mirror. Positioned at an invisible easel beyond the edge of the canvas, he holds palette and brushes in his right hand and a paintbrush in his left. The enormous, paint-smeared palette, which dominates the composition, foregrounds the apparatus of painting and the viscous materiality of paint. *Self-Portrait with Palette* inaugurated a series of self-portraits, but it is the only portrayal of Bazille as a painter. The unusually specific palette, whose pigments have been technically analyzed, mirror those used in the painting.[69] An inveterate dandy, Bazille is elegantly dressed in a high-collared, white shirt and black vest, rather than painter's garb. In January 1866, Bazille and Monet's halcyon séjour in rue de Furstenberg ended abruptly when a noisy masked ball precipitated their eviction for excessive noise.[70] Before quitting the premises, Bazille painted the Furstenberg studio as an *aide-mémoire* and a memento of a crucial twelve months that had affirmed his identity and vocation as a painter.

In July 1866, Bazille moved to a new studio, 20, rue Visconti, which he shared with Renoir and, periodically, Monet and Sisley.[71] He described it as convenient but small, with a very habitable bedroom.[72] Bazille painted a corner view of the cramped studio from an idiosyncratic raked angle, emphasizing the floor (fig.52). The somber, empty interior is dissected by the large, framed painting jutting out at far left and the angled bench in front of the fireplace intersecting with the painting. Although the 13 paintings displayed on the walls are sketchily rendered, several works by Bazille, including *Little Italian Street Singer* (1866) and *Young Woman with Lowered Eyes* (1866–7), can be identified. Monet is represented by *Rue de la Bavole, Honfleur* (*c.*1864) and several small seascapes; oddly, there are no works by Renoir. Besides his paintings, Bazille's presence is signalled by the palette in the lower left corner. The gloomy atmosphere accords with the dispiriting rejection of Bazille's and his colleagues' submissions to the 1867 Salon. The rejected paintings, notably Monet's *Women in the Garden* and Renoir's *Diana, the Huntress*, presumably remained in the studio, casting a virtual pall over the empty interior. The large, 'unseen' canvas on the easel may be Bazille's *Terrace at Méric*, which was also rejected.[73] In the *Studio on the Rue La Condamine*, Bazille prominently displayed paintings that had been rejected by the Salon jury. His dream of organizing independent, non-juried exhibitions for himself and his colleagues was not realized until 1874, when the first Impressionist exhibition was held in Nadar's studio.[74]

The rue Visconti studio was the site of the most intriguing instance of communal painting and artistic reciprocity. In November 1867, while Bazille and Sisley worked side by side on a heron still life, Renoir painted Bazille seated at the easel, engaged in painting his *Still Life with Heron* (fig.53).[75] To depict Bazille, Renoir adopted the same color palette that Bazille was using for the still life and likely borrowed his paints.[76] Viewed in profile, Bazille hunches over his canvas, holding a small rectangular palette in his left hand, as he delicately applies white paint to the heron with a small brush. In contrast to *Self-Portrait with Palette*, he is informally dressed in a brownish painter's smock and slippers. The close-up format captures Bazille's intense concentration and foregrounds the painting process. By painting Bazille's palette, using his colors, and reproducing the still life that Bazille was working on, Renoir created a double mise en abyme.

The three-way artistic interchange among Bazille, Renoir and Sisley is transcribed in paint in the closely related heron still lifes that Bazille and Sisley painted concurrently, which differ in subtle ways, and in Renoir's casual, full-length portrait of Bazille at work, which Manet admired and purchased.[77] Although Monet did not participate in the collective painting sessions, the winter landscape behind Bazille's head attests to his intimate connection with the studio's occupants.[78] Bazille, in turn, depicted Renoir at the easel, viewed from behind, working on a large canvas (*c.*1866–7). The charcoal drawing, previously attributed to Renoir's friend, Jules Le Coeur, has recently been attributed to Bazille.[79] Dressed informally in a worker's smock and

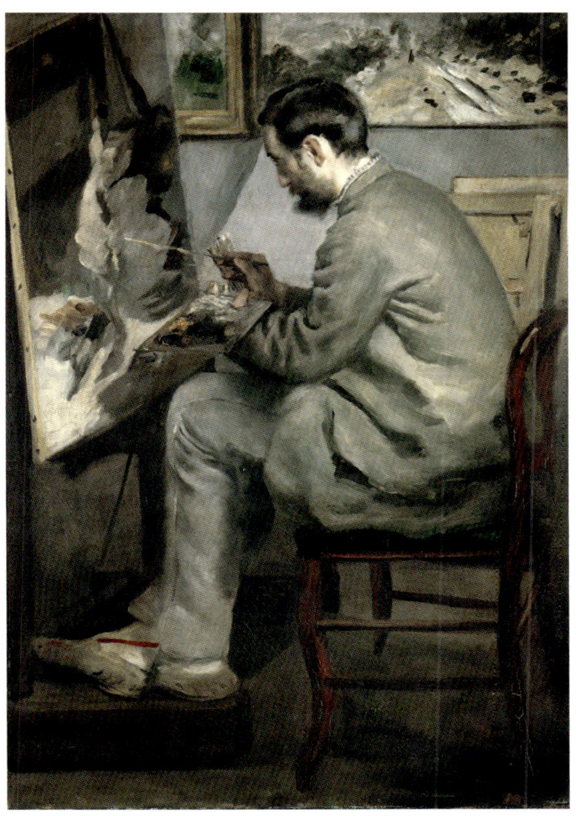

53. Pierre-Auguste Renoir, *Bazille Painting the Heron*, 1867, oil on canvas, 105 × 73.5 cm, Musée d'Orsay, Paris.

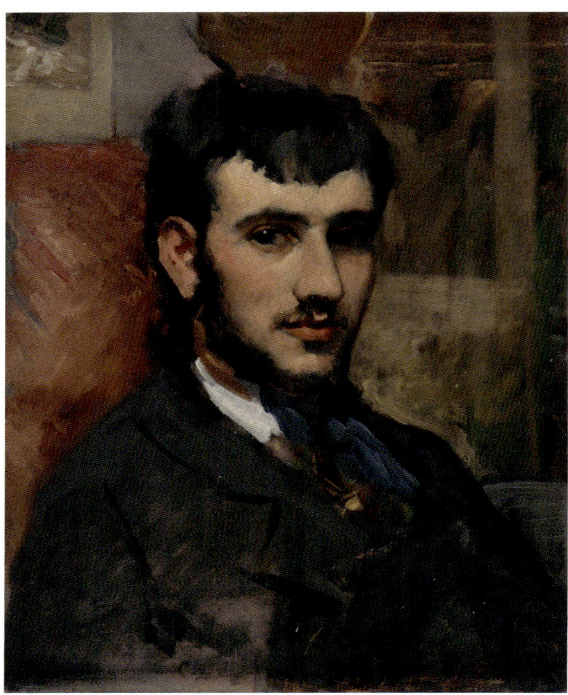

54. Frédéric Bazille, *Portrait of Renoir*, 1867, oil on canvas, 40.5 × 32.5 cm, Cleveland Museum of Art, Cleveland, OH.

slippers, Renoir rests his right knee on a chair while he paints. Completing the cycle of reciprocity, Bazille painted two contrasting images of Renoir in 1867: a small, full-length, perched nonchalantly on a chair, with his legs drawn up, and a more traditional, bust-length portrait in three-quarter view, seated on a rose-colored chair against a backdrop of paintings, presumably in the rue Visconti studio (fig.54). The stunning immediacy of Bazille's loosely painted portrait is strikingly different from Renoir's more self-contained, introspective depiction of Bazille painting. Both canvases attest to the camaraderie, communal painting practice and shared artistic aspirations that enlivened the rue Visconti studio. In May 1867, before leaving for southern France, Bazille made a small, commemorative painting of the studio, which he mentioned in a letter to his father.[80] When he returned to Paris in November, he rented a larger space in the Batignolles district on the Right Bank.[81]

THE RUE LA CONDAMINE STUDIO

In January 1868, Bazille and Renoir moved to a new studio at 9 rue La Condamine. It was near Manet's rue Guyot studio and the Café Guerbois, where the Batignolles group of artists and writers congregated.[82] Bazille was delighted with the spacious, modern studio and hoped to remain there for a long time.[83] *Studio on the Rue La Condamine* (fig.4), Bazille's most complex exploration of the studio topos, is the summation of his corpus of studio pictures and depictions of fellow artists. Unlike his earlier studio depictions, this painting exemplifies the Impressionist preference for airy, light-filled spaces with large windows. The light gray walls add to the overall luminosity and atmospheric clarity. Although *Studio on the Rue La Condamine* overlaps thematically with Fantin-Latour's *Studio in the Batignolles*, for which Bazille and his comrades posed in late 1869, it offers a counter-image of the modern studio as an informal, interactive artistic and social network rather than a formally staged collective portrait.[84]

Studio on the Rue La Condamine is animated by the dynamic arrangement of Bazille and his friends, who are casually scattered around the interior, engaging in conversation, inspecting paintings or playing the piano. The comfortable, pink sofa and the piano highlight the studio's hybrid artistic and social functions. Rather than an empty set piece, it is an interactive, collaborative stage. Art is thematized through the canvases displayed on the walls and the artists who inhabit the space. Standing to either side of the easel, Manet and Bazille are framed by the immense windows that look out on the cityscape and link the luminous studio interior to the world outside, making it synonymous with the painting of modern life. Viewed in profile, holding his palette and brushes, Bazille leans casually against the easel, obscuring *View of the Village* (1868), displayed on the easel, which Manet is discussing.[85] Initially, Bazille was not included, perhaps out of modesty or because his studio was already self-referential. Manet's extempore addition of Bazille's portrait made the painting more dialogic and altered its meaning by making Bazille the fulcrum of the composition. Before Manet's intervention, the red and green armchair, which also appeared in the *Studio on the Rue de Furstenberg*, and Bazille's paintings and palette would have been surrogates for the absent artist. Positioned for viewing the obscured canvas on the easel, the chair functions as a *repoussoir*; it invites viewers into the studio and directs their gaze. Around 1869, Bazille drew Manet, elegantly dressed in a suit and top hat, working at his easel, perhaps in the Condamine studio (fig.55).[86] Bazille's rapid sketch masterfully captures Manet's distinguished silhouette and posture as he paints and anticipates Manet's half-length *Self-Portrait with Palette*. In *Studio on the Rue La Condamine*, Bazille depicted Manet wearing a dark suit and bowler hat. Manet's improvised portrait of Bazille can be read as a clever riposte to Bazille's sketch of Manet at the easel, which creates a pictorial dialogue that reflects the painting's larger theme.

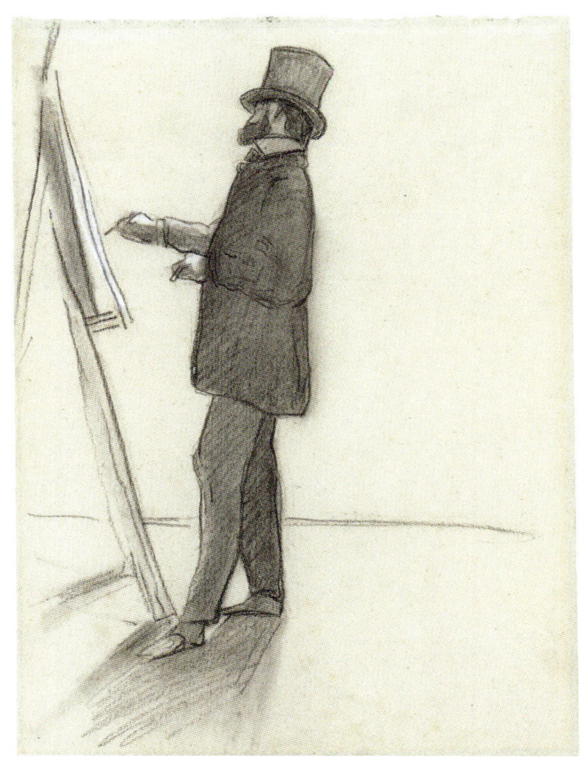

55. Frédéric Bazille, *Manet at His Easel*, c.1868–70, charcoal and white chalk on blue laid paper, 29.5 × 21.5 cm, Metropolitan Museum of Art, New York.

Studio on the Rue La Condamine is a composite image that assembles portraits of Bazille's friends in a luminous interior, conversing, playing or listening to music, thus constituting a sort of modern symposium. The figures, loosely adapted from individual portraits like the paintings on the walls, are a compendium of Bazille's own artistic development and the origins of Impressionism.[87] Bazille's small pastel study from 1869–70 of Edmond Maître and the poet Arthur Rimbaud likewise captures the studio's reflexive ambience.[88] Although Manet, Bazille and Edmond Maître (seated at the piano) are easy to recognize, the identities of the other three virtually interchangeable figures – dark haired, bearded and wearing dark suits – are disputed.[89] The figure standing behind Manet is most likely the critic Zacharie Astruc; the two men *en marge* (on the sidelines) on the stairway are probably Monet and Renoir, who also posed for Fantin-Latour's formal group portrait. Those identifications accord best with the logic of the groups, which are based on personalities, habitual activities and personal ties. Understood in this way, Bazille, Manet and Astruc are engaging in an artistic/critical dialogue, whereas Renoir and Monet are associated with the artistic/domestic space that they shared. Maître, a close friend, is aligned with music, Bazille's other passion. He and Maître played piano duets and attended concerts together. The depiction of Maître at the piano circles back to *Young Woman at the Piano* (1865–6), Bazille's first Salon submission, which was rejected in 1866 and believed lost. It was recently discovered hidden underneath *Ruth and Boaz* (1870).[90] The informal grouping in *Studio on the Rue La Condamine* suggests a compilation of different moments, or a suspended moment that, like a musical phrase, introduces the notion of time and duration.[91]

More specifically, the canvas charts Bazille's development as a painter and affirms the centrality of the studio to his artistic practice by showcasing his major figure paintings. These paintings include: *Fisherman with a Net* (1868), which was rejected from the 1869 Salon, on the left wall; the *Terrace at Méric* (1866–7), which was rejected in 1867, on the right wall; *View of the Village* (1868) on the easel; and *La Toilette* (1870), still in progress, hanging behind the sofa. Renoir's *Landscape with Two Figures*, which was rejected from the 1866 Salon, hangs above the sofa. Bazille's paintings dominate the studio; Monet, once preeminent, is only represented by a small still life. Despite its modest scale, *Studio on the Rue La Condamine* is an ambitious recasting of the studio as an interactive artistic and social space that is emblematic of Impressionist aesthetics and the painting of modern life. Finally, I would like to suggest that Bazille's studio functioned like a temporary theater set that could be adapted and repurposed for different activities by moving the furniture and rearranging the actors in space. It thus foreshadows Buren's characterization of the studio as a depot with paintings, some displayed, others piled against the wall – a depot that evolves over time, like the paintings themselves.[92]

CROSS-CURRENTS AND AFFINITIES: BAZILLE AND WHISTLER

Rather than contrasting *Studio on the Rue La Condamine* with Fantin-Latour's *Studio in the Batignolles*, it is more illuminating to consider how it corresponds and resonates with Whistler's *Artist in His Studio* (fig.56) – an oil sketch for a larger, unrealized painting for the Paris Salon, which was inspired by Velázquez's *Las Meninas*.[93] In a letter of 16 August 1865 to Fantin-Latour, Whistler described, 'a reunion of all of us . . . it shows the interior of my studio – porcelain and all. You are there, and [Alfred] Moore, the white girl sitting on the couch and the Japanese girl walking about! An apotheosis therefore of everything to outrage the Academicians.'[94] Whistler also noted the color scheme, himself in light gray, the women in white and flesh-colored dresses, Fantin-Latour and Moore in black, and a gray background. The painting was a pictorial riposte to Fantin-Latour's *Homage to Delacroix* and *Homage to Truth: The Toast*, exhibited at the 1864 and 1865 Salons, respectively, for which Whistler had posed. Although Whistler mentioned Fantin-Latour and Moore in his letter, they do not appear in the painting. Recent technical analysis has revealed a seated man in a dark jacket and hat underneath the 'Japanese girl'; however, the figure is incompatible with the composition, and there is no sign of a second figure.[95] Since the sketch differs from Whistler's description and was modified, his original concept remains a puzzle. Whistler's only other self-portrait with a painter's attributes is *Arrangement in Gray: Portrait of the Painter* (*c*.1872).[96]

During the 1860s, Whistler and Bazille were in Paris simultaneously and moved in the same artistic circles. Although it is not known if they were personally acquainted, Bazille undoubtedly saw Whistler's work at the Salon and knew him by reputation through Fantin-Latour, a close mutual friend.[97] Like *Studio on the Rue La Condamine*, *Artist in His Studio* is a multilayered, synthetic composition that is intertwined with Whistler's *Symphonies in White, Nos 1, 2* and *3*, where Joanna Hiffernan poses in a white dress, and *Princess from the Land of Porcelain* (1865), where a model in a pink kimono holds a fan.[98] *In the Studio* (1865), a related study, depicts the same view of Whistler's studio, with the porcelain cabinet at left, and two models, one of whom reclines, posing in the foreground.[99] *Artist in His Studio* also signals a shift in Whistler's artistic

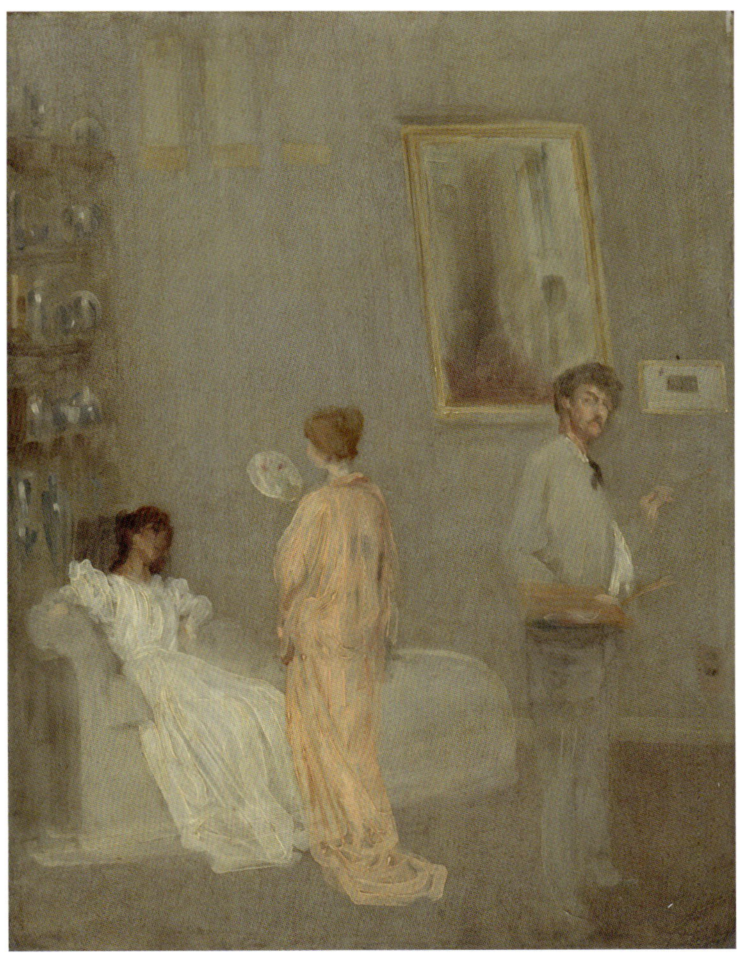

56. James Abbott McNeill Whistler, *The Artist in His Studio*, 1865–6, oil on canvas, 63 × 47.3 cm, Art Institute of Chicago, Chicago.

approach from an overt, artifact-based Japonisme to a subtle blending of Eastern and Western influences, and foreshadows the thinly painted tonal technique that he would perfect over the next decade.[100]

Artist in His Studio depicts Whistler's first Chelsea studio, no.7 Lindsey Row (now Cheyne Walk), which was near London's Battersea Bridge. Beginning in the 1860s, Whistler lived and worked at several nearby addresses and was closely identified with Chelsea.[101] His residences and studios were aesthetic models and backdrops for staging his artistic identity; they showcased his collections and actualized his ideas about interior design and displaying art.[102] In *Artist in His Studio*, Whistler's famous blue-and-white porcelain collection glistens at far left, alongside Japanese scroll paintings and a small, framed print, presumably by Whistler, at the far right. The spare but elegant interior subtly blends Eastern and Western aesthetic influences, reflecting Whistler's fascination with Japanese and Chinese art.[103] Whistler himself stands confidently in the foreground, holding a square palette and brushes in his right hand and brandishing a paintbrush in his left, with a large mirror directly behind his head. A woman in white, seated on the sofa, and a standing, kimono-clad woman, viewed from behind, holding a Japanese fan, face each other and appear to be conversing. Whistler, who wears a light gray suit that harmonizes with the studio walls, turns his back on the models and gazes out toward the viewer. His active pose, with the mirror behind him, recalls the pose of Velázquez in *Las Meninas*, but reversed, and no canvas is visible. Whistler is evidently painting his studio and his own portrait, reflected in reverse by the mirror. To do so, Whistler must have juxtaposed himself between two mirrors – one on the back wall and a second placed outside the picture frame – that would be in the viewer's space.[104] The muted reflective surface of the canvas itself is mirror-like. Thomas Way, who observed Whistler painting in his Tite Street studio, which had been designed by E.W. Godwin, described, 'a long, not very lofty room, very light, with windows along one side', a palette table and old Georgian mirror placed so Whistler could see his canvas and the model reflected in it.[105] *Artist in His Studio*, like *Studio on the Rue La Condamine*, is a complex meditation on the reflexivity of artist and studio and the practice of painting.

Despite Whistler's fame, information about his studios is fragmentary and incomplete – gleaned from contemporaneous descriptions, rare period photographs and cryptic clues in his paintings. Consequently, *Artist in His Studio* is doubly precious as a masterwork and as pictorial evidence. *Artist in His Studio* is the only surviving image of Whistler's studio, except for Walter Greaves's dubious pastiche, *Interior of the Lindsey Row Studio* (1869), which depicts Whistler posing in front of his iconic 1871 portrait of his mother.[106] Photographs of the dining room and drawing room, with its elegant Japanese decor, survive, but there are no photographs of the studio on the second floor at the back.[107] Whistler customarily hung muslin curtains in the rooms where he painted in order to get diffused light without definite shadows.[108] More than a literal representation, *Artist in His Studio* is a manifesto of art for art's sake that harmoniously amalgamates Whistler's porcelain collection and art with models in Asian and Western dress and with the artist, reflexively painting, thus blurring the boundaries between studio interior and domestic space and foregrounding the illusive sorcery of paint. Whistler's studios were typically plain workspaces devoid of decoration.[109] Jacques-Émile Blanche, who visited the Tite studio during the 1880s, emphasized the lack of decoration; he saw only a palette table with prepared colors, a black curtain and the backs of portraits that were in progress.[110]

Throughout Whistler's lifetime his studio was linked to his artistic identity and the Aesthetic movement. Fin-de-siècle critics like Gustave Geffroy envisaged Whistler's studio as a secluded refuge where he retreated into a private world of his own creation.[111] Although he alluded to Whistler's celebrity, Geffroy maintained that his true existence was solitary – like an alchemist. He poetically evoked Whistler's second-floor studio, cluttered with prints and canvases, where he reigned over a silent domain and created expressive harmonies of line and color. Whistler designed his homes as works of art that provided a frame for the paintings and prints displayed for visitors and that promoted his ideas about interior decoration and exhibition design.[112] Conceived as a public artistic manifesto and a token of friendship, *Artist in His Studio* remains an intimate, elusive aesthetic testament. While Whistler never painted the large canvas that he had envisaged, his 1895 letter to the art dealer Edward Guthrie Kennedy makes it clear that, for him, the sketch was a finished composition.[113]

The next chapter considers the gender and societal constraints that women faced when they pursued artistic careers, notably inadequate professional training and the lack of a studio. From Berthe Morisot to Marie Laurencin, most women artists worked in improvised domestic spaces rather than in professional studios.

4

Impromptu Studios

From Berthe Morisot to Marie Laurencin

> I'm often with you, my dear Berthe, in spirit; I'm in your studio and I'd like to escape if only for a quarter of an hour to breathe the atmosphere we lived in for so many years.[1]
>
> – Edma Pontillon to her sister, Berthe Morisot, 1869

> I don't think there has ever been a man who treated a woman as an equal, and that's all I would have asked, for I know I'm worth as much as they.[2]
>
> – Berthe Morisot, 1890

Although the studio has been linked to the identity and mystique of artists since the Renaissance, art has frequently been produced in makeshift spaces for various reasons. Surveying depictions of the artist's studio, there is a striking anomaly, which can be attributed to the conflicts and social and professional constraints that women artists faced due to ideologies of gender difference.[3] Whereas the studio was a common subject for male artists, it was unusual among female artists, who typically worked in improvised domestic spaces.[4] Even when successful artists, like Mary Cassatt, maintained independent studios, they rarely depicted them. Because the studio was gendered as a masculine space, it remained socially fraught for women, even if it was integrated into the domestic sphere. Women also contended with daunting obstacles to obtaining rigorous artistic training and pursuing professional careers. From Berthe Morisot to Marie Laurencin, most women artists worked out of their homes in impromptu studios. Beyond societal constraints and unequal access to artistic training, the economics of operating a studio in Paris was a further impediment. In 'L'Atelier' (1881), Realist novelist and critic Edmond Duranty estimated that a serious woman artist would spend around 1,000 francs per year on painting materials and frames, while maintaining a professional studio in Paris would cost 2,000–3,000 francs per year.[5] An individual studio thus cost more than many aspiring artists could afford; consequently, they frequently lived and worked in cramped, multipurpose spaces, or shared studios, as did Bazille, Monet and Renoir during the 1860s.

In 19th-century France, women's options for artistic training, especially working from the model, were extremely limited.[6] Until 1897, women were excluded from the École des Beaux-Arts, the premier art academy that was funded and administered by the State.[7] The only free art training available for women before 1897 was the École nationale gratuite de dessin pour les jeunes filles (Free Drawing School for Girls), which was sponsored by the city of Paris and was oriented toward earning a living from applied arts, such as embroidery or miniature painting.[8] Beginning in the 1850s, teaching studios for women like that of Madame O'Connell, opened in increasing numbers. The most viable training options for women were either studying privately with an established artist or enrolling at a private academy, such as Académie Julian, which had a separate women's section. Established in 1868, Académie Julian became a mecca for female art students. Charles Chaplin's influential, all-female studio was another alternative during the 1860s and 1870s. Mary Cassatt, Eva Gonzalès and Madeleine Lemaire were among the many women who studied there. Middle- and upper-class women, like Berthe Morisot, often took private painting and drawing lessons that were costly and were not intended to prepare them for professional careers.

Female artists were also constrained by strict gender and class divisions and by social mores that largely relegated women to the domestic sphere.[9] Talented painters, including the Morisot sisters, were deeply conflicted and struggled with a stark choice between conventional domesticity and an artistic career. Painting was viewed as a refined feminine accomplishment, much like playing the piano – an amateur hobby rather than a serious profession. Even prominent women artists who exhibited publicly usually worked out of their homes. Consequently, they were restricted to small-scale works and were likely to work in pencil, gouache or watercolor, which were portable and less messy than oil painting.[10] The artist's studio, which was perceived as a male workplace and associated with bohemianism and sexual license, was not considered respectable for middle- and upper-class women. Mirroring the paucity of studio depictions, the improvised domestic spaces where women artists typically worked are poorly documented.[11] The principal exception is Rosa Bonheur, whose unparalleled financial success enabled her to construct purpose-built studios in Paris and later at Thomery.

Due to their inadequate professional training and marginal position within the artistic establishment, women also faced challenges when they sought to exhibit their work publicly. In terms of technical skill and level of ambition, there was an enormous gap between amateur and professional artists that was difficult to surmount.[12] During the Second Empire, the percentage of women artists exhibiting at the official Salon ranged from 4.9% to 8.9%. By 1872, it had risen to 14%.[13] Although the number of women exhibiting at the Salon increased substantially when watercolors were accepted after mid-century, few women pursued public careers or actively marketed their work. Even women whose works were accepted felt disenfranchised at the Salon, which had no female jurors until 1898.[14] Not surprisingly, works by women were often poorly displayed and were rarely awarded medals or purchased by the French government. The Union des femmes peintres et sculpteurs (Union of Women Painters and Sculptors), which Bonheur called 'sisters of the brush', was founded in 1881 by sculptor Madame Léon Bertaux to unify support for women artists and to implement non-hierarchical, collective exhibitions where women could display and market their work unimpeded.[15] The first Salon des femmes (Women's Exhibition) was held in January 1882, and the Union became an influential public arts organization. Independent-minded artists, including Morisot, Cassatt and Lemaire, eschewed the Union. Instead, they preferred to exhibit with male peers at the official Salon, in specialist societies or alternative venues (such as the Impressionist exhibitions and the Salon des Indépendants), or shows organized by dealers, such as Durand-Ruel and Georges Petit.[16]

To better comprehend the combined impact of gender and of professional and societal constraints, this chapter examines the careers of five women artists from different backgrounds and generations and working in a variety of mediums, stretching from aristocratic amateurs to members of the avant-garde.

The first section focuses on two prominent, aristocratic amateurs, Adèle d'Affry, Duchess of Castiglione-Colonna, and Princesse Mathilde Bonaparte. The sections that follow survey the artistic training and careers of Berthe Morisot, Rosa Bonheur and Marie Laurencin. Despite their dissimilar personal and socioeconomic circumstances and their stylistic diversity, the systemic societal and professional obstacles that they encountered in pursuing their artistic goals are strikingly similar. Although details vary, they all contended with gender-specific hurdles and constraints, including limited access to professional training and studio space, diminished exhibition and marketing opportunities and lack of official public recognition. As artists, they struggled against gender hierarchies and social conventions, performing a delicate personal and professional balancing act.

BETWEEN STUDIO AND SALON: ARISTOCRATIC *FEMMES-ARTISTES*

Overcoming societal and professional barriers, the Swiss-born Adèle d'Affry, Duchess of Castiglione-Colonna (known professionally as 'Marcello') became a successful, critically acclaimed sculptor during the Second Empire.[17] She received prestigious private and public commissions and counted the imperial family among her patrons. Widowed at 20, she studied sculpture in Rome with Heinrich Maximilian Imhof and modeled a self-portrait and a bust of her late husband from memory in Imhof's studio (1857).[18] Socially prominent and financially independent, Marcello's artistic career commenced in 1859, when she arrived in Paris and set up her studio at 1 rue Bayard, in a building owned by Delacroix's cousin, Léon Riesener. Unable to train at the École des Beaux-Arts because of her gender, she copied the Old Masters at the Louvre and studied sculpture and anatomy privately. She obtained special permission to attend cadaver dissections at the École pratique de médecine, which necessitated dressing as a man.[19] Marcello maintained close ties with the sculptors Jean-Baptiste Carpeaux and Auguste Clésinger, whom she met in Rome. She befriended leading painters, including Delacroix, Manet, Morisot, Mariano Fortuny and Courbet, who painted her portrait in 1870. In 1874 at La Tour-de-Peilz, she shared a model with Courbet and stimulated his interest in sculpture.[20]

Unusually for a woman of her rank, Marcello received serious training in drawing, painting and sculpture. From an early age, she was fascinated by Michelangelo. Like most women sculptors, she was known primarily for portrait busts, although she also produced full-length figures, like *La Pythie* (Pythian Sybil, 1870) – her masterpiece, which was purchased for the Paris Opéra. The portrayal of heroic women was a major theme across her sculptures. In 1863, she made her debut at the Salon under the male pseudonym 'Marcello', not wishing her gender or title to impact the reception of her sculpture.[21] Her three submissions, especially *Bianca Capello*, which critics deemed worthy of a Florentine Renaissance master, were a triumph, and her career was brilliantly launched. At the 1867 Paris Exposition Universelle, Marcello staged a mini-retrospective with seven female busts and a full-length *Hecate* (1866), which had been commissioned by Napoleon III. Unlike Courbet and Manet, who showed their work in private pavilions outside the official exhibition, Marcello's femme-centric display, comprised entirely of female figures, was shown in the Exposition's Pontifical States section.[22] Her *Bianca Capello* and *Abyssinan Chieftan* were the only works by a female sculptor on view at the Musée du Luxembourg in 1873.

Prominent at court and well connected in the art world and in elite Faubourg Saint-Germain salons, Marcello led a double life as an aristocratic socialite and a professional artist. Cultivating an aristocracy of the mind, she surrounded herself with a distinguished coterie of artists, musicians and government officials, including Adolphe Thiers, and enjoyed an unusual degree of autonomy due to her aristocratic pedigree and

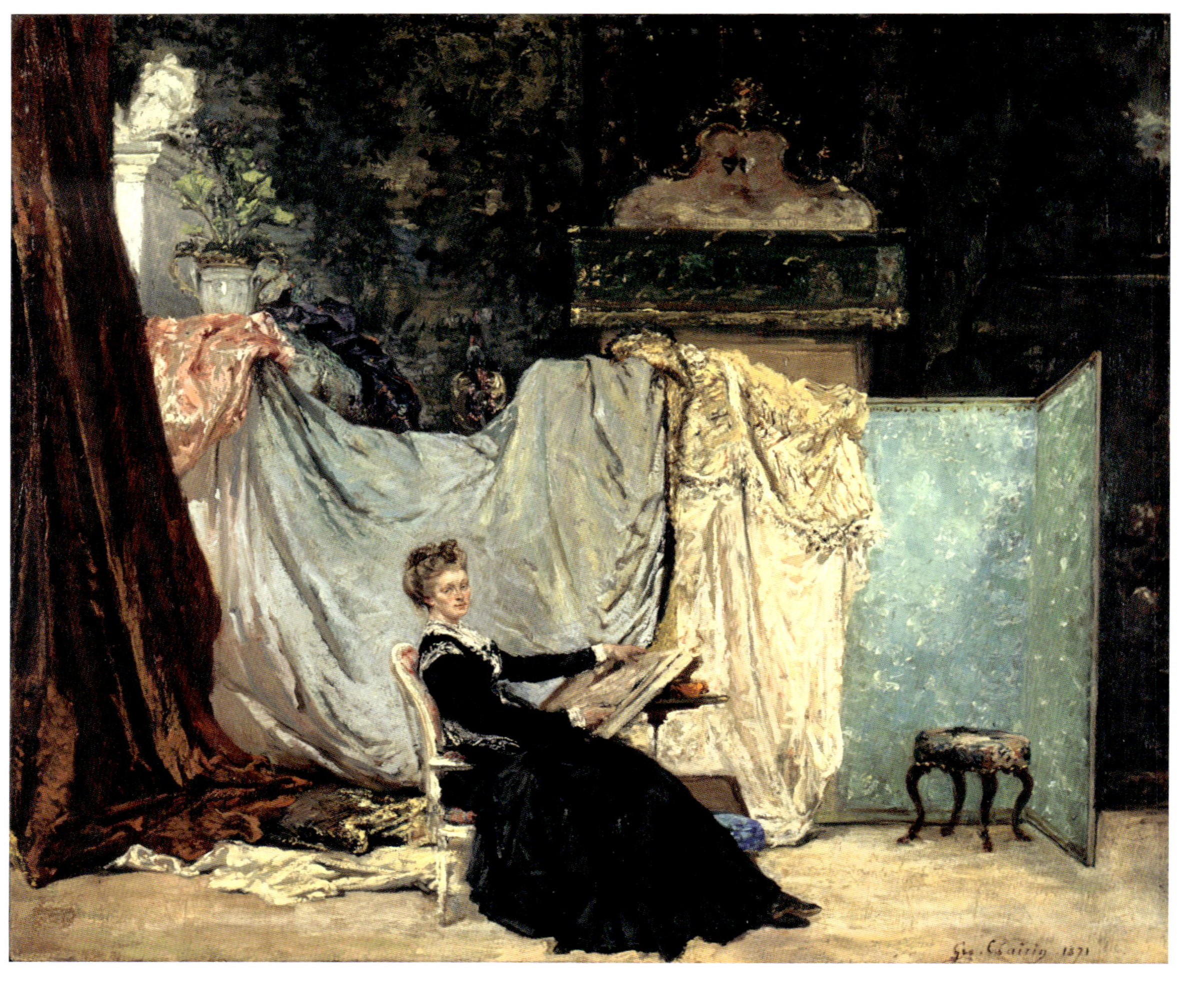

57. Georges Clairin, *Marcello in Her Studio at Givisiez*, 1871, oil on canvas, 64.5 × 77 cm, Musée d'art et d'histoire, Fribourg.

widowhood. Marcello was an influential friend and role model for Berthe Morisot at the outset of her career.[23] A painter and a sculptor, she painted Orientalist subjects and portraits, including one of Morisot in 1875.[24] In 1874 Marcello submitted her painting titled *The Feschi Conspiracy*, which was inspired by Friedrich Schiller, to the Salon; however, much to her chagrin, the jury rejected it. Critics expressed surprise that Marcello was not designated *hors concours* (outside of competition) at the Salon or officially honored with medals for her sculpture.[25] In her diary, Marcello confessed that she was 'a bluestocking, an artist, a woman of her own mind, that is to say, a tyrant'.[26] Considering her sculptures to be her true progeny ('*ses filles*', or 'her daughters'), she proactively fashioned her posthumous legacy by bequeathing a collection of her work to Fribourg to establish a museum, which opened in 1881.

Adeptly negotiating hierarchies of class and gender as well as professional obstacles, Marcello achieved success and official recognition in the male-dominated arena of sculpture, while retaining her feminine identity and exalted social position in private life. However, this delicate balancing act came at a personal cost, as evidenced in her letters and her carefully constructed public persona. No images of Marcello as a sculptor survive. Adolphe Dallemagne's portrait photograph (*c.*1866–7) for the Galerie des artistes contemporains portrays her in *toilette de bal* (formally dressed for a ball) with no reference to her art.[27] Georges Clairin's *Marcello in Her Studio at Givisiez* (1871) is the only representation of her as an artist (fig.57). Wearing an elegant, lace-trimmed black dress, she sits in a mysterious shadowy interior, silhouetted against an artfully draped, textile backdrop and screen, and works on a small drawing or pastel. In 1875, Marcello declined Manet's offer to paint her portrait for the Salon, presumably to avoid controversy. Édouard-Théophile Blanchard's full-length portrait, exhibited at the 1877 Salon, portrays Marcello wearing an ornately embroidered silk shawl over a décolleté, black velvet evening gown with a train, in an eclectic interior, decorated with textiles and *objets d'art*, that may be her studio (fig.58). Blanchard's portrait was intended to perpetuate the memory of 'a serious artist' and 'femme du meilleur monde' (high-born society woman) who seamlessly melded the aristocratic, the artistic and the bohemian.[28] Posed like a Spanish dancer, Marcello stands in profile, her head turned toward the viewer, holding a closed fan in her left hand. Her portfolio, resting on a chair, and the bronze copy of *The Gorgon* (1865), which she gave to Blanchard in exchange for the portrait, discreetly allude to her artistic vocation.

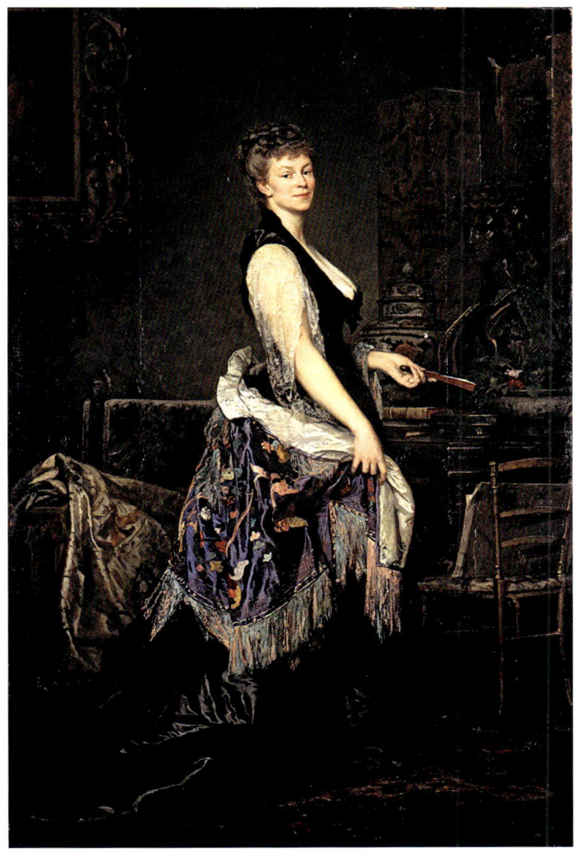

58. Édouard-Théophile Blanchard, *Portrait of Marcello, Duchess of Castiglione-Colonna*, 1877, oil on canvas, 245.5 × 161 cm, Musée d'art et d'histoire, Fribourg.

Princesse Mathilde Bonaparte, amateur artist and *salonnière* for over half a century, followed a more conventional trajectory. The studios in her Paris and country residences were integral to her artistic persona and a social nexus.[29] She painted every day, often in the company of friends, and regularly worked from the model. Besides her quasi-religious devotion to painting, she manifested her identity as *femme-artiste* by exhibiting at the Salon (1859–70) and by forging ties with numerous artists whose studios she frequented.[30] Like many women artists, Princesse Mathilde studied painting privately under Ernest Hébert and Eugène Giraud and primarily drew and worked in watercolor. She exhibited portraits, Orientalist studies and copies after the Old Masters at the Salon. Her ambitious, large-scale watercolors, which were painted from nature, were admired for their rich color and vigorous technique. Also a collector and patron, she donated works to French museums including the Musée du Luxembourg and the Château de Versailles. By exhibiting at the Salon and strategically placing

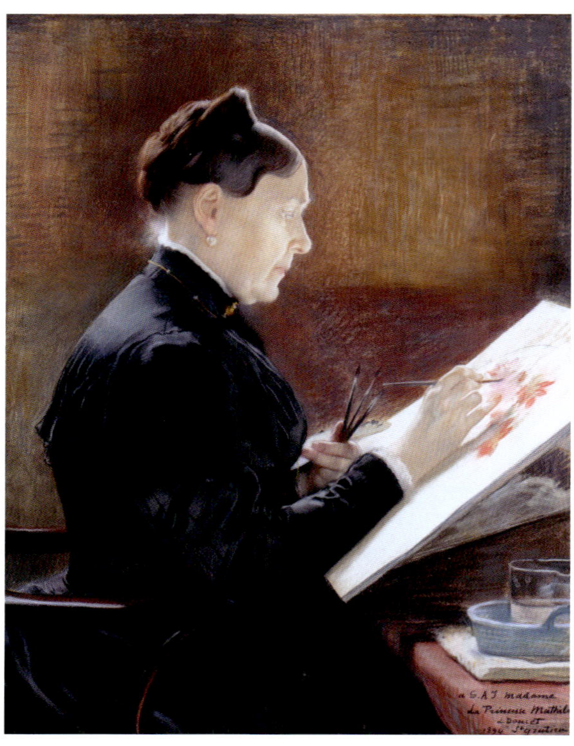

59. Henri-Lucien Doucet, *Portrait of Princesse Mathilde*, 1894, pastel, 92.4 × 73.1 cm, Musée national des Châteaux de Versailles et de Trianon, Versailles.

her works in public collections, she gained artistic recognition and assured her posthumous legacy.[31]

Exceptionally for a woman of her eminence, Princesse Mathilde was depicted as an artist in paintings and photographs, some of which were reproduced.[32] In a watercolor (*c.*1850), Eugène Giraud discreetly portrayed her from behind; we see her seated at the easel, holding a porcelain watercolor palette in her left hand and drawing a masculine profile on a large sheet of paper. Dallemagne's photograph (*c.*1866), created for the Galerie des artistes contemporains, represents Princesse Mathilde as a painter, holding palette and brushes, with a cartel identifying her. Her elegant dress, pearl necklace and pendant earrings highlight her dual persona of painter and princess. During the same session, Dallemagne also photographed her in *grande toilette*, wearing a diadem. Henri-Lucien Doucet portrayed her in old age in an intimate, half-length pastel portrait, seated at her drawing table in her Saint-Gratien studio, painting flowers in watercolor (fig.59).[33] As she delicately wields her brush, her intense concentration is almost palpable. Her august profile, irradiated against the somber background, accentuates the reality effect. Edmond de Goncourt termed the portrait, which was unveiled after dinner in the rue de Berri salon, a perfect likeness.[34] Princesse Mathilde particularly prized Doucet's informal portrait, which appeared on the cover of *L'Illustration* in 1903. She distributed reproductions of it to close friends and bequeathed the original to the Château de Versailles.

In her elegantly appointed salon-atelier at the Hôtel de Bragance, 24 rue de Courcelles, Princesse Mathilde received members of the literary and artistic elite, notably Gustave Flaubert, the Goncourt brothers, Charles-Augustin Saint-Beuve, and numerous artists, including Alexandre Cabanel, Paul Gavarni, Jean-Léon Gérôme and Carpeaux, to name a few. During the 1860s, at the height of her salon's success, she consecrated Wednesdays to writers and Fridays to artists.[35] Charles Giraud, Eugène's younger brother, meticulously documented the storied salon-atelier in a series of paintings, one of which was exhibited at the 1857 Salon.[36] In this painting Princesse Mathilde's drawing table and easel are enshrined at the center of the grand drawing room, and a work in progress is displayed on the easel, highlighting her love of art.[37] The opulent interior opens onto a veranda and is adorned with precious art objects and family portraits, including that of Napoleon.

Complementing the imposing salon-atelier on the main floor, Princesse Mathilde designed a smaller, more intimate workspace under the eaves – a private sanctuary devoted to painting, where she spent countless hours and admitted only close friends.

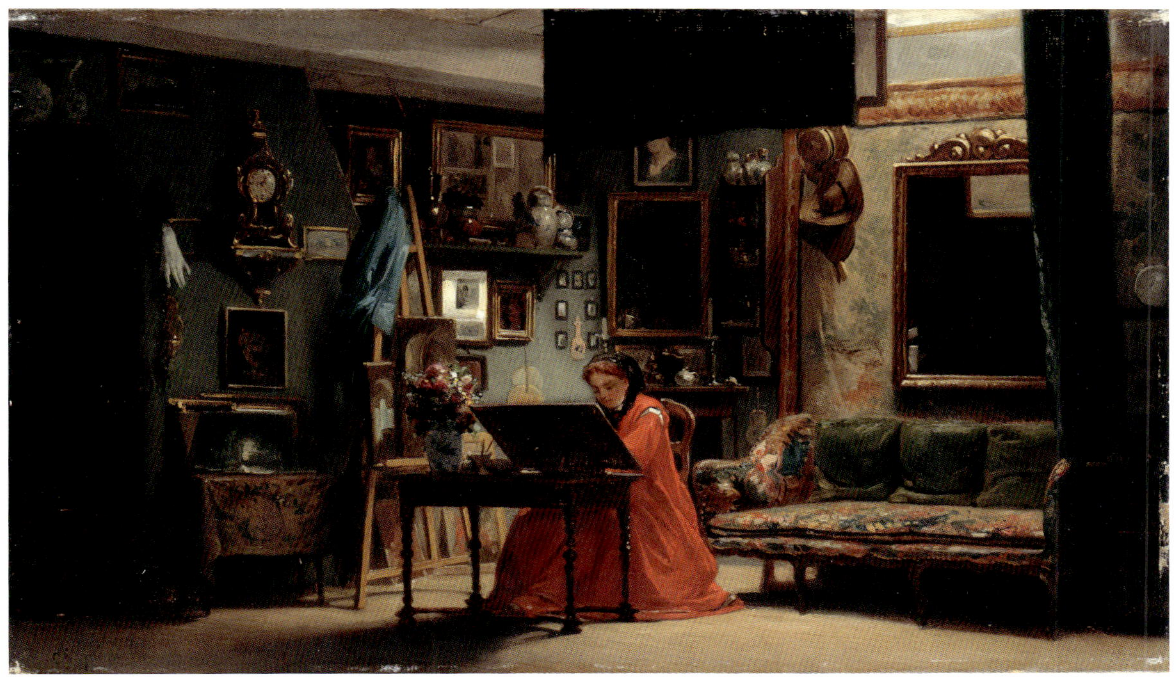

60. Charles Giraud, *Princesse Mathilde in Her Studio*, 1850s, oil on canvas, 30 × 51 cm, Musée du Château de Compiègne, Compiègne.

Charles Giraud's *Princesse Mathilde in Her Studio* (1850s, fig.60), depicts her *petit atelier*, which was heated by a little stove; the walls are covered with her studies, and paintings are stacked haphazardly on the floor. Princesse Mathilde, wearing a bright red *robe de chambre* (dressing gown), sits at her drawing desk. Behind her are a Louis XV mirror and a comfortable settee.[38] Her elegant *deshabille* and the refined 18th-century furnishings evoke the rarefied atmosphere of the Ancien Régime. The existence of replicas suggests she may have given copies of Giraud's painting to friends. Her intense absorption in her work and the studio setting testify to her dedication to painting and underscore her self-identification and reinvention as a *femme-peintre* after she moved to Paris.

Princesse Mathilde was instrumental in launching the fashion for the salon-atelier – a hybrid artistic and reception space for elite entertaining. After the collapse of the Second Empire, she moved into a smaller townhouse on rue de Berri, where she created a large drawing room by linking a greenhouse and a dining room and resurrected her legendary salon. At the turn of the century, young Marcel Proust frequented her salon, and she makes a cameo appearance in his *Within a Budding Grove* (1918). On 25 February 1903, Proust published a historical account of her salon in *Le Figaro* under the pseudonym 'Dominique', which recreated one of her celebrated soirées.[39] Proust was profoundly moved by the aged Princesse Mathilde and her salon, which he envisaged as a *lieu de mémoire* – a living repository of human and literary history that bore the indelible imprint of the luminaries who had once gathered there and miraculously embalmed the vestiges of its glorious past.

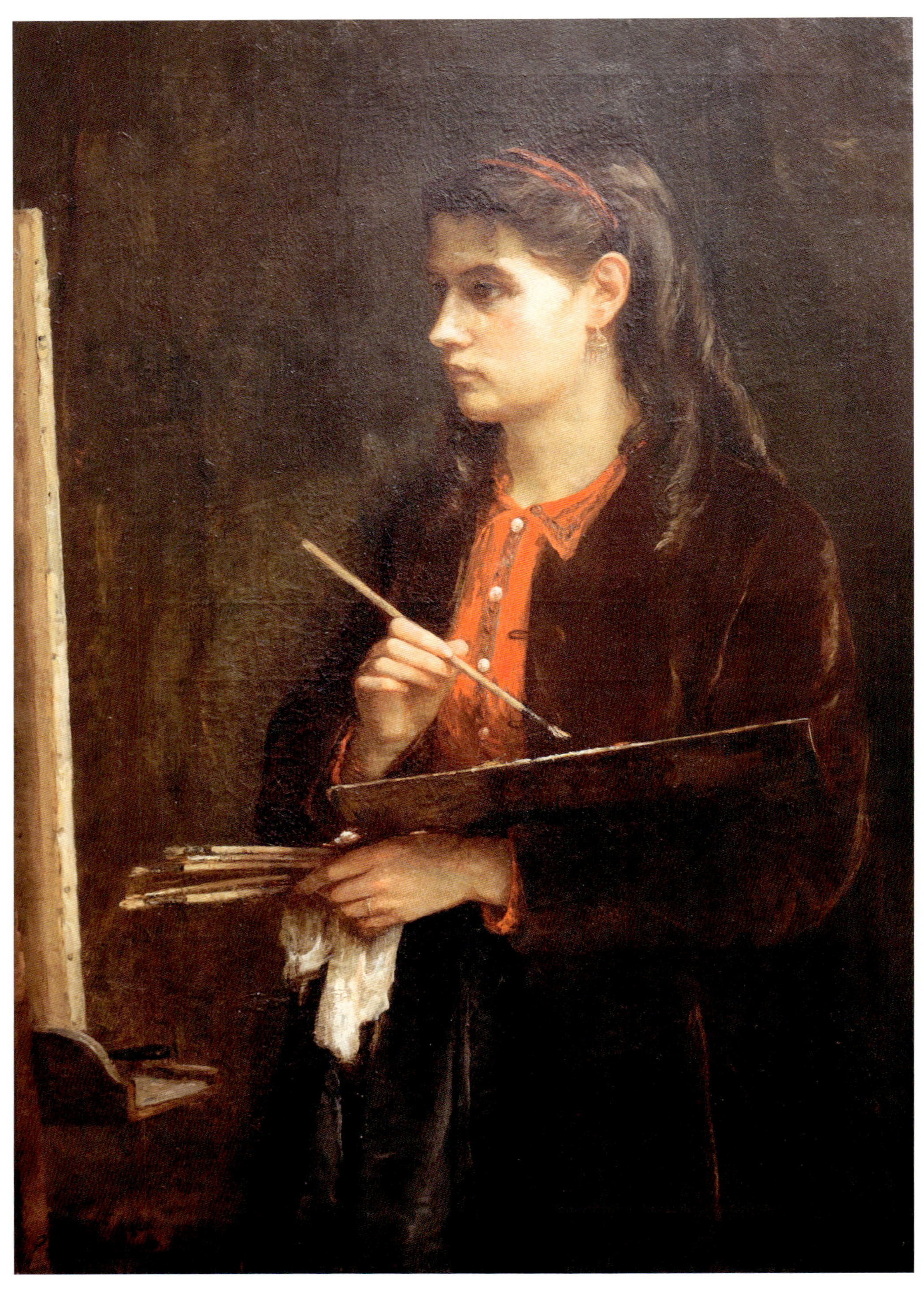

61. Edma Morisot, *Portrait of Berthe Morisot at the Easel*, *c.*1865, oil on canvas, 100 × 71 cm, private collection.

AGAINST THE ODDS: BECOMING AN IMPRESSIONIST PAINTER

For most of her career, Berthe Morisot worked without a proper studio. Independent-minded and determined to become a painter, Berthe and her sister, Edma, studied privately with Joseph Guichard and made copies after the Old Masters at the Louvre. They were chaperoned by their mother, who disregarded Guichard's warning that, with temperaments like theirs, his teaching would make the sisters painters rather than talented amateurs.[40] During the early 1860s, both sisters studied plein-air painting under Corot and Achille Oudinot and were inspired by Daubigny's example to try painting from small boats.[41] In 1864, Morisot's father constructed at considerable expense a studio pavilion for his daughters in the garden of their rue Franklin residence.[42] The studio gave Morisot a space of her own where she could escape domestic obligations and paint without interruptions. Although her parents were unusually supportive, the studio fostered independence, which led to familial tensions.

Edma's marriage in 1869 left Morisot bereft of companionship, alone in her dogged pursuit of painting. When the family moved to a new apartment at 7 rue Guichard in 1873, Morisot relinquished her precious studio and was reduced to working in her bedroom.[43] In his youth, Jacques-Émile Blanche visited Morisot's provisional workspace in the family apartment. Devoid of bric-a-brac and art objects, except for a few studies and a treasured sketch by Corot, Blanche nonetheless recognized it as 'the studio of a great artist'.[44] Unfortunately, he was unable to see any paintings, since Morisot destroyed almost all her work out of dissatisfaction at that time.

There are no images of the rue Franklin studio, which was rectangular and had high windows on two sides. Furnished with a red sofa and a pouffe, it overflowed with canvases at various stages of completion.[45] Morisot's emerging identity as an artist is captured in the portrait that Edma painted around

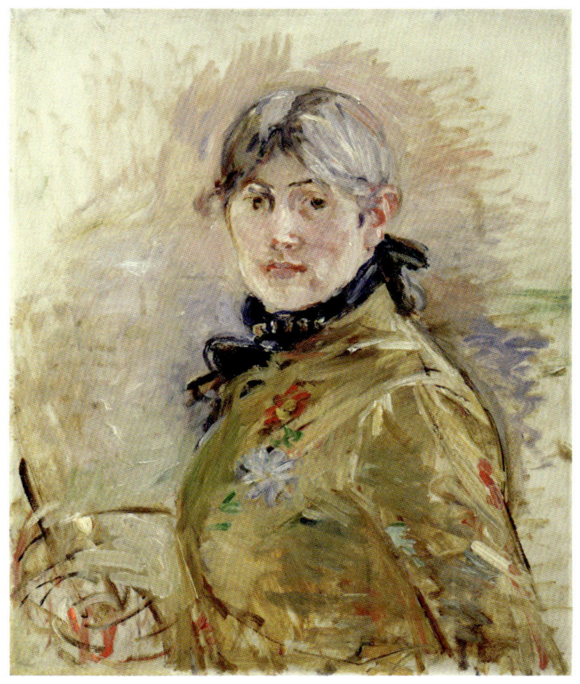

62. Berthe Morisot, *Self-Portrait*, 1885, oil on canvas, 61 × 50 cm, Musée Marmottan Monet, Paris.

1865, shortly after their mutual debut at the 1864 Salon (fig.61). The undated canvas is a tangible record of the studio that they shared from 1864 until 1869. Berthe, wearing a loose brown smock and red blouse, stands at the easel, her head turned to the left, holding her palette and brushes. Silhouetted against a dark background, her face and hands are illuminated. Her serious expression and fierce concentration evoke her determination to pursue a painting career. The canvas that she is painting is hidden; only the edge of it catches the light. Edma's three-quarter length portrait lacks the studied pose and elegant femininity of Manet's *Portrait of Eva Gonzalès* (fig.18). By depicting Berthe at work in a format typically used for self-portraits, Edma created a self-reflexive double portrait that testifies to and commemorates their years of camaraderie and shared artistic ambitions. In 1869, Edma wistfully wrote: 'I'm often with you, my dear Berthe, in spirit; I'm in your studio and I'd like to escape if only for a quarter of an hour to breathe the atmosphere we lived in for so many years'.[46]

Through social connections and ties with artists including Corot, Marcello and Puvis de Chavannes, Morisot built a professional network that expanded her artistic and intellectual horizons. From 1864 to 1873, she exhibited regularly at the official Salon. In 1867, she began placing her works with dealers, notably Louis Martinet, Alfred Cadart and Durand-Ruel. By exhibiting her work at the Salon as well as in private galleries, Morisot gained professional exposure and began to attract the notice of collectors.[47] She was respected by her male peers, especially Manet (for whom she posed in the late 1860s and early 1870s), Fantin-Latour, Monet, Degas and Renoir, all of whom became personal friends. Degas invited her to participate in the first Impressionist exhibition. After 1874, Morisot abandoned the official Salon and boldly cast her lot with the fledgling Impressionist movement. Rather than vying for institutional recognition at the Salon, she found her niche outside the official art establishment. Consequently, she was free to focus on depicting modern interiors and landscapes and to experiment with painting techniques.

After Morisot married Eugène Manet in December 1874, she painted whenever and wherever she could – either outdoors or, more frequently, in her bedroom or living room. In the house that she and Manet built at 40 rue de Villejust in 1883, Morisot designed an elegant, ground-floor salon-atelier, where she received guests and painted. The high-ceilinged, light-filled salon was tastefully decorated with Japanese screens, Japanese prints, Empire furniture and paintings.[48] Contemporaneous photographs offer glimpses of the marble mantel, surmounted by a mirror, and the art covering the walls. A nearly invisible closet, where Morisot's painting materials could be stored at the end of the day or whisked away when visitors arrived unexpectedly, was concealed behind a wall.[49] Like many women artists, Morisot did not separate her art from her domestic life; rather, her art was subsumed into her domestic world. Presiding as wife, mother, painter and hostess in the salon-atelier, she blurred traditional gender divisions and effaced distinctions between domestic space and workspace.[50] In 1890, after more than three decades as a painter, Morisot finally got a studio of her own in the attic of La Blotière, a rental property at Mézy. After her husband's death in 1892, she and her daughter, Julie, moved to a new apartment at 10 rue Wéber, where Morisot created a top-floor studio from repurposed maids' rooms.[51]

Except for the portrait by her sister, the only depiction of Morisot painting is a half-length, rapidly brushed self-portrait at the easel (fig.62). The brilliant light and vibrant palette suggest that it was painted in the Villejust salon-atelier with its south-facing window. Morisot represented herself at close range in the traditional attitude used for self-portraits, asserting her parity with her male counterparts.[52] Her hand is blurred, thematizing the act of painting. Around 1885, Morisot began keeping notebooks to jot down ideas and impressions as part of an intensified process of self-examination.[53] In three related self-portraits from 1885, which were only discovered after her death, she took stock of herself and rehearsed her identity as a woman painter.[54] Although she is dressed identically in all three, the portraits reveal dueling aspects of her persona and underscore the disjunction between her private and professional roles.[55] The two painted self-portraits, the second of which is a double portrait with Julie, highlight her technical virtuosity and rapid brushwork and confidently convey her identity as a woman and a painter on her own terms.[56] The third self-portrait is a psychologically probing pastel, which scrutinizes Morisot's partially shadowed face. In this haunting image, Morisot appears anxious and vulnerable rather than self-assured. The disarray and emotional rawness of the picture recall Manet's *Berthe Morisot in a Mourning Hat* (1874), which he painted shortly after her father's death. The unfinished *Self-Portrait with Julie*, which resembles the 1885 *Self-Portrait*, depicts Morisot posing in the studio, with Julie at her side. Emphasizing her maternal identity, this double portrait presents a more conventional feminine image and suggests a balance between the personal and the professional. Morisot also drew portraits of herself and Julie, one of which she reworked as a print, and in 1887, she painted a small full-length double portrait with a rapid sketch of Julie.[57]

During the 1880s, Morisot often depicted domestic interiors with servants or nursemaids going about their daily activities, which closely mirror her own surroundings, and, like her self-portraits, they are technically daring and experimental and break with convention.[58] Due to the gendering of Morisot's style as quintessentially feminine, which began during her lifetime, together with her focus on female subjects, self-effacing personality and disinterest in self-promotion or marketing her art, critics have until recently underestimated her central role in the Impressionist movement.[59] Writing for *Le Temps* in 1877, Paul Mantz observed, 'The truth is that there's only one Impressionist in the rue Le Peletier group: that is Berthe Morisot'.[60] Morisot participated in all the Impressionist exhibitions, except in 1879, when Julie's birth prevented her from exhibiting. She was a friend and confidant of Degas, Monet, Renoir and Stéphane Mallarmé, who attended the artistic soirées that she hosted on Thursdays at her home on rue de Villejust. Through the concerted efforts of Duret and Mallarmé, Morisot's *Young Woman in a Ball Gown* (1879) became the first Impressionist painting to enter the Musée du Luxembourg in 1894.[61]

BREAKING THE MOLD: A STUDIO OF ONE'S OWN

Rosa Bonheur was a trailblazer of female autonomy and professional and financial success. Trained from an early age by her father, Raimond, who was a drawing master and an ardent Saint-Simonian, she began making copies in the studio and rapidly progressed to painting landscape and animal studies from nature.[62] She rounded out her artistic education by copying Old Masters at the Louvre and studying anatomy at the Roule slaughterhouse.[63] Unlike many women artists, Bonheur received comprehensive training and was encouraged and nurtured by her artist-father, although her childhood was darkened by financial hardship and her mother's death when she was 11. After her father remarried, Rosa and her younger siblings worked beside him in a studio, which had a large window, a stall for animal models and a bird cage.[64] In 1841, at 19, Bonheur made her debut at the Salon and exhibited regularly thereafter until 1855. A member of the Realist generation, she adhered to the principle of direct observation from nature. Critics lauded her scrupulous technique and verisimilitude, and she rapidly gained renown as an *animalier*. With *Ploughing in the Nivernais* (1849), her artistic career was launched.

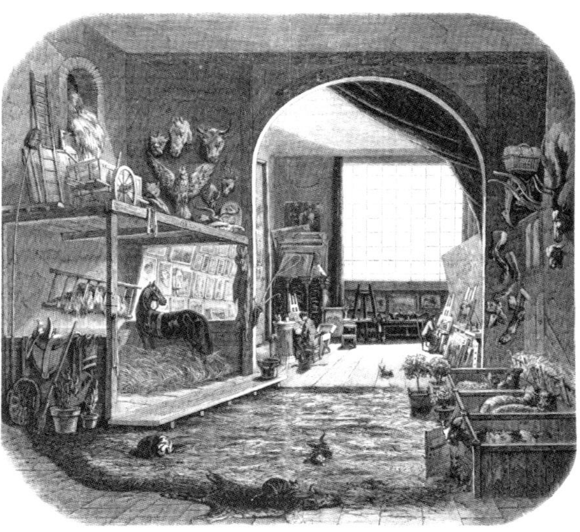

63. Studio of Rosa Bonheur, in *L'Illustration*, 1852, engraving, 20.5 × 23.7 cm, University of California, Berkeley, CA.

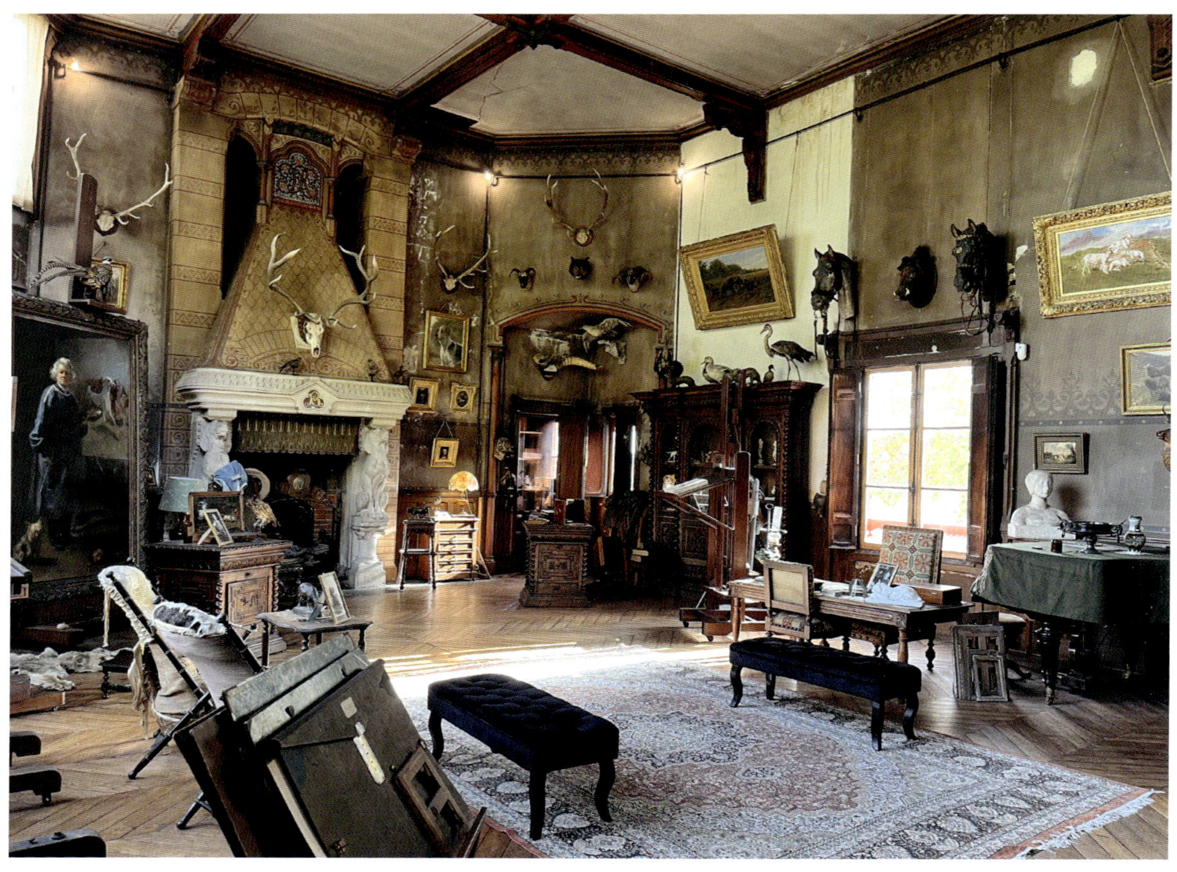

64. Studio of Rosa Bonheur, Château de By, Thomery, *c.*1860.

Commissioned by the French government, Bonheur's timeless evocation of traditional rural life triumphed at the 1849 Salon.[65] The Tedesco brothers, her principal Paris dealers, and the London-based dealer Ernest Gambart, who became a lifelong friend, aggressively marketed her work and besieged her with orders, ensuring her financial success.[66]

In 1849, Bonheur left home to set up her own studio in the rue de l'Ouest, a tranquil artists' colony near the Luxembourg Gardens. Her picturesque, rustic atelier was featured in *L'Illustration* in 1852 (fig.63), confirming her rising artistic stature. The high-ceilinged, wood-floored studio was illuminated by an immense, multi-paned window at the rear and adjoined a barn-like space housing horses and livestock that facilitated painting animal subjects.[67] The *L'Illustration* print depicts Bonheur and her companion, Nathalie Micas, working in the studio, which was crammed with easels and stacks of paintings. At the right Bonheur, her hair cropped short like a young man's, sits at the easel before a vast canvas, surrounded by studies of horses. The accompanying article extolled Bonheur's talent and industriousness and mentioned her studies for *Horse Fair,* which she called her 'Parthenon Frieze'. Bonheur's first independent studio set the pattern for the larger, more elaborate studios that she would occupy for the rest of her career.

In 1853, Bonheur moved into a spacious, purpose-built studio in the rue d'Assas; designed by art

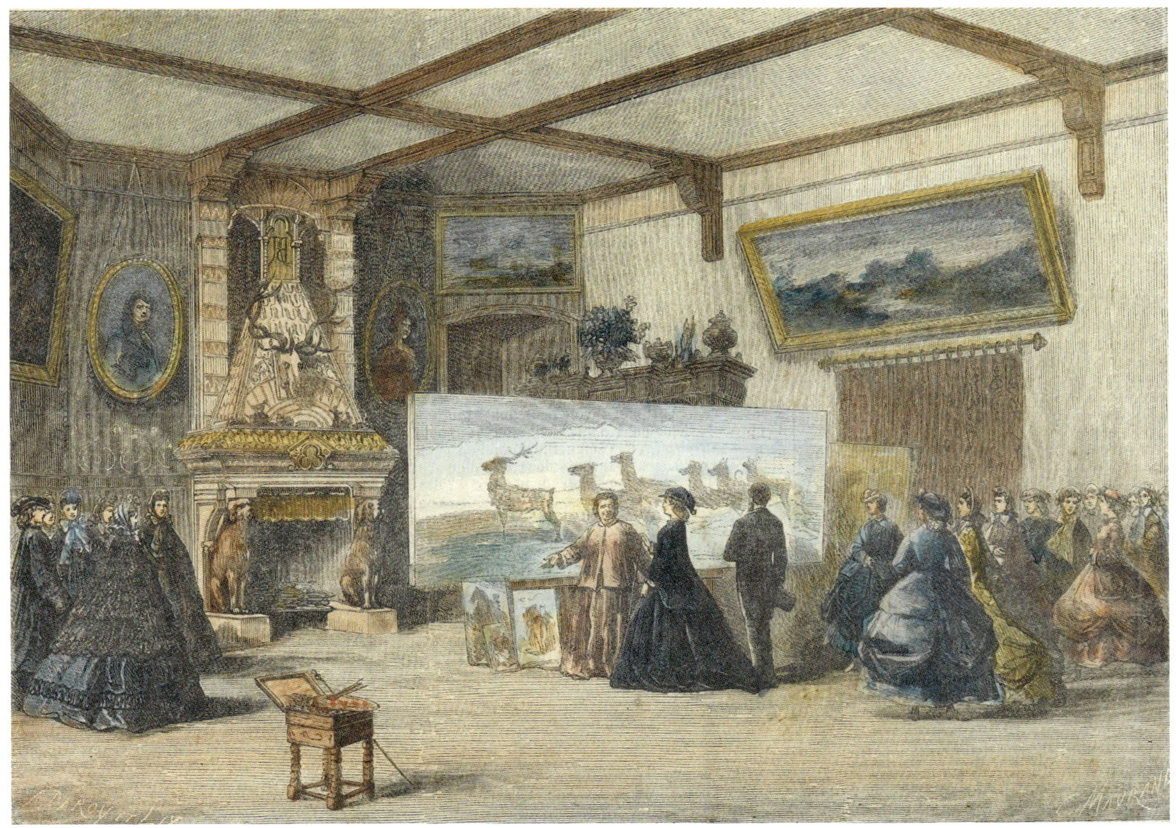

65. Charles Maurand (after Isidore-Laurent Deroy), *Empress Eugénie Visiting Rosa Bonheur in Her Studio*, 1864, colored wood engraving, 16 × 22 cm, Château de Fontainebleau, Fontainebleau.

connoisseur Georges Meusnier, it had a courtyard and extensive gardens.[68] Although no images survive, various visitors, including Eugène de Mirecourt and Armand Baschet, described the studio. Tastefully furnished and papered in green velvet, the studio was on the second floor.[69] On Fridays, Bonheur received artists, writers, musicians and fashionable society, even members of the court, at her studio, which doubled as a salon.[70] The property included a garden with palisaded stables and a menagerie of farmyard animals and fowl that roamed freely in a fenced enclosure. Baschet observed that Bonheur's domain could almost 'be taken for a real model farm'.[71] Visitors admired the menagerie and the well-proportioned, light-filled studio. Paintings, sketches, casts and trophy heads decorated the walls; the floor was carpeted with exotic animal pelts. Easels and works in progress, scattered around the room, completed the animal-themed decor.[72] Attracted by Bonheur's artistic celebrity, visitors were also intrigued by her unconventional appearance and eccentric lifestyle, from her cropped hair to her masculine dress and her habit of riding astride through the streets of Paris. At Chevilly outside Paris, Bonheur repurposed an old barn, used as a second studio and to house additional livestock.[73]

Horse Fair, Bonheur's *magnum opus*, made her the most famous female artist of the 19th century and an international celebrity. The immense canvas, measuring

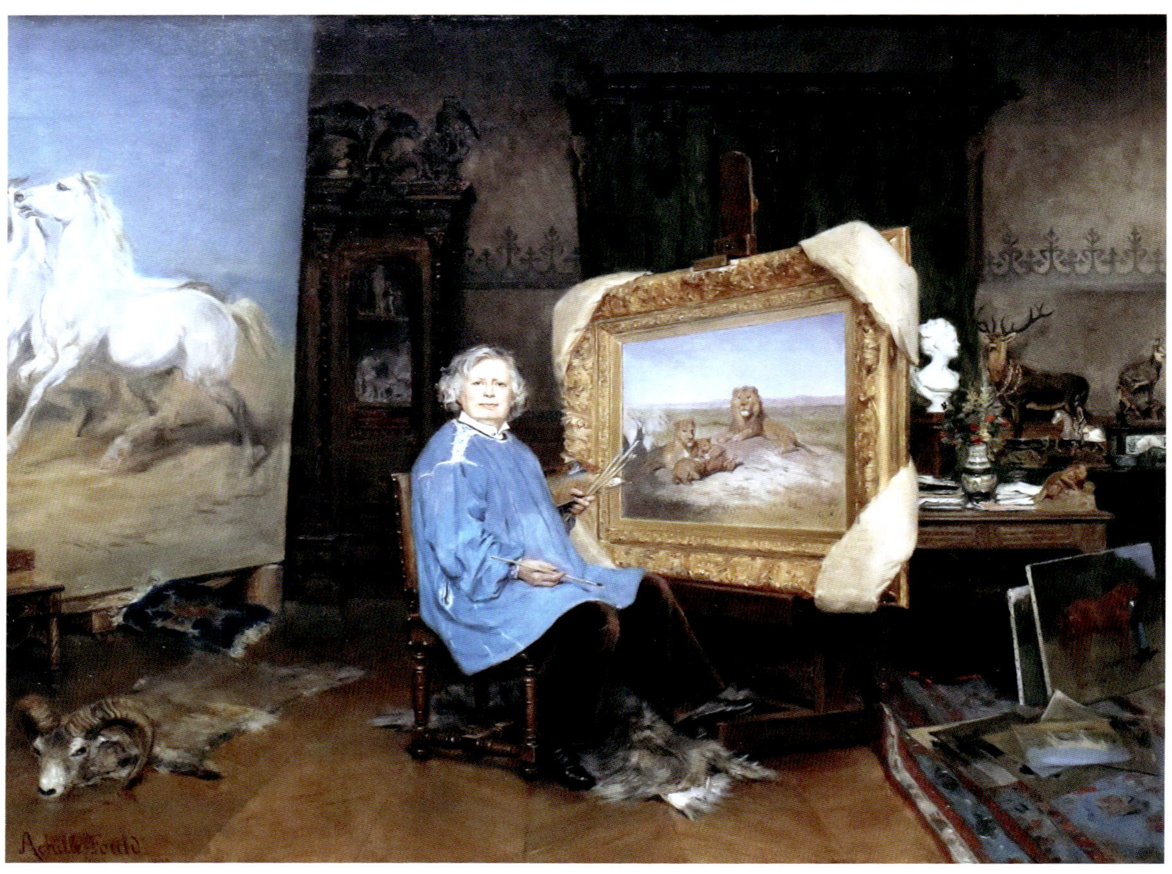

66. Georges Achille-Fould, *Rosa Bonheur in Her Studio*, 1893, oil on canvas, 91 × 124 cm, Musée des Beaux-Arts, Bordeaux.

2.4 × 5 m, depicts the Boulevard de l'Hôpital horse market and demonstrates Bonheur's extraordinary mastery of animal anatomy on an epic scale. Critically acclaimed and popular at the 1853 Salon, *Horse Fair* was compared to paintings by Géricault. After the Salon, it was exhibited in Ghent and Bordeaux, but did not find a buyer. In 1855, Gambart purchased the canvas from Bonheur for the princely sum of 40,000 francs and had it engraved.[74] In 1856, *Horse Fair* was exhibited at Pall Mall Gallery in London. Bonheur toured England and Scotland, and she and her painting were a sensation.[75] Although *Horse Fair* was not acquired by the Bordeaux Museum as Bonheur had initially hoped, Cornelius Vanderbilt purchased it in 1887 and donated it to the Metropolitan Museum in New York, where it remains one of the most popular paintings on view.[76]

In 1860, Bonheur and Micas abandoned the Paris art world and moved to the bucolic Château de By in Thomery, near Fontainebleau – a move that was financed by the sale of *Horse Fair*. Bonheur constructed an elegant addition, featuring a spacious, light-filled studio on the second floor, where she could work on large-scale paintings.[77] The studio, which was custom built by Louis-Jules Saulnier, had a huge, north-facing window as well as a south-facing window, to provide as much natural light as possible for painting (fig.64).

Besides this 'grand studio', which Bonheur called her 'sanctuary', there was a small adjoining photographic studio and a billiard room that was used as a winter studio. From her garden, Bonheur could access the forest; accompanied by her dogs and pet monkeys, she took walks and sketched.[78] She kept a changing menagerie of domestic and wild animals and set up a dissection laboratory to further her study of anatomy.

On 14 June 1864, Empress Eugénie, who admired Bonheur's work, made a surprise studio visit and commissioned a painting.[79] Bonheur's fragmentary autobiography recounts scrambling to slip a skirt over her flannel knickerbockers and put on the black jacket that she wore for formal occasions, before the Empress arrived. On 8 June 1865, the final day of her regency, Eugénie made a second visit to award Bonheur the Legion of Honor. She pinned the cross to Bonheur's jacket and embraced the new chevalier.[80] In bestowing it, Eugénie pointedly asserted, 'Genius has no sex'.[81] Her first impromptu visit, which was recorded in Charles Maurand's engraving after Deroy and published on 25 June 1864 in *Le Monde illustré*, anticipated the formal presentation (fig.65). In the engraving, the Empress and artist stand at the center of the studio in front of Bonheur's enormous *Family of Deer* (1865), and her paint box is visible in the left foreground. Thronged with fashionably dressed attendants in crinolines, the studio is recast as a ceremonial reception hall and imperial stage for Eugénie's official consecration of a female painter. The first woman to be honored for artistic talent, Bonheur was promoted to the rank of officer in 1894 – another first.

For almost four decades, Bonheur worked tirelessly in her By studio, where she received family, friends and visitors, ranging from collectors and dealers to the Empress and Buffalo Bill Cody, who visited in September 1889. His Wild West troupe of 115 Native Americans, 48 cowboys and a menagerie of buffaloes, mustangs and horses performed at the 1889 World's Fair, enthralling Parisians and also Bonheur, who haunted the encampment and made numerous sketches

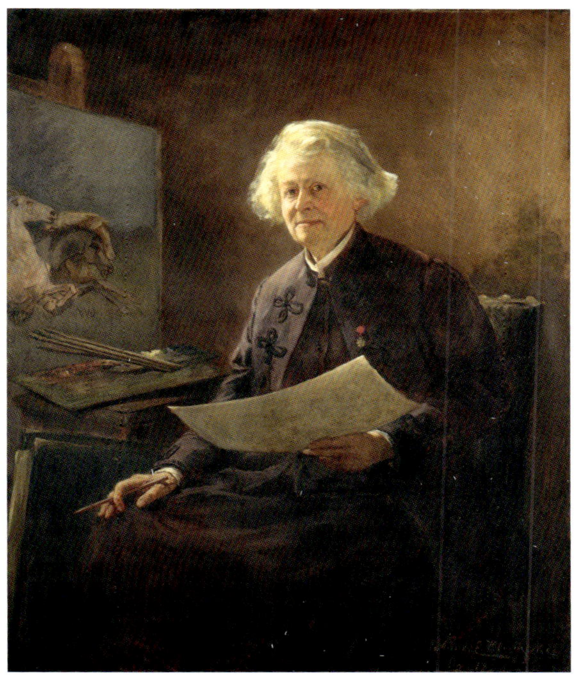

67. Anna Klumpke, *Portrait of Rosa Bonheur*, 1898, oil on canvas, 117.2 × 98.1 cm, Metropolitan Museum of Art, New York.

and paintings, including a small equestrian portrait of Cody riding his favorite horse.[82] From the sculpted dogs supporting the mantel, executed by her brother Isidore, to trophy heads and taxidermized pets to studies and works in progress, animals permeate the studio, which is now a museum. Recently restored and preserved exactly as Bonheur left it, the studio is a time capsule and a moving memorial to her lifelong dedication to art – 'a tyrant' that demanded 'heart, brain, soul, body' and that she was wedded to for life.[83] (fig.64). The By studio was depicted in contemporaneous prints and photographs and late portraits of Bonheur. Paul Chardin's lively drawing (1870) shows Bonheur painting at the easel, surrounded by dogs, assorted fowl and the tall ladder that she used for large canvases.[84] Material artifact and *lieu de mémoire*, the By studio functioned as a palimpsest of Bonheur's life as a painter.

Édouard Dubufe's three-quarter length portrait, which was exhibited at the 1857 Salon, depicts Bonheur holding a crayon in her right hand and a portfolio in her left, with a landscape behind her. Although her hair is cropped, she is demurely clad in a black dress and white lace collar. Dissatisfied with the portrait's blandness, Bonheur proposed replacing the table against which she was leaning with her favorite bull, and Dubufe agreed. Bonheur's arm is draped over the bull, which dominates the canvas, transforming it into a collaborative double portrait that highlights her lifelong love of animals. Recalling Paulus Potter's celebrated *Bull* (1647), Bonheur showed off her technical prowess, claiming her place in history as a preeminent *animalier* and her illustrious male predecessor's equal. Dubufe received 8,000 francs for the portrait; Bonheur earned 7,000 francs for the bull.[85]

During the 1890s, three women artists closely tied to Bonheur – Consuélo Fould and Georges Achille-Fould (daughters of her friend, Princess Stirbey) and Anna Klumpke – painted the aging artist in the By studio. In 1893, Bonheur posed for the Foulds. Consuélo's London publisher commissioned her to paint Bonheur's portrait as a pendant to Dubufe's portrait.[86] Echoing Dubufe, Consuélo depicted Bonheur at three-quarter length, in a dark painting smock with a white collar. Bonheur holds a large palette and brushes in her left hand and rests her right hand on the head of one of her beloved dogs, which she had painted, thus emphasizing her empathy for animals and skill in painting them.[87] Her austere dress, erect posture and serious expression are characteristics more typically found in masculine professional portraits. Critics, including her biographer, Roger-Milès, associated the superiority of Bonheur's art with masculine qualities.

Achille-Fould's *Rosa Bonheur in Her Studio*, which was exhibited at the 1893 Salon, uses standard tropes for depicting male artists, thus underscoring Bonheur's professional persona (fig.66). Wearing her work costume – a blue smock and trousers, Bonheur sits at the easel, holding her palette and brushes, before a painting of a lion family. At the left, the edge of an unfinished canvas, *Wheat Threshing in the Camargue*, is visible, recalling her celebrated *Horse Fair*. Bonheur herself painted the pictures that appear in Achille-Fould's portrait, making it a creative collaboration and mise en abyme, in which the artist/subject (re)painted the works that surround and define her.[88] Devoid of feminine referents, the studio is furnished like a typical masculine workspace – replete with animal skin rugs and taxidermies, evoking the hunt. As in Chardin's drawing of Bonheur's studio, paintings and studies are scattered, but there are no live animals. Bonheur, unsmiling, gazes sternly out at the viewer, asserting her artistic vocation and making the case for female genius and friendship. The portrait was purchased by friends of Bonheur for the Bordeaux Museum. In 1898, Bonheur commissioned Anna Klumpke to paint her portrait (fig.67).[89] Bonheur, who was increasingly frail, sits at the easel, holding a pencil in her right hand and a drawing or print in her left, with her palette and brushes and a sketch of horses nearby. Posing for posterity, she is formally dressed in a long black skirt and frogged jacket, topped with a stiff white collar – the Legion of Honor displayed on her left lapel. In this memorial portrait, Bonheur is benevolently portrayed as a 'grande dame' of French painting, rather than in working attire, as in Achille-Fould's transgressive image, which asserts her preeminence by subverting gender hierarchies.

* * *

Although the careers of Bonheur and Morisot overlapped chronologically, their paths diverged. Artistically precocious and financially independent by her twenties, Bonheur flouted gender norms. Her cropped hair, masculine dress and unconventional personal life contrast with Morisot's cultivated upper bourgeois upbringing, elegant femininity and conventional domestic world. Although both women benefited from familial support and access to professional artistic training, their careers were nonetheless circumscribed by gender. Whereas Morisot's upper-class background made it socially unacceptable for her to become a painter, Bonheur was driven from an early age to earn her living from art. Bonheur gained success as an *animalier*, a genderless but predominantly male genre that was grounded in precise anatomical and naturalistic detail. Her meticulously crafted animal paintings were produced in quantity, aggressively marketed and widely disseminated as prints. Morisot, who focused on depictions of women, intimate interiors and landscapes, was more daring artistically, forging an independent path as an Impressionist.

For contemporaries, like Duranty and Mallarmé, Morisot's delicately nuanced paintings encapsulated her quintessential femininity. Her femininity continues to be a double-edged sword that essentializes her art and her Impressionist style but risks ghettoizing her and diminishing her reputation. In many ways, Morisot remained heiress to the amateur pictorial tradition, rather than a professional artist in the usual commercial sense.[90] The non-hierarchical Impressionist movement, which privileged intimate modern subjects, provided a congenial milieu for pursuing her radical painting experiments. By liberating her from academic constraints, Impressionism allowed her to achieve more than she could have in the official art world. Harnessing her professional and domestic identities, Morisot challenged academic and gender hierarchies by producing small-scale masterpieces in impromptu studios. Because most of Morisot's work remained in her studio, the full extent of her artistic achievement was not evident until the 1896 posthumous retrospective. Her daughter, Julie, and husband, Denis Rouart, promoted Morisot's art, assuring her posthumous reputation through exhibitions of her work and scholarly publications, and her reputation continues to increase in the 21st century.

Despite Bonheur's success, her traditional approach and naturalistic style gradually fell out of favor. When she died in 1899, Klumpke, her end-of-life companion and universal legatee, inherited everything, including the Château de By and her paintings.[91] As 'faithful keeper of the flame', Klumpke preserved Bonheur's studio and published a biography/catalogue raisonné in 1908. The major 2022 Bonheur retrospective and recent restoration of her studio signal a renewed interest in her career and work. Born a generation apart, Bonheur and Morisot are emblematic of the challenges that 19th-century women artists encountered and the delicate balancing acts that they performed in negotiating their intertwined personal and professional lives, with or without a studio. As Marie Laurencin's career demonstrates, women artists continued to face systemic challenges at the turn of the century.

'BETWEEN PICASSO AND ROUSSEAU': VANGUARD *FEMME-PEINTRE*

The distinctively feminine art of Laurencin which, like that of Morisot, focuses on intimate representations of women, stubbornly resists classification. Her elegantly stylized, femme-centric style and pastel palette are frequently disparaged as excessively feminine, and she has been faulted for not measuring up to her Cubist colleagues, Pablo Picasso and Georges Braque.[92] Unlike Bonheur and Morisot, Laurencin received only spotty and haphazard training. The illegitimate daughter of a single mother who worked as a seamstress, she grew up in a cloistered feminine environment that shaped her lifelong love of everything feminine.[93] Her artistic vocation was a fortuitous accident. An indifferent student at the Lycée Lamartine, she enrolled at the Sèvres factory in 1901–3 to study porcelain painting and attended the free Drawing School for Girls. From 1903 to 1904, Laurencin attended Académie Humbert, where she befriended Francis Picabia, Georges Lepape and Braque, who admired her accomplished draftsmanship.[94] A 1904 photograph depicts students, including Laurencin, working from the model.

Laurencin's originality emerged in a series of

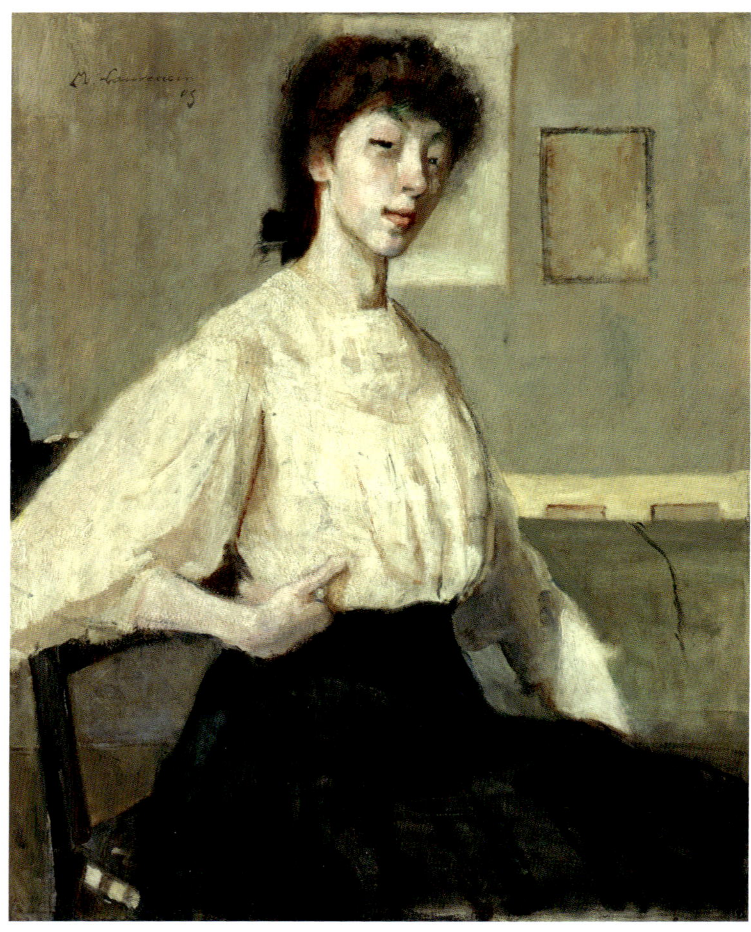

68. Marie Laurencin, *Self-Portrait*, 1905, oil on canvas, 92 × 73 cm, Musée de Grenoble, Grenoble.

psychologically revealing self-portraits in which she interrogated her features and her identity and experimented with a range of styles. Throughout her career, she used her art to explore her inner psyche and feelings.[95] Henri-Pierre Roché, patron and lifelong friend, noted, 'In front of the easel, she is searching for herself'.[96] Laurencin made numerous self-portraits during the early 1900s, wrote poems and kept a journal. *Self-Portrait* (1905, fig.68) demonstrates her assimilation of academic painting, but her assertive pose and provocative gaze signal her artistic independence.[97] Deploying an austere palette of gray, black and off-white, she poses in three-quarter view, her right arm akimbo, in a rigorously structured studio space. Her head is framed by the pictures on the wall, but she is not painting. Demurely dressed in a white blouse and dark skirt, her ambivalent expression and feline sensuality complicate the image. The small, full-length *Marie Laurencin Painting* (1906) is strikingly different in ambience and style. Fauve color and Picasso's influence permeate the vibrant canvas. Wearing a white dress and an embroidered, fringed apron, Laurencin perches on a green sofa, like an exotic bird, and wields her palette and brushes. Unlike her 1905 self-portrait, she works here in a domestic space, as she habitually did. The primitivizing image reduces her features to a stylized mask and boldly asserts her identity as *femme-peintre*.

For most of her career, Laurencin worked in hybrid domestic spaces. Until 1913, she lived with her mother. During the early 1900s, she went to Louis Jouas-Poutrel's studio several times a week.[98] Throughout her itinerant Spanish exile (1914–19), after she married Baron Otto von Wätjen, she worked sporadically in makeshift spaces. A 1914 photograph taken in Madrid depicts Laurencin in a bedroom/studio, surrounded by her paintings, with a skull and a guitar serving as decor. After separating from von Wätjen, she resettled in Paris in 1921 and briefly occupied an apartment at 19 rue de Penthièvre, which had a studio.[99] In 1928, Laurencin purchased a spacious light-filled apartment at 1 rue Savorgnon de Brazza, with a view of the Eiffel Tower. As was her habit, she worked at home, temporarily setting up her easel in different rooms and meticulously tidying her painting materials at the end of the day, like Morisot.[100] When her apartment was requisitioned in 1944, she moved to a small pavilion at 11 rue Masseran. Since there was no space for painting, Laurencin rented a studio nearby – at 15 rue Vaneau. The only independent studio that she ever had, the rue Vaneau studio was a workspace and refuge for Laurencin.[101] The long narrow studio, accessed by a crooked staircase, was furnished with bookcases and a comfortable armchair near her easel. Photographs from the 1940s and 1950s depict Laurencin working here, often wearing a painting apron, while other photographs show her impeccably dressed, posing more formally with her paintings. In one photograph, she leans against the easel, which displays a painting of a young woman, her hand on her hip, reprising the pose of *Self-Portrait* (1905).

During the years leading up to World War I, Laurencin was an avant-garde insider. Part of the Bateau-Lavoir coterie, she attended the legendary Rousseau banquet in Picasso's studio (1908). Laurencin met Picasso in 1907 in Clovis Sagot's gallery, and a few days later, he introduced her to the poet, Guillaume Apollinaire.

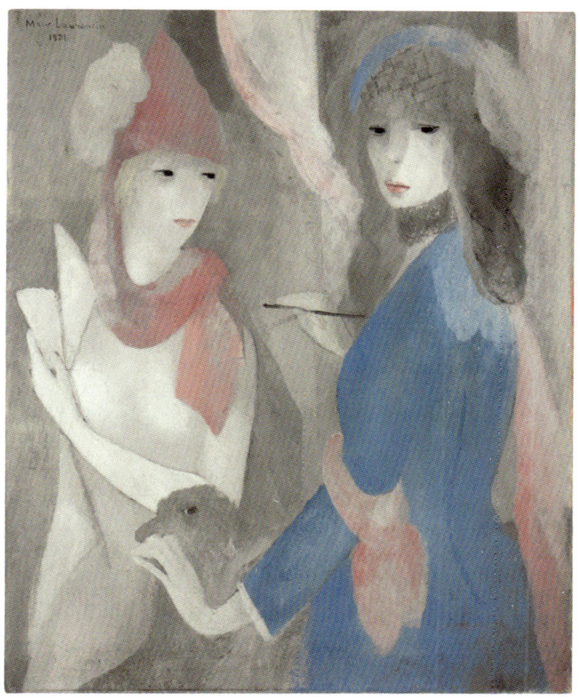

69. Marie Laurencin, *Woman Painter and Her Model*, 1921, oil on canvas, 81 × 65 cm, private collection.

Their tumultuous love affair, which lasted from 1907 until 1913, profoundly shaped the artistic vision of Laurencin and Apollinaire. Douanier Rousseau's double portrait, *The Muse Inspiring the Poet* (1909), depicts the couple in an exotic landscape as mirror images or alter egos of each other, paying homage to their creative partnership. Throughout her career, Laurencin was linked to writers and celebrated by poets from Jean Moréas to Apollinaire to André Breton. In *Les Peintres cubistes* (1913), Apollinaire situated Laurencin artistically between Picasso and Douanier Rousseau.[102] During 1908–9, she painted two self-reflexive group portraits that pay homage to Picasso and Apollinaire: *Group of Artists* (1908) and the more ambitious *Apollinaire and His Friends* (1909).[103] The radical simplification, sharply defined contours and primitivizing style reflect the dual influences of Picasso and Rousseau. In *Group of Artists*, Laurencin poses between Picasso and Apollinaire, who is reading. Laurencin and Apollinaire, flanked by smaller figures of Picasso and Fernande Olivier, dominate the composition. The expatriate collectors Gertrude and Leo Stein purchased *Group of Artists*, which was displayed at 27 rue de Fleurus until Gertrude Stein sold it to Claribel Cone in 1925. *Apollinaire and His Friends* enlarges the cast, adding the poets Marguerite Gillot and Maurice Cremnitz and three female graces. Apollinaire, flanked by Picasso, is enthroned at the center in an idyllic landscape, with the Pont de Passy behind his head. Laurencin, wearing a blue dress, sits in the foreground, affirming her prominent position in the Parisian avant-garde.

Although Laurencin's adoption of Cubist principles in works like *The Young Women* (*c.*1910–11) was more instinctive than doctrinaire, she participated in the Maison Cubiste at the Salon d'Automne and the Puteaux Group's Salon de la Section d'Or in 1912. She exhibited with Robert Delaunay at Galerie Barbazanges in 1912 and showed seven works in the groundbreaking New York Armory Show in 1913. Paradoxically, Apollinaire's lavish praise and designation of Laurencin as a scientific Cubist damaged rather than advanced her reputation. Despite her vanguard credentials and artistic success in prewar Paris, Laurencin's idiosyncratic art remains outside the Modernist mainstream. Married to a German national, she was exiled from France during World War I, which interrupted her career and isolated and disenfranchised her.

When she returned to Paris in 1921, Laurencin enjoyed a second wave of success as a fashionable society portraitist and a set and costume designer, notably for *Les Biches*, which the Ballets Russes staged in 1924. As her style evolved during the 1920s, her dreamlike feminine universe increasingly incorporated animals. In *Femme peintre et son modèle* (*Woman Painter and Her Model*, 1921, fig.69), Laurencin explored the artist/model theme that Picasso obsessively investigated in paintings and in his *Suite Vollard* etchings (1930–37), but gave it a distinctly feminine twist. Rather than linking the creative process to the male sexual drive, both artist (Laurencin) and model are women who mirror and closely resemble each other, suggesting a more reflexive, collaborative template of artistic creation. The delicate, ethereal figures in subtle shades of pink, blue and gray that she favored in the 1920s are steeped in poetic melancholy. *Femme peintre espagnole* (*Spanish Woman Painter*, 1930) portrays Laurencin clothed in a red dress and pearls, seated at the easel painting an *amazone* (horsewoman). After World War I, Laurencin collaborated with leading writers and designed numerous book illustrations. Following in Bonheur's footsteps, she received the Legion of Honor in 1937. She continued to exhibit at Paul Rosenberg's gallery, but her work became increasingly formulaic. By her death in 1956, she was largely forgotten.

Beginning in the 1980s, interest in Laurencin's art revived, as evidenced in a growing body of scholarship, the opening of the Marie Laurencin Museum in Nagano-Ken, Japan in 1983 and Laurencin's first retrospective exhibition in France at the Musée Marmottan in 2013.[104] Although Apollinaire celebrated Laurencin for her distinctively feminine style, her pastel palette and femme-centric subjects marginalized her and have continued to divide feminist critics. Too often she has been ghettoized as Apollinaire's muse and unfairly measured against the yardstick of Picasso and doctrinaire Cubism. Laurencin's idiosyncratic style and mythologizing of the feminine have excluded her from the vanguard narrative.[105]

Through the careers of five women artists from different social backgrounds whose careers spanned the Second Empire to the early 20th century, this chapter provides a dynamic snapshot of the systemic obstacles that women artists continued to face and makes the case for recalibrating the mythos of the studio in relation to gender and social mores.

The concluding chapter examines the studio's evolving role as a refractive self-portrait and a metaphor for art-making in the work of Matisse and Picasso.

5

The Refracted Studio

Matisse and Picasso

The work is the emanation, the projection of self. My drawings and my canvases are pieces of myself. Their totality constitutes Henri Matisse. The work represents, expresses, perpetuates. I could also say that my drawings and my canvases are my real children.[1]

– Henri Matisse, 1952

It's not enough to know the works by an artist, you also have to know when he did them, why, how, under what circumstances. Some day there'll be a science ... that deals with human creativity . . . and I want to leave as complete a record as possible for posterity.[2]

– Pablo Picasso, 1943

This chapter investigates the studio's heightened significance as a refracted self-portrait and metaphor for art-making for Matisse and Picasso. Focusing on their divergent artistic approaches through the lens of the studio, I bring together a growing body of research on their studio practices. Before revolutionizing art at the turn of the century, both artists had received extensive academic training.[3] Interrogating their individual and professional identities and the creative process, they represented their studios and themselves experientially and metaphorically or conceptually throughout their careers. Picasso's and Matisse's self-portraits and studio pictures are complemented by studio photographs that promote them as iconic modern masters.[4] Beginning in the early 1900s, Picasso photographed himself and his friends at the Bateau-Lavoir and at his Montmartre and Montparnasse studios.[5] The Musée Picasso's 5,000 photographs illuminate the multipronged role of photography as a creative catalyst, an observational device and an archive for documenting Picasso's artistic practice and oeuvre, including works in progress.[6] Though less abundant, photographs of Matisse shaped his public image and reveal how he transformed his Nice studios, using textiles and decorative objects.[7]

Focusing on the 1900s to 1920s, the chapter surveys both the studio's central place in Picasso's and Matisse's creative process and art production at pivotal moments in their careers and their evolving relationship to their studios over time. Their shared preoccupation with artist and model as subject and metaphor generates a rich pictorial dialogue that is emblematic of their antithetical personalities and approaches to art.[8] Picasso's and Matisse's depictions of their studios,

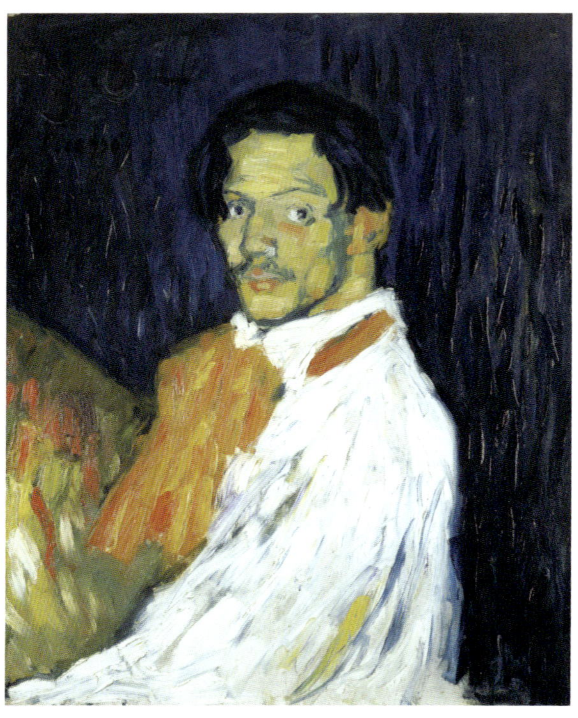

70. Pablo Picasso, *Yo, Picasso (Self-Portrait)*, 1901, oil on canvas, 73.5 × 60.5 cm, private collection.

produced over several decades, will be contextualized to elucidate the studio's material and metaphorical significance and role in shaping their public images. Analyzing an array of examples, from early self-portraits to Matisse's groundbreaking *Red Studio* and Picasso's radically abstracted studio paintings, I argue that for Matisse and Picasso, the studio functioned to an unprecedented degree as a laboratory of the artist's mind – a refracted self-representation and metaphor for the complexities of the creative process that encapsulated their individual and professional identities. A brief epilogue at the end of the chapter, considers how Picasso's and Matisse's personal relations and engagement with the studio morphed and intensified as they confronted their own mortality and contemplated their posthumous legacies.

The studio and the artist/model relationship preoccupied both Matisse and Picasso, but their studio practices and workspaces differed strikingly. For Matisse, the studio was an aesthetic sanctuary and refuge and, increasingly, an immersive environment and stage for his creativity. Late in his career, he referred to the objects and textiles in his studio as a 'working library' and described objects as 'actors' that took on different roles.[9] For Picasso, the studio was an experimental laboratory and social nexus – a crossroads of his life – and a launching pad.[10] In the studio, Matisse was concerned primarily with investigating pictorial problems of color and space, whereas Picasso considered the studio a conceptual frame for exploring emotions and reactions to people and events in invented scenarios. In later years, he looked to the Old Masters, notably Velázquez, Delacroix and Manet, as a testing-ground for demonstrating his artistic prowess and preeminent position in the annals of art history. Not surprisingly, Matisse's and Picasso's studios reflected their antithetical personalities and working methods and differed materially. From the outset, Picasso's studios were messy – littered with junk and painting paraphernalia – thus mirroring the calculated disorder of his daily life. On her first visit to the Bateau-Lavoir, Fernande Olivier was struck by the squalor and chaos of Picasso's sparsely furnished studio, with easels, canvases, tubes of paint and paintbrushes scattered across the floor.[11] In contrast, Matisse's bright quai Saint-Michel studio was orderly and tastefully furnished, reflecting his refined taste and disciplined creative process.[12]

Although Matisse was 12 years older than Picasso, both artists struggled to establish their reputations in the rough and tumble Paris art world of the early 1900s.[13] They exhibited at the same galleries, but did not meet until 1906, when the Steins began collecting their work. Picasso and Matisse became lifelong rivals and frenemies; they perpetually kept a wary eye on each other and engaged in a competitive artistic exchange that can be best characterized as a protracted chess match.[14] In 1907, they exchanged pictures at a tense dinner in Picasso's Bateau-Lavoir studio. Their choices were unexpected and revealing. Picasso selected Matisse's simplified, childlike *Portrait of Marguerite*, and Matisse chose Picasso's brutally sculptural *Pitcher, Bowl and Lemon*; both painted in 1907.[15] Picasso later observed, 'No one has ever looked at Matisse's paintings more carefully than I; and no one has looked at mine more carefully than he.'[16] Their contrasting personalities and divergent approaches are evident in their self-portraits from 1900–01.

Picasso's flamboyant *Yo, Picasso* (1901), which was exhibited at Ambroise Vollard's gallery, announced his arrival with blazing fanfare (fig.70).[17] Matisse's infrequent self-portraits were more reticent; they were private, self-exploratory works rather than public statements.[18] Exceptionally, in 1900, Matisse painted a pair of self-portraits that reveal dueling aspects of his persona: a restrained professional self – workman-like, with sleeves rolled up versus an expressionist self – unhinged and gripped by his turbulent imagination.[19] *Self-Portrait in Shirtsleeves* (fig.71) portrays Matisse at three-quarter length as he works on a canvas, seen from the back. Head tilted, he gazes up appraisingly. The color and paint application are controlled and systematic, echoing the structured composition. The other, more intense self-portrait employs a darker, more expressive palette and jagged, frenzied brushwork. Depicted bust-length, Matisse's abruptly cropped body emerges from a stark, indeterminate background. His unfocused expression and the agitated brushstrokes suggest uncertainty or anxiety. Contrasting with Matisse's uneasy self-interrogation, *Yo, Picasso* boldly asserts the 19-year-old prodigy's self-assurance and boundless ambition.[20] Wearing a dazzling white shirt and flaming orange scarf, he poses theatrically with an oversized brilliantly colored palette, confronting the viewer. In the preparatory sketch, Picasso depicted himself full-length, painting at the easel. Cropped to half-length in *Yo, Picasso*, he fills and animates the canvas. The high intensity palette, feverish brushwork and defiant, riveting gaze proclaim Picasso's arrival in the vanguard of modern painting.

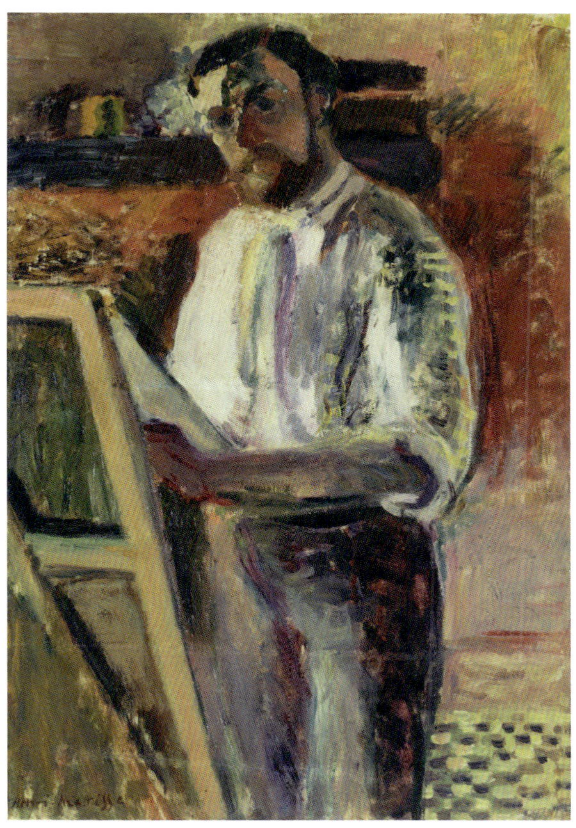

71. Henri Matisse, *Self-Portrait in Shirtsleeves*, 1900, oil on canvas, 64 × 45 cm, private collection.

PICASSO'S EARLY STUDIOS, MONTMARTRE TO MONTPARNASSE

Picasso's obsession with the studio surfaced early in his juvenilia – such as the imaginary sketch of a painter's studio that he made at 13.[21] His first studio was in Barcelona, near La Llotja art school. He later shared studios with fellow artists in Barcelona and Madrid. In 1900, Picasso traveled to Paris for the Exposition Universelle, where *Last Moments* was exhibited, and briefly shared a Montmartre studio with Carles Casagemas and Manuel Pallarès. Returning in 1901

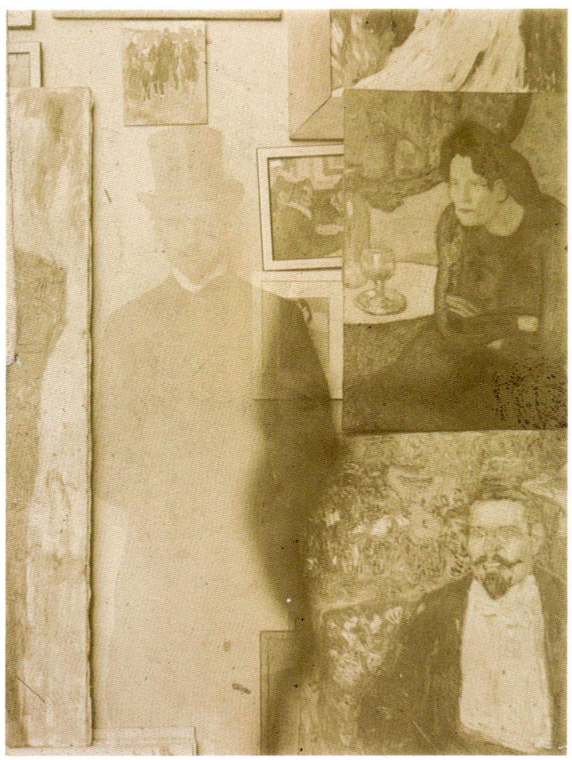

72. Pablo Picasso, *Self-Portrait in the Studio*, 1901–2, 12 × 9 cm, photograph, Picasso Archives, Musée national Picasso-Paris, Paris.

for his exhibition at Vollard's gallery, he stayed in a top floor studio/bedroom at 130ter boulevard de Clichy in Montmartre, which is documented in contemporaneous photographs, notably *Self-Portrait in the Studio* (fig.72), an eerie double exposure that includes a montage of paintings: *Yo, Picasso* (cropped) at the upper right, *Absinthe Drinker* and Gustave Coquiot's portrait below and *Group of Catalans in Montmartre* at the upper left. Picasso's ghostlike portrait, dressed in a black suit and top hat, is superimposed over the left half, highlighting his fascination with doubling and with photography's uncanny transformative properties.[22] Picasso wrote: 'This photograph could be entitled "The strongest of walls open at my approach"'.[23] Layering his phantasmagoric self-portrait over recent paintings, Picasso evokes his multifaceted identity as artistic sensation, dapper habitué of Montmartre cabarets and Catalan bohemian.[24] In another photograph, he poses at the easel, surrounded by friends with *Woman with a Cape* and a small portrait, believed to depict Vollard, in the foreground.[25] The table, laden with bottles and brushes, and the paint box and palette at Picasso's feet thematize the practice of painting. In the photograph, which depicts the same corner of the studio as *The Blue Room*, the large window at the left is reflected in the mirror at the upper right.

Blue Room (fig.73), one of Picasso's most complex early Blue Period paintings, is a self-referential depiction of his Clichy studio and a model bathing that has broader metaphorical implications for his professional identity and engagement with French art.[26] Henri de Toulouse-Lautrec's *May Milton* poster (1895) is prominently placed on the back wall next to a Catalan seascape that invokes the absent artist and his Catalan roots. By appropriating the poster and replicating it in paint, Picasso demonstrated his technical mastery and affiliation with the Parisian avant-garde.[27] Scientific analysis has revealed an unidentified, pensive male figure underneath *Blue Room*, which elucidates Picasso's studio practice. The surface irregularities visible under raking light indicate that he rotated the canvas 90 degrees and quickly painted over the figure.[28] *Blue Room* is the first of a series of studio pictures in which art and daily life coalesce. Although the layout with the window at the left echoes the studio photograph, *Blue Room* is more elaborately furnished and domesticated; it contains a large cupboard, striped divan and brightly colored rug. With the Degas-inspired model bathing in a metal tub, the interior is more reminiscent of a private room in a brothel than the bare-bones studio recorded in photographs, suggesting that it is an imaginative reinvention. Demonstrating his rapid assimilation of Impressionism and Post-Impressionism, from Degas to Rodin to Lautrec, the canvas interrogates Picasso's individual and professional identity via his studio, reflexively recasting it as a hybrid, metaphorical space.

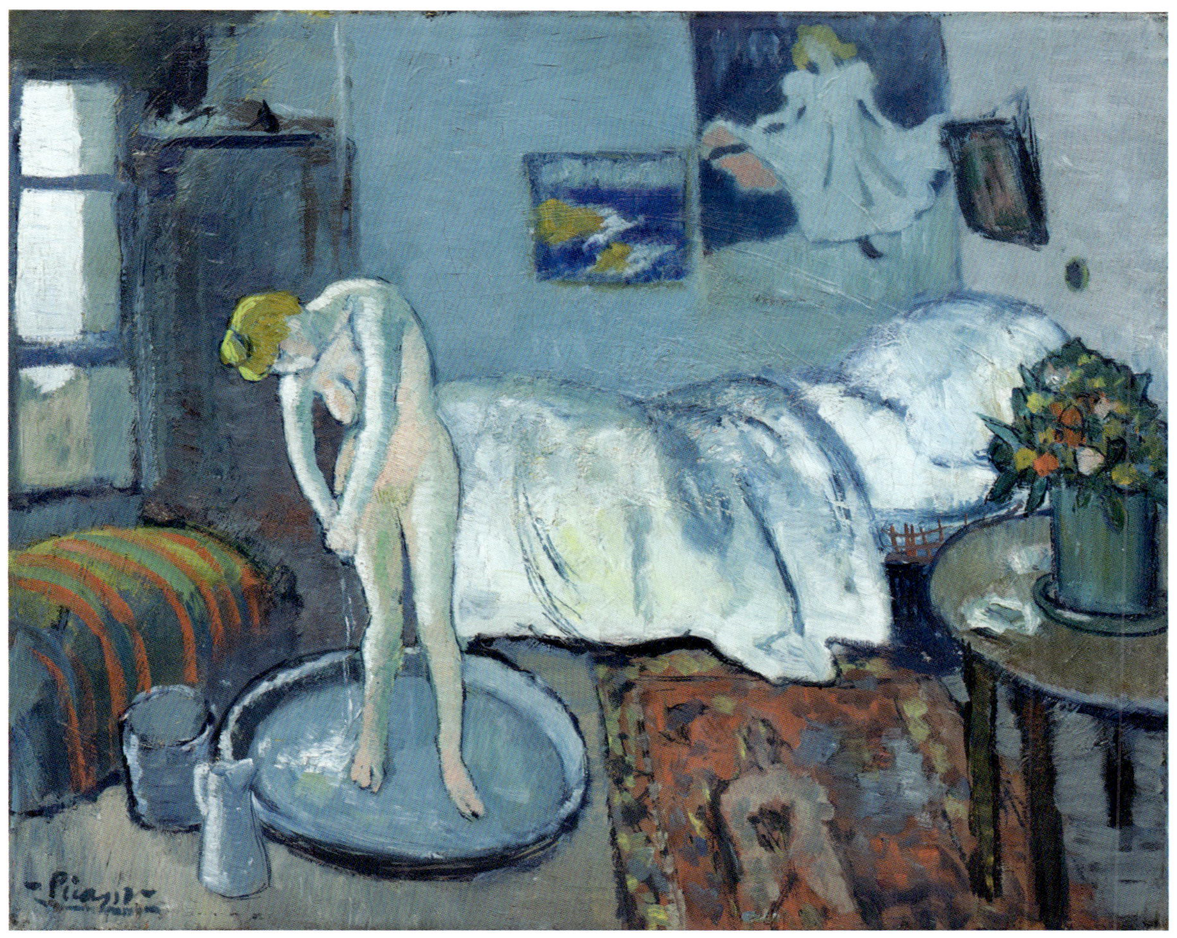

73. Pablo Picasso, *The Blue Room (Le Tub)*, 1901, oil on canvas, 50.5 × 61.6 cm, The Phillips Collection, Washington, DC.

La Vie (*Life*, fig.74), painted in Barcelona in 1903, bookends the Blue Period and provides further clues about Picasso's creative process and multilayered artistic identity. Almost everything about this compendium of Blue Period themes, which was painted over *Last Moments* (1899), is enigmatic – its alterations during the painting process, dense nexus of autobiographical references and metaphorical and allegorical meanings, encompassing the sacred and profane, love and death and the stages of life.[29] We do know that the painting depicts an artist's studio and that the male figure was initially a self-portrait. An easel and two paintings fill the space between the life-size figures of a nude couple embracing at the left and an older woman cradling an infant at the right. Picasso made four preparatory studies, in which he experimented with compositional variations and alternative gestures and poses.[30] X-radiographs reveal the most significant change during the painting process – the substitution of Casagemas's features for those of Picasso – transforming it from a self-portrait to a memorial to Casagemas, who committed suicide in 1901 over a failed love affair. Picasso began painting *La Vie* in his la Riera de Sant Joan studio in Barcelona in May 1903, but it is unclear when he completed it. Sebastian Junyent's somber portrait of Picasso (1903–4) portrays him posing in front of the painting in the studio.[31] Like other Blue Period paintings, *La Vie* addresses melancholy and social marginalization, but it focuses specifically on artistic alienation and despair, emotions embodied in the tragic figure of Casagemas, who haunted Picasso.[32]

Picasso's later self-portraits are mostly projections or surrogates rather than unequivocal self-depictions, except for *Self-Portrait with Palette* (1906), which shows him as a working artist.[33] After settling in Paris in 1904, he photographed himself and his friends in his studios, beginning with the Bateau-Lavoir, and used photographs in painting portraits. Both personal and documentary, the photographs highlight the studio's roles as social nexus, where the world came to him, and as experimental laboratory and gallery.[34] Although Picasso rarely painted self-portraits in his Cubist years, he took elaborately staged photographs of himself in his studio with his works – for instance, *Self-Portrait in the 11, boulevard de Clichy Studio* (1910) and the heroic series in the 5bis rue Schoelcher studio (1914–16) in Montparnasse that exalt him as both protean creator and genius. In *Self-Portrait in Front of Man Leaning on a Table*, Picasso poses theatrically, holding paintbrush and palette; paint cans, brushes and jars litter the floor. The Schoelcher studio, which he described as 'big as a church', overflowed with hundreds of stacked up canvases.[35]

During his Synthetic Cubist period, Picasso revisited the studio theme in two diametrically opposed canvases.[36] *Painter and His Model* (fig.75), which was painted during the summer of 1914 in Avignon and only discovered after his death, alludes to earlier masters, notably Cézanne and Courbet. Using the studio as a portmanteau linking past and present, Picasso essayed a classicizing Ingresque style that foreshadowed his postwar Neoclassical phase. The seated Cézanne-like figure of the artist is summarily outlined.[37] Only the nude model, holding a towel, believed to depict Picasso's companion, Eva Gouel, and part of the back wall are painted.[38] A palette hangs from a trompe-l'oeil nail on the back wall. The figure arrangement, the model's pose and the landscape painting in progress recall Courbet's *Painter's Studio* (fig.3) – a paradoxical 'Realist allegory' that thematized artistic representation and the studio as conceptual space and praxis.

Picasso's reductivist *Harlequin* (fig.76) depicts the artist in *commedia dell'arte* garb, holding a blank white palette or painting in his left hand. The gray shadow on the palette's right side may be a profile of Picasso, possibly echoing Matisse's abstracted self-portrait holding a palette in *Goldfish and Palette* (1914–15). According to John Richardson, Jean Cocteau, who desperately wanted Picasso to paint him as Harlequin, visited the artist wearing a harlequin costume that Picasso kept and used for this painting.[39] Initially conceived as a dancing couple, the composition was condensed into a solitary abstracted Harlequin/painter.[40] The austere canvas is a 'ground zero' depiction of the artist in the studio, who is reduced to a rebus of geometric fragments on a black ground, identifiable only by the easel and palette. The somber harlequin has also been interpreted as an allegory of loss since it was painted against the shattering backdrop of war and Eva Gouel's death in December 1915.[41]

MATISSE'S STUDIOS: QUAI SAINT-MICHEL AND ISSY-LES-MOULINEAUX

From the outset, the studio was a privileged subject and site for reflexivity in Matisse's art that was variously represented: empty, as in *Studio Interior*; with a model posing, as in *Studio, Quai Saint-Michel*; or, more rarely, with the artist working, with (or without) a model.[42] Matisse's existence was organized around his studio, and he lived between its walls. Late in his career, he observed, 'A painter exists only in terms of his pictures'.[43] At moments of crisis and transition, Matisse turned to depictions of his studio, notably in 1911. During his early years in Paris (1894–1908), he lived and worked in a compact top floor studio at no.19 quai Saint-Michel.[44]

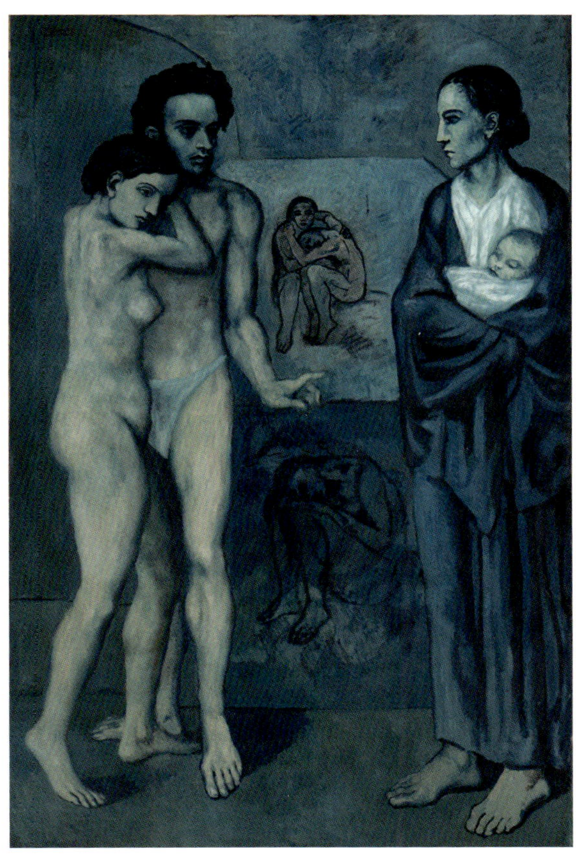

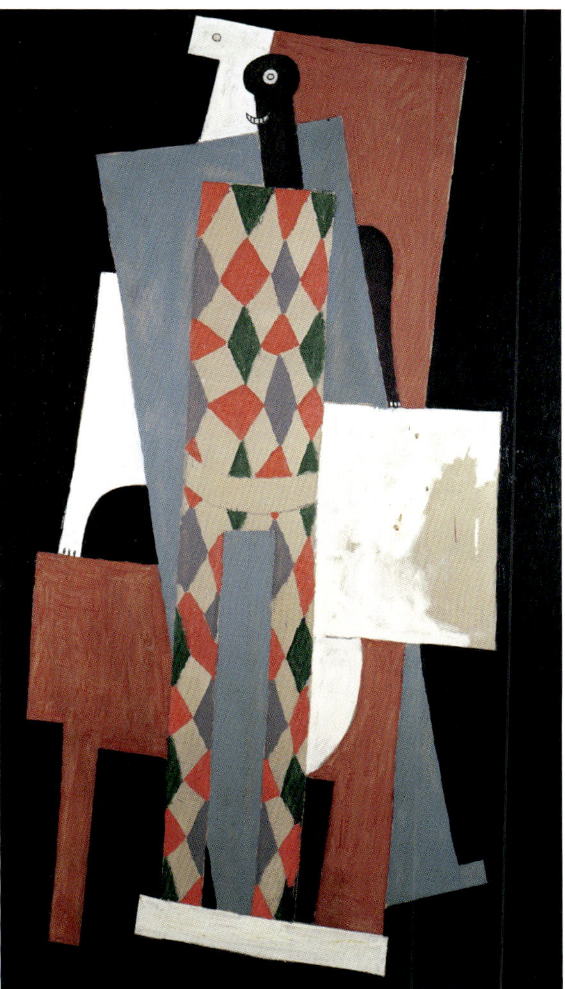

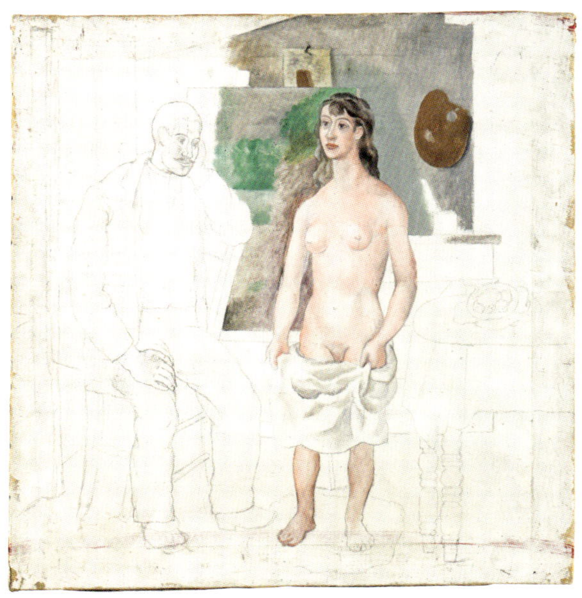

74. (top left) Pablo Picasso, *La Vie*, 1903, oil on canvas, 196.5 × 129.2 cm, Cleveland Museum of Art, Cleveland, OH.

75. (left) Pablo Picasso, *The Painter and His Model*, 1914, oil and pencil on canvas, 58 × 55.9 cm, Musée national Picasso-Paris, Paris.

76. (top right) Pablo Picasso, *Harlequin*, 1915, oil on canvas, 183.5 × 105.1 cm, Museum of Modern Art, New York.

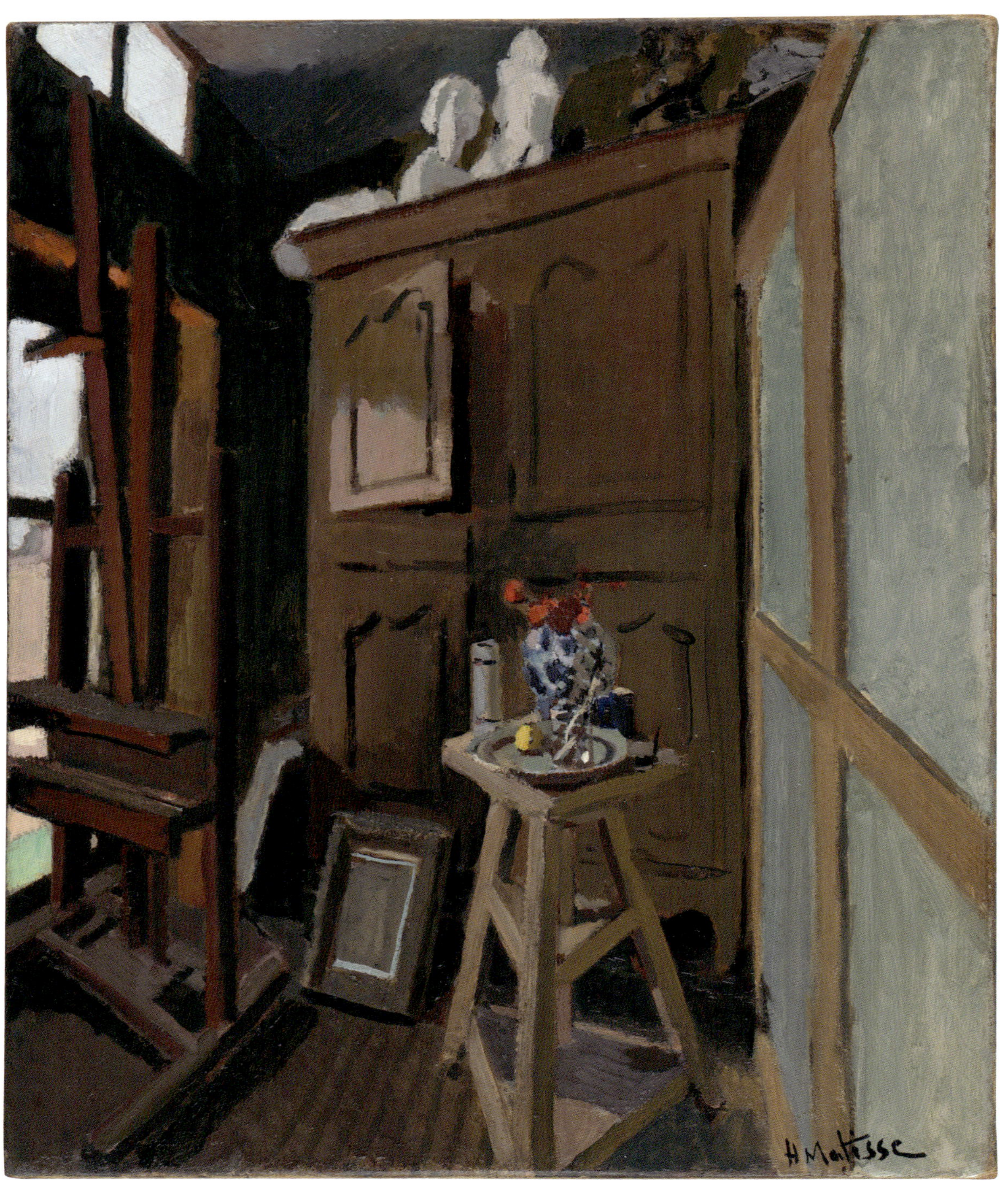

77. Henri Matisse, *Studio Interior*, c.1903–4, oil on canvas, 55 × 46 cm, Tate, London.

Studio Interior (*c*.1903–4, fig.77) underscores the seriousness of Matisse's artistic vocation and preoccupation with the creative process. It depicts a corner of his studio; there is a still life at the far right, and various plaster casts, including *Bust of a Woman*, *Serf* and *Jaguar Devouring a Hare* (after Antoine-Louis Barye), are displayed on top of the cabinet. Below are a framed figure study and an elegant still life arranged on a sculpture stand.[45] An early instance of Matisse's inclusion of sculpture and paintings in his studio pictures, the canvas demonstrates the significance that he attached to both media. The view of the Seine through the window is obscured by a wooden easel that is in dialogue with the large canvas seen from behind at the right – a leitmotiv in studio depictions. Though cramped, the studio is tastefully furnished and personalized, as all Matisse's studios would be. *Studio Interior* forms a pair with *Studio under the Eaves* (1903), which depicts the makeshift attic studio in Bohain where Matisse took refuge during a financial crisis.

In 1909, Matisse and his family moved to a spacious house in Issy-les-Moulineaux, outside Paris, and he constructed a large, custom-built studio on the adjoining lot. This demountable, shed-like structure is an early prototype of the functional, industrial-type studios and exhibition spaces favored by artists today. The studio was square: 10 m on each side, 5 m high and roughly 92.9 m^2. It had an iron framework, sloping sheet metal roof, a large skylight and a wall of windows on the north-facing side. The interior was lined with unpainted wood paneling and had a wood plank floor. Surviving photographs and paintings, like *Still Life with Geraniums* (1910), which shows blue, painted walls, give an idea of the interior. Financed by Russian collector Sergei Shchukin's 1909 commission for *Dance* and *Music*, Matisse's Issy studio provided space for painting the massive canvases.[46] Bazille's *Studio on the Rue La Condamine* (fig.4), which was displayed at the 1910 Salon d'Automne where *Dance* and *Music* were also exhibited, conceivably spurred Matisse to explore a new type of studio picture focusing on his art.[47] Matisse's monumental studio interiors did not develop in isolation; they evolved from, and expanded on, earlier still lifes incorporating artworks, including *Still Life with Dance* (1909) and the *Spanish Still Lifes* (1910–11), which reveal the impact of the groundbreaking Islamic art exhibition that he saw in Munich in 1910. To Matisse, Persian miniatures opened new pictorial possibilities for combining the imagined and the seen in an intangible space where drawing and color worked in tandem.[48] *Seville Still Life* features a vibrant medley of predominantly pink- and green-patterned furniture and textiles against a deep pink background that prefigures *Pink Studio*.

In January 1911, Shchukin commissioned Matisse to paint three decorative panels the same size as *Harmony in Red* (1908) for an antechamber in the Trubetskoy Palace in Moscow, leaving the subject up to the artist.[49] Rather than a standard theme, such as the four seasons, Matisse painted four 'symphonic interiors': (as Alfred Barr baptized them): *Pink Studio*, *Painter's Family*, *Interior with Aubergines* and *Red Studio*, which introduced a new level of ambition and visual complexity.[50] In *Pink Studio* and *Red Studio*, Matisse reinvented and amplified the conceptual and decorative parameters of the studio picture, fusing the real and the imaginary in an autonomous pictorial space that was at once literal and reflexive or metaphorical. Examining the floor plan of the Issy studio with the aid of Matisse's studio pictures, we can identify Matisse's vantage point and discover correspondences between the canvases, which depict four of the same artworks and provide an overlapping panoramic view of the studio.[51] By representing his studio on a grandiose scale, Matisse was asserting its cardinal significance as workspace, gallery, projection of the artist's mind and lodestar of the creative process.

THE PINK AND RED STUDIOS

Pink Studio (fig.78), the first of Matisse's symphonic interiors, was exhibited at the 1911 Salon des Indépendants before it entered Shchukin's collection.[52]

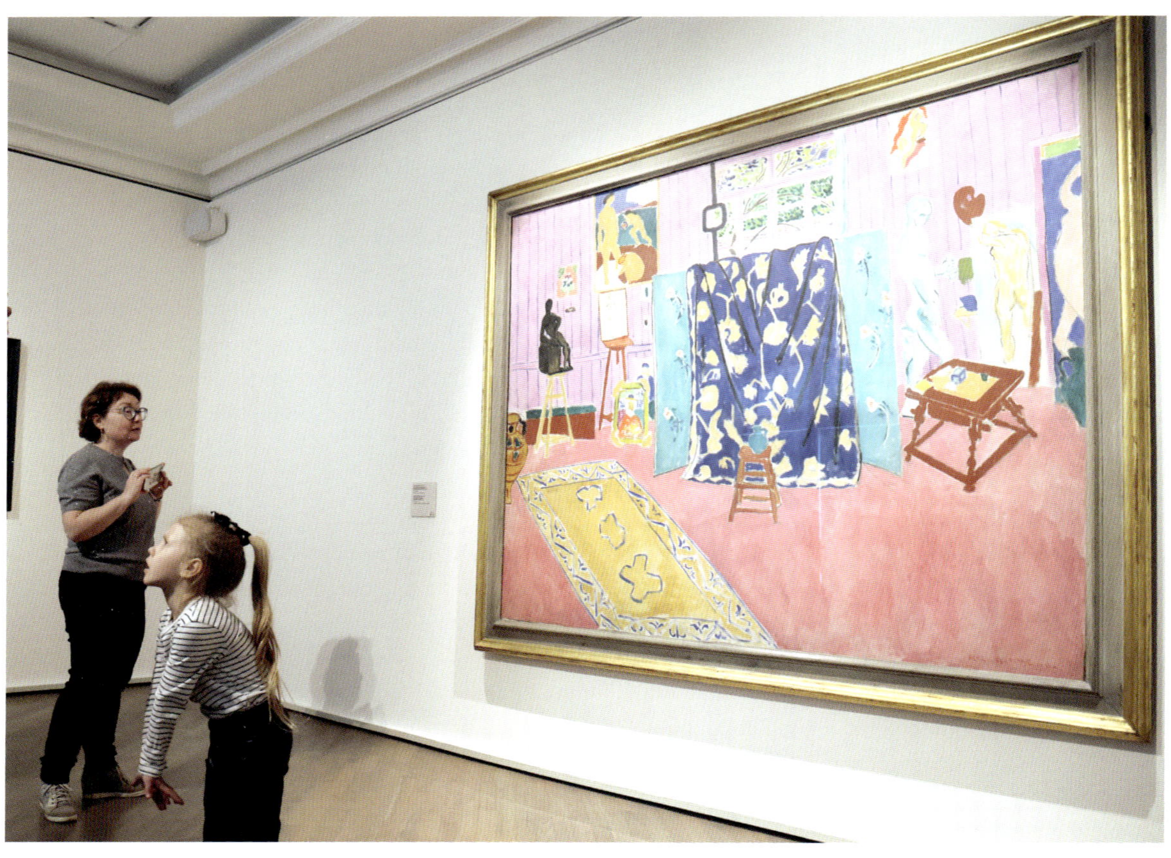

78. Installation shot of Henri Matisse's *Pink Studio*, 1911, oil on canvas, 182 × 222 cm, Pushkin Museum of Fine Arts, Moscow. On display as part of *After Impressionism: Russian Painting in Dialogue with New Western Art*, at Pushkin Museum of Fine Arts Moscow, 2023.

Its brilliantly orchestrated palette is dominated by pinks and greens, and the composition is anchored by the folding screen at the center. Draped over the screen is the blue and cream coverlet that appeared in the *Seville Still Lifes*. Paintings and sculptures, focusing on the human figure and that were created between 1906 and 1911 are displayed along the back wall to either side of the screen. Although Matisse depicted what was in his field of vision, he reimagined the studio through the mind's eye and the lens of Persian miniatures, metamorphosing it into an immaterial space defined by color.[53] The light pink, paneled walls are accented with blue lines, while the plank floor is an expansive field of brilliant pink. Devoid of figures, the studio is animated by paintings and sculptures, including full-scale casts of the *Mars Borghese* and *Back I* and a slice of *Dance I* at the far right. The skewed perspective, subtle layering of space and decorative patterning reflect the influence of Persian miniatures. *Pink Studio* is the culmination of a series of ambitious still lifes that forged an intensified dialogue between Matisse's studio and his artistic output and initiated a new type of pictorial space premised on color and the decorative.[54] Discussing the impact of Persian miniatures on his work, Matisse explained how they showed him 'the full possibility of my sensations' and suggested 'a larger and truly plastic space'.[55] When Matisse traveled to Russia in November 1911, he installed *Pink Studio* with *Painter's Family* in the antechamber of the Trubetskoy Palace.

Pink Studio, Matisse's innovative exploration of the studio interior/still life and the picture within the picture, foreshadowed his daring rehang of the Rose Salon in the ornate Trubetskoy Palace – a total work of art that, like a musical score, was based on a rhythm of chromatic resonances and dissonances.[56] *Pink Studio's* structural and chromatic balance is grounded in the ideas about color equivalence and synthetic balancing of tones and hues that Matisse formulated in 'Notes of a Painter' (1908).[57] *Pink Studio* reprises the pink and green palette of Fauve works, such as *Young Sailor II* (1906), visible behind *Girl with Green Eyes* (1908) at lower left. The brilliant green vase, displayed on a red sculpture stand at the center, is an eye-catching punctum that, like the red palette on the back wall and the black stove pipe protruding behind the folding screen, asserts its material presence in the insubstantial, decorative mise en scène. The thematic dialectic of art and reality is echoed in the formal dialectic of color and drawing.[58] Matisse began by outlining forms in pencil on the canvas and then colored them with almost no repainting or impasto. The perspective is skewed and contradictory; it invites us to enter the studio space through the diagonal recession of the yellow rug, but also obstructs our passage with the screen.

Like the harmony of colors and patterns, the placement of textiles and ceramics and grouping of artworks appears premeditated, especially the juxtaposition of the *Mars Borghese* with the painted cast of *Back I* and *Dance I*, creating an artistic *pas de trois*. Virtually all of the works depicted, including *Le Luxe II*, *Cyclamen*, *Young Sailor II* and *Dance I*, exist in more than one version or are multiples implicitly, like *Decorative Figure* and the plaster casts. When creating related pairs, Matisse used the same size of canvas, but pushed the concept further in his second more fully realized version, thus interjecting the notion of time and underscoring the studio's dynamism as a creative laboratory in constant flux.[59] That is illustrated by *Luxe II* (1907–8), *Young Sailor II* (1906) and *Cyclamen* (1911), which appear in both *Pink Studio* and *Red Studio* but are reconfigured spatially. In *Red Studio*, *Luxe II* is literally 'repainted'. Matisse's two depictions of the Issy studio follow the same template. Painted sequentially from different vantage points, the *Studios* offer alternative visions – what could be termed 'studio variations' – that contrast with and complement each other. In *Red Studio*, Matisse pushed the concept further and radically reconceived pictorial space.

Matisse spent the summer of 1911 at Collioure, where he painted *Large Nude* and *Interior with Aubergines*, the third symphonic interior, using a darker palette and distemper rather than oil.[60] *Interior with Aubergines*, the most exuberantly decorative, depicts the Collioure studio – a storage area under the roof, illuminated by a large window. Like *Pink Studio*, *Interior with Aubergines* is anchored by the central folding screen and patterned textiles, but it is more complex and spatially disorienting, suggesting a hall of mirrors.[61] It was preceded by *Open Window*, which depicts the same interior, sketchily painted in a pink and green palette, recalling *Pink Studio*.[62] Part of *Luxe I* is visible at the upper left, and several smaller works can be seen at right. The still life elements in *Interior*, including the titular aubergines, are reflected in miniature in the obliquely placed mirror, but the scale and spatial orientation are distorted, adding to the visual ambiguity. Although none of Matisse's paintings appear here, the profusion of rectangular forms mimic picture frames, and the view out of the window resembles a landscape painting. A crouching *écorché* on the table and a sculpture on the mantel are swallowed up in the vibrantly patterned visual field.[63] Shchukin did not purchase either *Interior with Aubergines* or *Large Nude*, which exceeded the specified dimensions.

Matisse finished painting *Red Studio* (fig.79) in December 1911. Begun earlier that fall, he had repainted it in Venetian red by the end of December.[64] Identical in size to *Pink Studio*, it was clearly intended to be

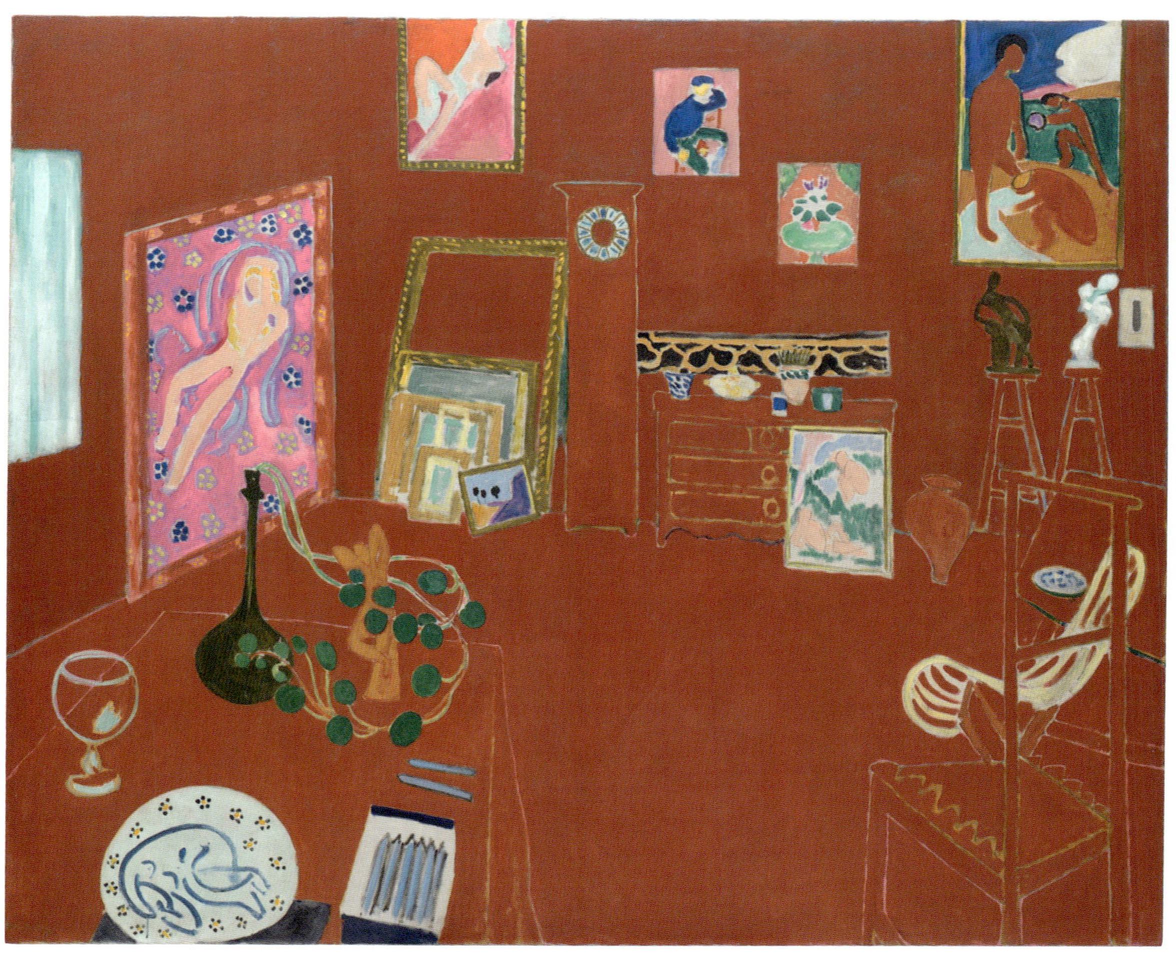

79. Henri Matisse, *The Red Studio*, 1911, oil on canvas, 181 × 219.1 cm, Museum of Modern Art, New York.

a pendant. As with *Pink Studio*, he began with an under-drawing and made minimal revisions during the painting process. *Red Studio* presents a semicircular snapshot of the Issy studio, to the left of the view shown in *Pink Studio*, that starts with the tabletop still life arrangement in the left foreground and concludes with the straight-backed chair on the lower right, which directs the viewer's gaze and evokes the absent artist.[65] Unlike *Pink Studio*, *Red Studio* has no focal point. Instead, the eye moves freely around the expanse of red that subsumes everything, except the individual artworks, which retain their autonomy. 11 works by Matisse and various objects and pieces of furniture, including a grandfather clock with no hands and a chest of drawers, populate the dematerialized space. The artworks (all in Matisse's possession and created from 1898 to 1911), include paintings, sculptures in different media – terracotta, plaster and bronze – and a painted ceramic plate. The studio doubles as a retrospective gallery that traces Matisse's artistic development over a decade, from the naturalistic Corsican landscape (late 1890s) at the lower left to the radically reductivist

Large Nude and *Jeannette IV* at the far right, both from 1911. Directly observed and subjectively reimagined, *Red Studio* reveals a complex dialectic of absence and presence that is encapsulated by the 'ghost' furniture, which is both real and ethereal.

The Issy studio was a fluid space that mutated over time and housed a changing cast of artworks, some complete, others, like *Large Nude*, in progress. *Le Luxe II* is depicted hanging above *Decorative Figure* in both *Pink Studio* and *Red Studio*. However, in *Red Studio*, the relative scale and viewing angle have shifted, and the figure study on the right sculpture stand has been replaced with a cast of *Jeannette IV*. In *Le Luxe II*, the figures are overpainted in Venetian red, like the studio itself, giving them a primitive aspect. *Young Sailor II*, propped on the floor in *Pink Studio*, is hung centrally in *Red Studio*, catty-corner to *Cyclamen*. *Large Nude*, which Matisse kept reworking, differs from the version depicted in a photograph from fall 1911; here it appears vertical rather than horizontal, which accentuates its similarity to *Nude with White Scarf*.[66] Rather than focusing on the artist working, Matisse thematized the studio as a gallery that was reflexively defined by the art on display. The only references to art-making processes are the box of crayons on the table, connoting drawing, and the paintbrushes on top of the chest of drawers.[67] Though modeled on *Pink Studio*, *Red Studio* more radically reconceptualizes the studio picture and envisions the painted surface as autonomous in a new way – a red wall punctuated by paintings – and a projection of the artist's mind in which the individual artworks are the central protagonists.[68]

Red Studio was born when Matisse applied a layer of Venetian red over the initial version of the painting, covering walls and floor to create an abstract space defined by color alone. Although the red flattens the pictorial space, the foreshortening of the table and the diminishing scale, indicating distance, create an illusion of recession. Before Matisse's audacious transformation, the painting's palette was closer to that of *Pink Studio*. Recent technical analysis has revealed that the walls were originally cobalt blue, the floor bright pink and the furniture painted in ocher.[69] Paint samples show distinct paint layers; the original color is intact underneath the red. When *Red Studio* was unframed, vestiges of the original colors were also discovered along the edges of the canvas. Variations in the red in different areas of the canvas and in the colored outlining of the furniture, moreover, are visible to the naked eye.

It is unclear exactly when, or why, Matisse decided to paint the canvas red. In *Dance and Music* (1909–10), he employed expansive fields of color, but they delineated earth and sky. The most intriguing precedent is his reworking of *Harmony in Red*, which Shchukin had commissioned as a *Harmony in Blue* for his dining room. In a 6 August 1908 letter to Shchukin, Matisse explained that upon completing the painting, he exhibited it in his studio to gauge the effect. Dissatisfied with the blue tonality that he judged insufficiently decorative, he repainted the canvas red before delivering it to Shchukin.[70] Discussing the principle of expressive color in 'Notes of a Painter', Matisse noted that a change in color harmony completely modifies a picture.[71] In *Harmony in Red*, the blue paint underneath the red overpainting transformed the color, creating a startling violet-tinged red. Although Shchukin's response to Matisse's reworking is not recorded, he accepted *Harmony in Red* and displayed it.

After completing *Red Studio*, Matisse notified Shchukin, who asked the price and requested a watercolor sketch; Matisse sent the sketch, together with a description of the painting, on 1 February 1912. Although the main elements of the canvas are present, the washed-out sketch does not convey the intensity and immersive effect of the red. 'The whole is Venetian red', Matisse wrote, explaining that it was a precise color and warmer than ocher red. He added that red was the harmonic link with the greens, blues, pinks and yellows, 'representing the paintings and other objects placed in my studio'.[72] Oddly, he did not mention that *Red Studio* and *Pink Studio* form a pair. On 14 February 1912, Shchukin wrote, 'the painting must be very interesting,' but 'preferred [Matisse's] paintings with figures' and declined to purchase it. *Red Studio* remained in Matisse's studio, where Shchukin could have seen it when he visited in July. Three foreign visitors published accounts of Matisse's studio, two of which discuss *Red Studio*.[73] Vilma Balogh, who visited between late 1911 and early 1912, described, 'Matisse's latest painting on an easel, awaiting his finishing touches. Its Pompeiian red background binds together the interior and the details of the Master's atelier', and noted the synergy between his paintings and sculptures.[74] Viewing *Red Studio*, Ernest Goldschmidt was captivated: 'My attention was particularly caught by a large painting depicting a few simple, everyday pieces of furniture against a red-brown wall. The objects had about them a wondrous, visionary character, and yet appeared absolutely truthful'.[75] He observed that the uniform expanse of red made the objects on the wall come alive and that all the other colors were codependent.

Red Studio made its public debut in 1912 at Roger Fry's second Post-Impressionist exhibition at Grafton Galleries in London. Matisse was the featured artist, with 19 recent paintings, eight sculptures and a handful of prints and drawings.[76] The powerful impact of Matisse's canvases, including *Red Studio*, can be gleaned from Fry's small, snapshot-like sketch of the gallery where 17 of them were displayed. The four paintings depicted on the back wall of *Red Studio* (*Nude with White Scarf*, *Young Sailor II*, *Cyclamen* and *Le Luxe II*) were also included in the exhibition, virtually reconstructing the Issy studio and the art it contained, and foreshadowing the Museum of Modern Art's 2022 *Matisse: The Red Studio* exhibition. Although Matisse garnered attention from the press, none of his paintings sold. 11 Matisses, including *Red Studio*, were exhibited at the 1913 Armory Show in New York, which traveled in a reduced version to Chicago and Boston.[77] After its high-profile international debut, *Red Studio* vanished until 1927, when it dramatically resurfaced in London at the Gargoyle, a fashionable Soho nightclub. Purchased by the wealthy young owner, David Pax Tennant, *Red Studio* presided over the Gargoyle's glittering mirrored ballroom during the late 1920s and 1930s.[78] In 1928, Tennant purchased a second major Matisse, *Studio, Quai Saint-Michel* (1916), which was displayed in the bar.

QUAI SAINT-MICHEL RETROUVÉ

In 1914, Matisse re-established his studio at 19 quai Saint-Michel, on the floor below his previous studio. He depicted his new studio in a series of rigorous, Cubist-inflected canvases that probed the relationship between interior and exterior spaces. *Goldfish and Palette* (1914–15) includes an abstracted self-portrait with his palette, contemplating a goldfish bowl.[79] Only the palette and the painting in progress are legible, creating a mise en abyme that thematizes the creative process. During 1916–17, Matisse painted two related studio pictures that focus on contemplation and representation of the model and signal a turning point in his art and studio practice. In November 1916, he started collaborating with a new model, called Lorette or Laurette, who posed more than fifty times (1916–17).[80] Working serially, he experimented with varied poses and formats.

Matisse painted *Studio, Quai Saint-Michel* (1916, fig.80) at a transitional moment, before vacating the building where he had spent more than two decades. Prefiguring his odalisques of the 1920s, it depicts a corner of his studio with a nude model (Lorette) reclining on a bright red, floral-patterned bedspread. The Phillips painting was preceded by a more naturalistic, over life-size study of Lorette sleeping, which Matisse reduced and simplified.[81] In *Studio, Quai Saint-Michel*, the model's body is delineated by thick dark outlines; her legs are cropped above the ankle. A large window overlooking the Seine on the right, which offers an expansive view of the Palais de Justice and Sainte-Chapelle, links the Paris cityscape to the studio interior. The connection is accentuated by the bridge's

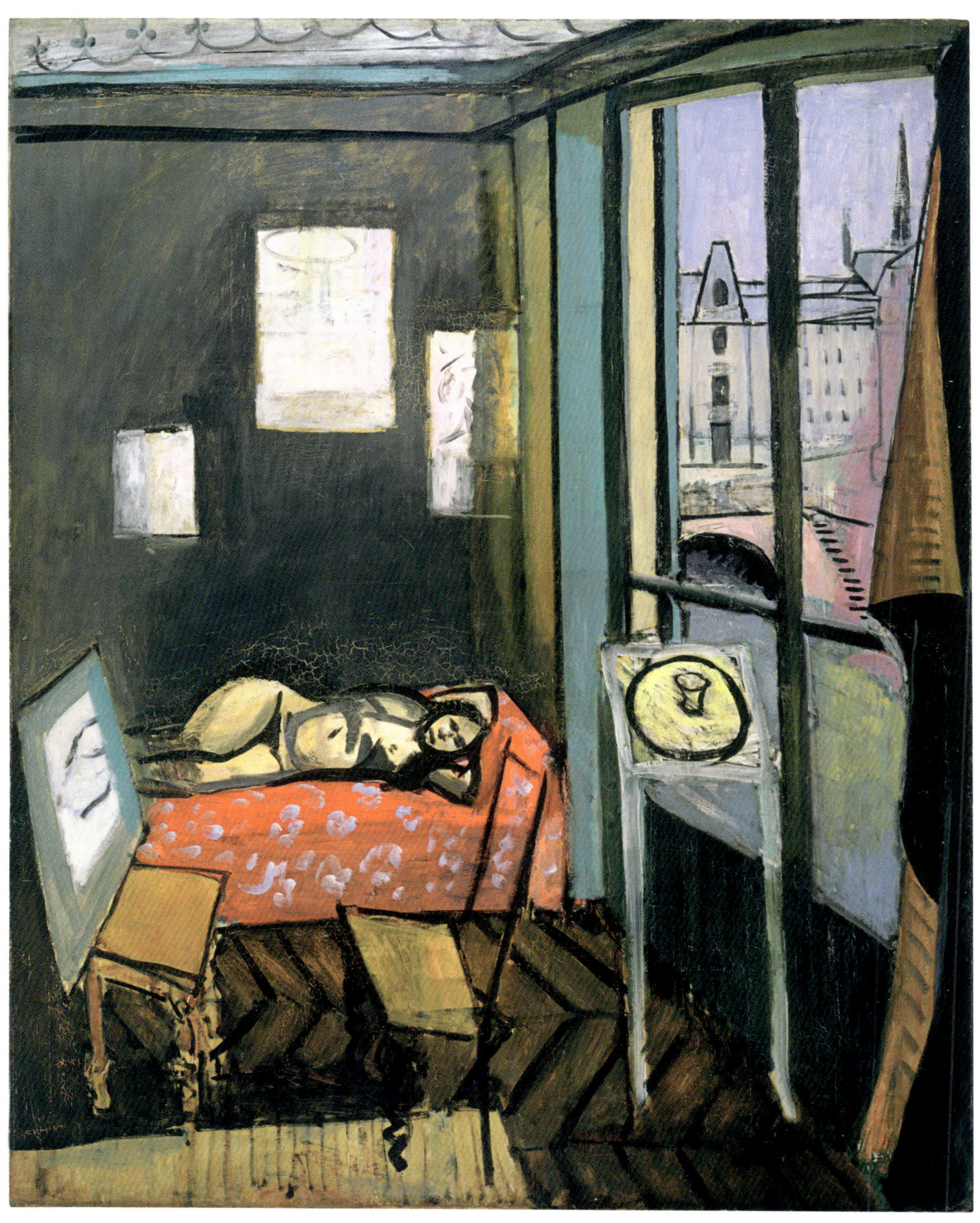

80. Henri Matisse, *Studio, Quai Saint-Michel*, 1916, oil on canvas, 148 × 116.8 cm, The Phillips Collection, Washington, DC.

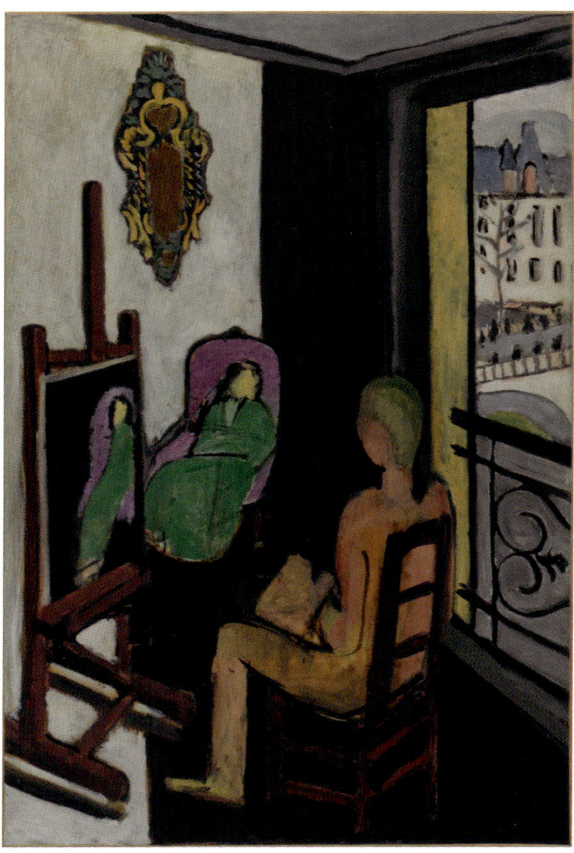

81. Henri Matisse, *The Painter in His Studio*, 1916–17, oil on canvas, 146.5 × 97 cm, Musée National d'Art Moderne, Centre Georges Pompidou, Paris.

pinkish tones, which echo the curtain, and the blue and gray tonalities both inside and outside the window. Matisse made a rapid compositional sketch that he modified during the painting process. Some changes, especially around the model, are visible to the naked eye.[82] Painted five years after *Red Studio*, *Studio, Quai Saint-Michel* heralds Matisse's focus on the female nude, thematization of the model and intensified engagement with the studio as a fictive performative space.

Painter in His Studio (also known as *Painter and His Model*, fig.81), which forms a pair with *Studio, Quai Saint-Michel*, depicts the same corner from a slightly different angle. The view through the window has shifted and narrowed and the studio is separated from the world outside by the balcony's ornamental grillwork. Matisse is depicted working from the model, but he is viewed impersonally from behind, as if in the third person.[83] He sits at the easel, holding his palette in his left hand; however, his right hand and paintbrush are concealed. He is painting *Lorette in a Green Robe* (1916), which is shown in progress on the easel, creating a double mise en abyme in which the canvas appropriates and mirrors the portrayal of the model in the studio, and the 'actual' painting is reproduced in miniature on the easel. The robot-like figure of the artist, depicted in three-quarter view from behind, appears oddly inanimate; both artist and model are faceless and inconsistent in scale.[84] As with *Studio, Quai Saint-Michel*, Matisse painted a larger study of the model, which he modified and simplified in *Painter in His Studio*. The interior is painted black, like the background of *Lorette in a Green Robe*, which foregrounds the studio's role as a theatrical set.

The decor, furnishings and ambience differ in these two studio depictions. The stark black and white interior of *Painter in His Studio* provides a foil for the artist's easel and the ornamental Baroque mirror on the back wall. The curved, pink Voltaire armchair sets off the model's vibrant green robe and contrasts with the artist's rigid posture and straight-backed chair. In *Studio, Quai Saint-Michel*, a rectilinear white table, with a plate and flowerpot, is in front of the window (where the artist sits in *Painter in His Studio*); the empty chair before the reclining model indicates where the artist would be. The pictures on the wall are puzzling, flesh-toned ciphers with random markings, thus equating painting with the model's flesh. The dark brown wall is crowned with an ornately patterned ceiling or molding that is absent from *Painter in His Studio*, and the parquet floor and furniture are accentuated with thick dark lines. The most intriguing conundrum is the framed square propped up on the chair, contiguous with the model's truncated body. The square, which reflects or represents the model's legs, can be read as a mirror or as a painting in progress. Either way, it suggests the tension between perception and reality. No palette or painting materials are shown; the left chairback is an impromptu support for the mirror or canvas. Matisse's divergent depictions suggest that they are also metaphorical representations in which he meditates on the creative process through the reflexive lens of the studio. Via the multilayered relationship of artist and model, both canvases explore the overlapping of painted image and actuality and the complex dialectics of absence and presence.

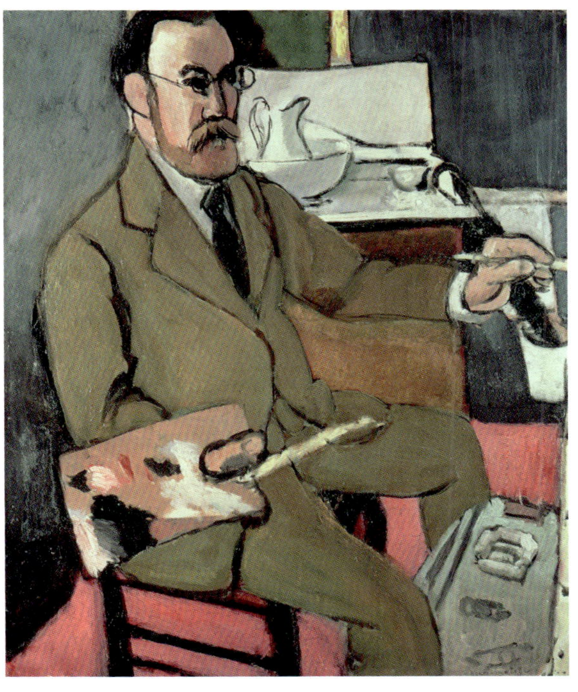

82. Henri Matisse, *Self-Portrait*, 1918, oil on canvas, 65 × 54 cm, Musée Matisse, Le Cateau-Cambrésis.

STUDIO VARIATIONS: 1920S AND BEYOND

During the 1920s, Matisse's and Picasso's preoccupation with the studio and artist/model theme deepened and intensified, although they approached them from different perspectives and their art developed along opposing tracks. A key distinction is the presence or absence of the model in the studio. Matisse relied on the model's physical presence for inspiration, whereas Picasso rarely worked from the model directly, relying instead on memory and imagination.[85] Both artists were photographed working in their studios, revealing the occult process of creation, which simultaneously humanized and mythologized them as artistic icons. After 1918, Matisse spent much of the year in Nice, which reoriented his art in terms of style and subject.[86] His tightly controlled *Self-Portrait* (fig.82), painted shortly after his arrival at the Hôtel Beau Rivage, signals the transition.[87] Matisse sits rigidly at the easel, with his suitcase wedged between his legs, holding his palette and brush, in a cramped, ad hoc workspace. The pose recalls *Painter in His Studio*, but flipped 180 degrees and seen from the front. Viewed close-up, his body cropped abruptly below the knee, he is reflected in reverse in the wardrobe mirror as he paints.[88] His hands appear enormous, especially his paint-smeared thumb emerging from the palette. This is Matisse's last painted self-portrait; however, his image appears occasionally in studio depictions. Although the impersonal setting, suitcase and umbrella give the scene an improvisational feel, it is nevertheless a forthright, professional image of the artist at work that signals his determination and the return to a more traditional approach to the figure and pictorial space.[89]

Tired of working in hotel rooms, Matisse rented a third-floor apartment in an ornate 18th-century building at 1 Place Charles-Félix in fall 1921. The apartment had two studio spaces with sea views. He used the larger studio for painting and drawing and the smaller, corner one for sculpture.[90] Matisse transformed his Nice studios into imaginary environments, resembling stage or film sets, that could be manipulated

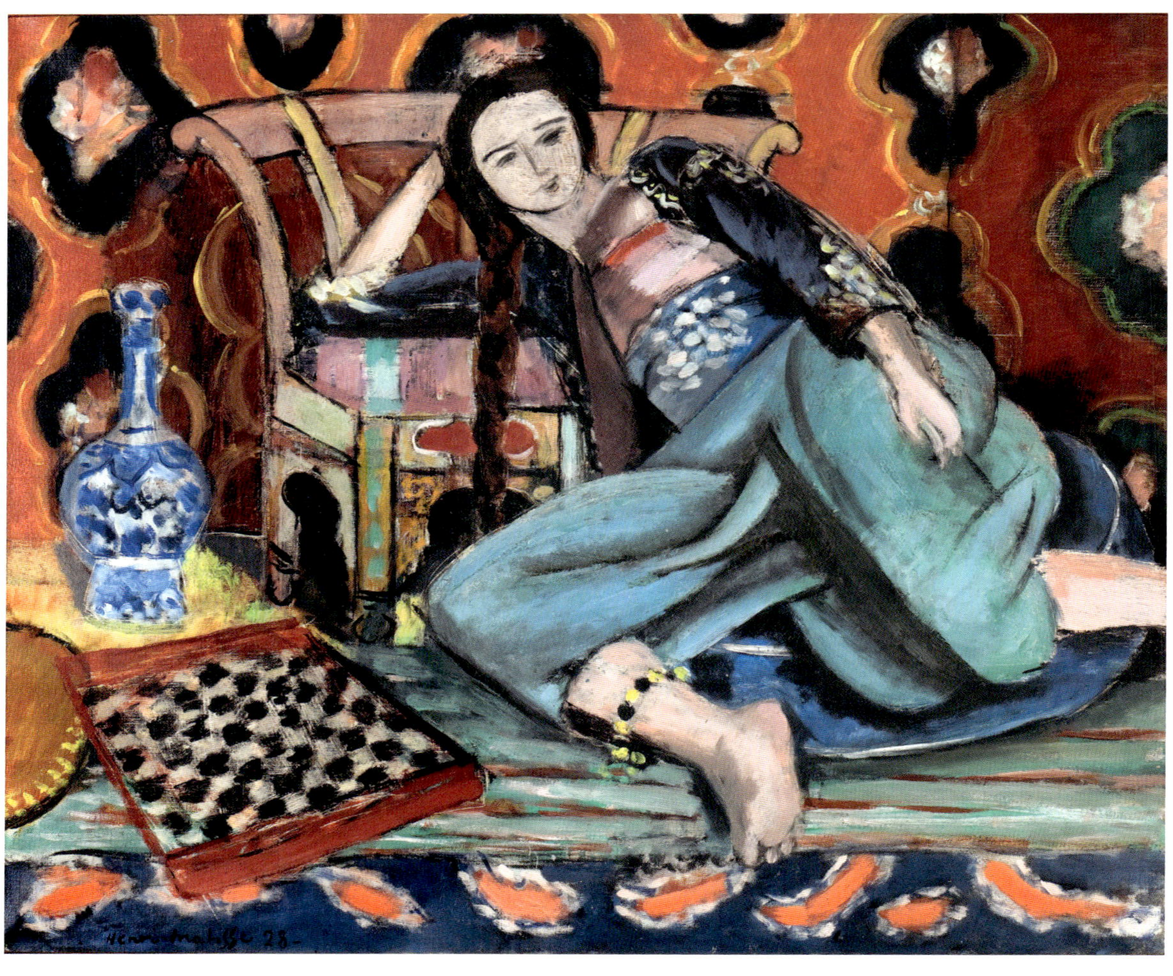

83. Henri Matisse, *Odalisque with Armchair*, 1928, oil on canvas, 60 × 73 cm, Musée d'Art Moderne de Paris, Paris.

at will by deploying textiles and portable screens as well as exotically costumed models and props to create a multilayered, pictorial reality for his odalisque series.[91] The studio metamorphosed into an ornamental, sensory universe, overflowing with textiles and exotic objects – a combination of archive and toolbox that Matisse called his 'working library'.[92] He rearranged and replenished his collections and used them in composing his paintings. Although his studios gave an impression of munificence, he furnished them from junk shops.[93] In a 1951 interview, Matisse observed that objects were, like actors, able to play different roles in different pictures.[94] His creative process relied on close collaboration with individual models – like Henriette Darricarrère, who posed from 1920 to 1927 and excelled at role-playing. In 1939, Matisse explained, 'My models . . . are never just "extras" in an interior. They are the principal theme in my work. I depend entirely on my model'.[95]

Photographs of Matisse working from the model show the elaborate settings and exotic objects that he orchestrated to stage paintings like *Odalisque with*

Armchair (fig.83). A 1928 photograph (fig.84) records the theatrical artifice of the Place Charles-Félix studio. Zita, the same model who appears in *Odalisque with Armchair*, is shown here lounging on a raised platform in an alcove, framed by patterned textiles, while Matisse, seated at the left, paints her. In *Odalisque with Armchair*, she reclines against a colorful, inlaid, octagonal chair of North African origin. Dressed in loose harem pants and an embroidered top, she is surrounded by vibrant textiles and exotic props, including a blue and white vase and a chessboard.[96] Her right arm is interlaced with the chairback, which is painted a pinkish flesh tone, thus conflating odalisque and chair. Through the harmonious synchrony of colors and patterns, model and decoration coalesce, and the boundaries between figure and setting blur.

In 1927, Matisse moved to a larger fourth-floor apartment, with panoramic views and a wraparound balcony. There were two studios that faced the sea: one with a window wall and false-tile, painted walls that he used for painting and the other with false-marble walls, as well as an interior studio and storage area where he occasionally worked.[97] The main studio, with its immense south-facing window overlooking the Baie des Anges, was a giant light chamber or camera aperture, whose reflective white walls amplified its luminosity.[98] The almost blinding southern light was the antithesis of the cool northern light traditionally favored by artists. Matisse painted his studio repeatedly, sometimes with a model posing, as in *Nude in the Studio* (1928), sometimes empty, as in *The Studio in Nice* (1929, fig.85), where the large easel and female torso on the sculpture stand evoke the absent artist, who has momentarily stepped out. A *brasero* (brazier), which was a recurring motif in odalisque paintings, is depicted at the far left. Like other paintings by Matisse from the late 1920s, *The Studio in Nice* is saturated with light, which seems to emanate mysteriously from thin, translucent veils of paint. In *Nude in the Studio*, the model appears ephemeral, as if she is dissolving in the brilliant light. Seated at the easel, Matisse is reflected in the mirror at the right, creating a complex interplay of absence and presence, illusion and reality.

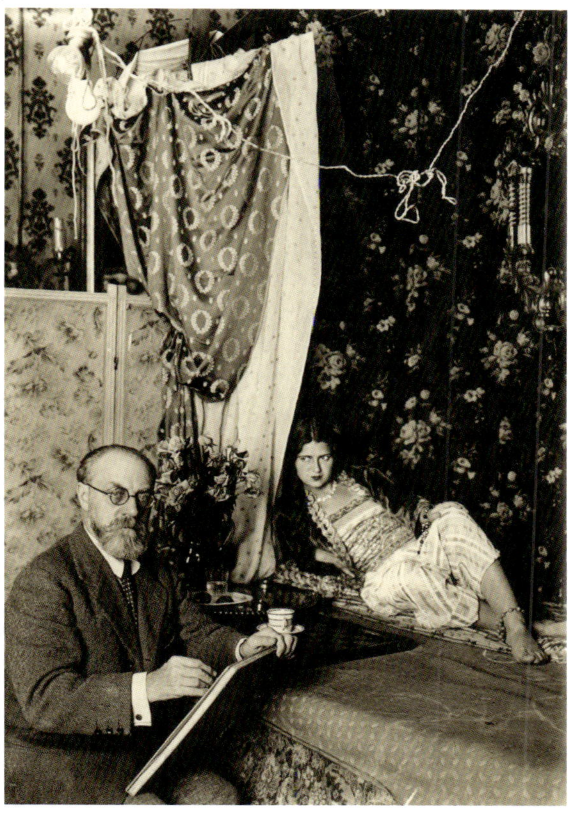

84. Anonymous photographer, *Matisse Painting the Model Zita*, 1928, photograph, unknown dimensions, National Gallery of Art, Washington, DC.

After Picasso married Russian ballerina, Olga Khokhlova, in 1918, his art and lifestyle changed dramatically.[99] In December, the Picassos moved to an elegant apartment at 23 rue La Boétie – the center of the art trade – and began frequenting fashionable society and the Parisian intelligentsia.[100] Picasso set up his studio in small rooms overlooking the street. In spring 1920, he recorded his studio – filled with stacks of pictures and painting paraphernalia – in three pencil drawings.[101] One drawing depicts a jumble of easels, palettes and paints

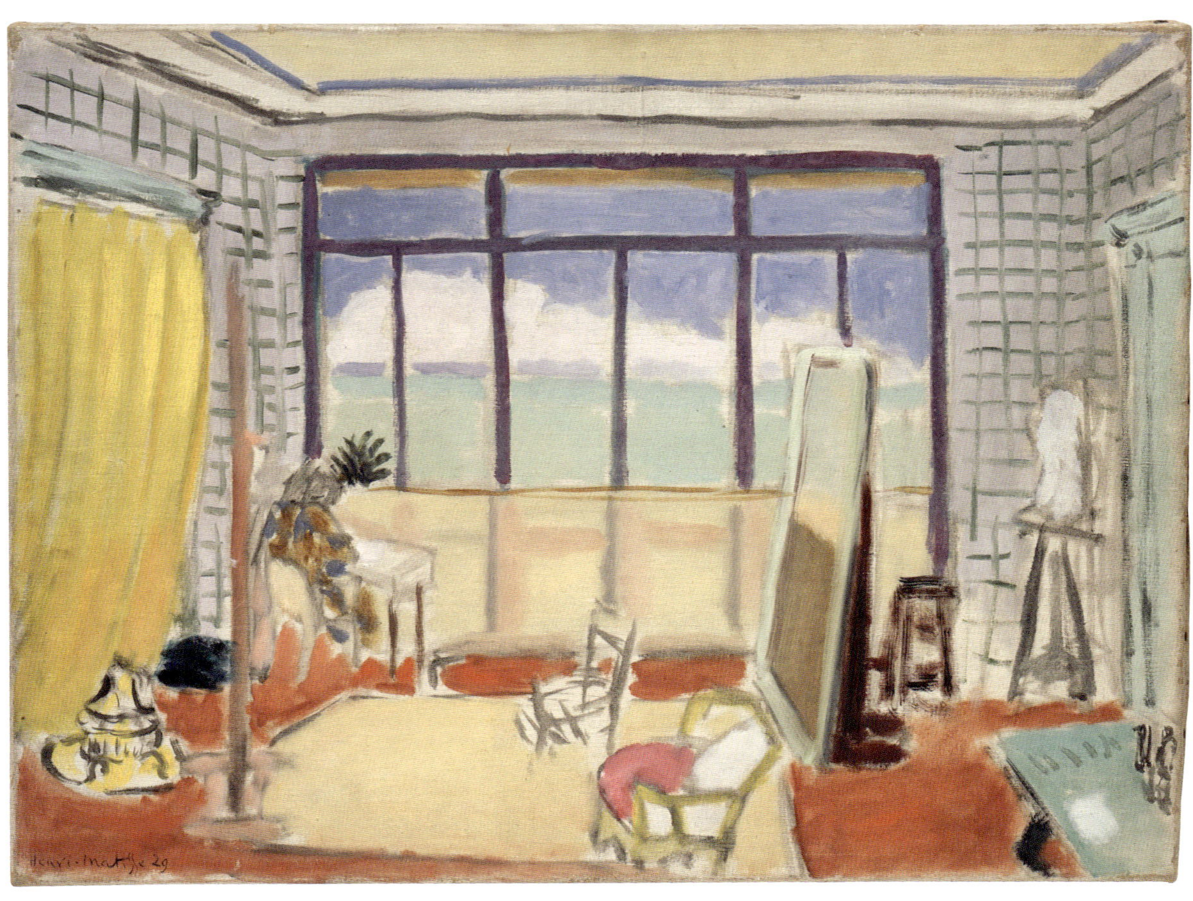

85. Henri Matisse, *The Studio in Nice*, 1929, oil on canvas, 46.5 × 61 cm, Museum Berggruen/Nationalgalerie/Staatliche Museen, Berlin.

scattered around the floor, while another shows the window and a wooden chair surrounded by palettes and a portfolio – a reminder of the absent artist. The orderly, elegantly furnished rooms in the rest of the apartment, where Olga presided, contrasted with Picasso's chaotic workspace. In 1925, he rented the floor above their apartment and used it exclusively as a studio, expanding his workspace and increasing his autonomy.[102]

In 1932, the Surrealist review *Minotaure* commissioned Brassaï to photograph Picasso's studios. He described the La Boétie complex of studios as, 'four or five rooms . . . transformed into a combination junk shop and old-curiosity shop', which were crammed with papers, stacks of pictures, books and cigarette packs and covered with a thick layer of dust.[103] *Minotaure*'s 1933 inaugural issue was mostly devoted to Picasso's sculpture.[104] Brassaï's striking photographs of the Paris and Boisgeloup studios accompanied André Breton's hagiographic essay, 'Picasso dans son élément', which poetically conjured his creative inner sanctum and extolled him as a protean demiurge.[105] Referring to Brassaï's photographs of the La Boétie studio, Breton invested the clutter and detritus surrounding Picasso with weighty existential significance, loftily invoking the mystery of human creation and the delectation of the perishable and ephemeral.[106]

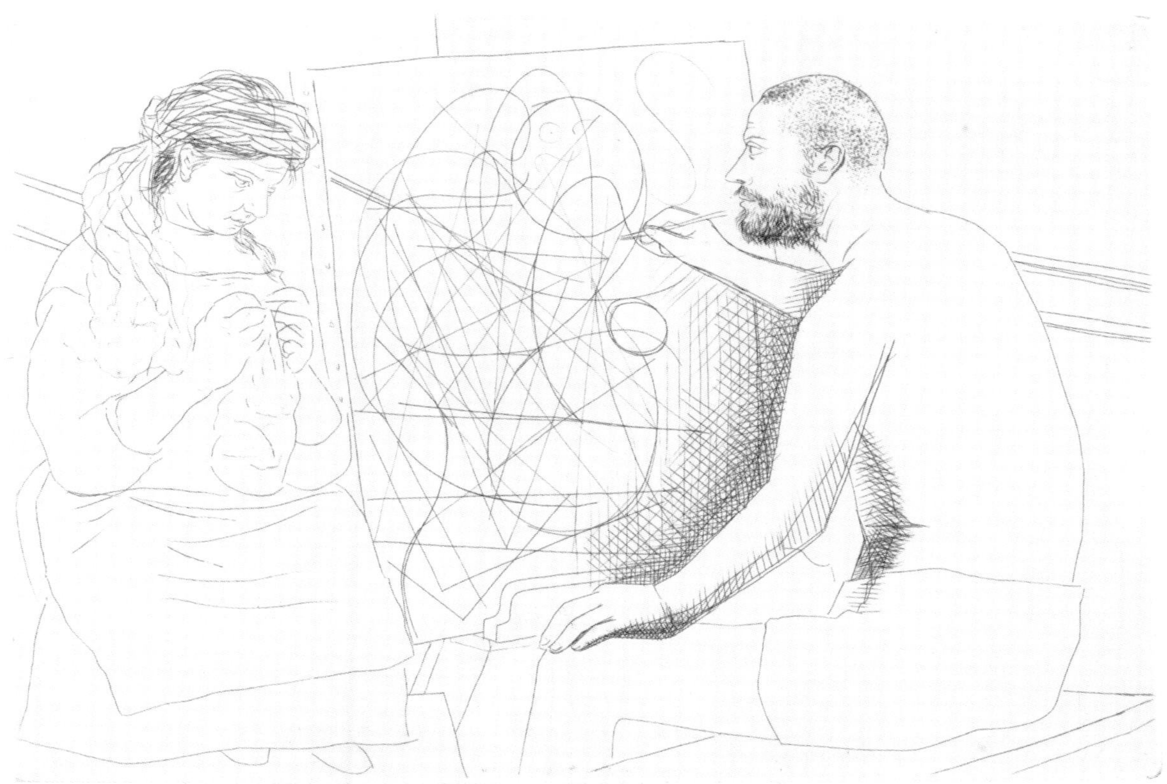

86. Pablo Picasso, *Painter and Model Knitting*, 1927, in Honoré de Balzac, *Le chef-d'oeuvre inconnu*, Vollard, Paris, 1931, etching, 19.3 × 27.8 cm, Museum of Modern Art, New York.

ARTIST AND MODEL

Picasso investigated the studio theme through the polymorphic relationship of artist and model in a protracted, pictorial meditation on the creative process that culminated in the *Suite Vollard* (1937).[107] The 1926 commission to illustrate Honoré de Balzac's *Le chef-d'oeuvre inconnu* (*The Unknown Masterpiece*) was a catalyst for Picasso's heightened preoccupation with the reciprocity of artist and model. Vollard's luxury edition, with 13 etchings by Picasso, was published in 1931. Picasso adopted a classicizing style in the etchings. Rather than illustrating the text, he produced a set of variations on the artist/model theme by modifying the position of artist and model and, at times, conflating their identities.[108] The fourth plate depicting the artist at the easel, painting a clothed model, absorbed in her knitting, relates most directly to Balzac's text (fig.86). The painting on the easel is an illegible tangle of lines and circles, underscoring the discrepancy between the model and the artist's portrayal and, thus, the problematics of representation – central tropes in Balzac's parable about painting. Picasso identified with and was haunted by Frenhofer, the failed artist at the center of Balzac's tragic fable about genius, artistic rivalries and the limits of painting. After he was commissioned to paint a mural for the Spanish Pavilion at the 1937 Paris World's Fair, Picasso rented an immense studio under the eaves at 7 rue des Grands-Augustins on the Left Bank. His initial sketches,

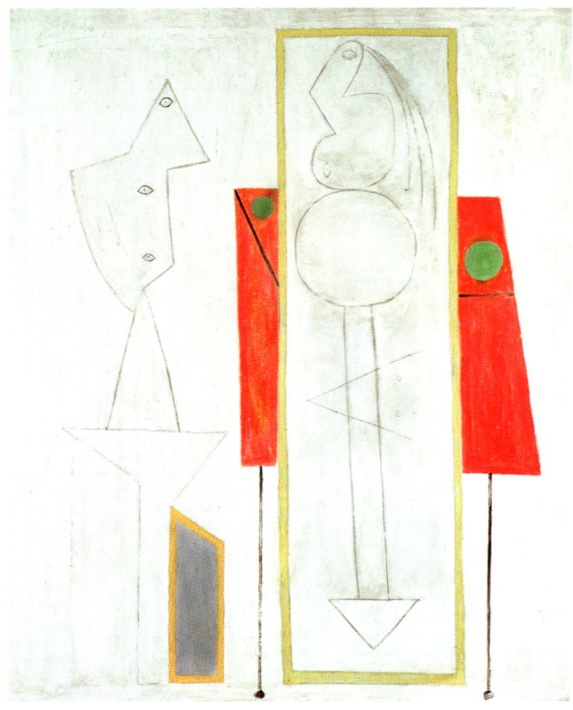

87. Pablo Picasso, *The Studio (L'Atelier)*, 1928, oil on canvas, 161 × 129.9 cm, Peggy Guggenheim Collection, Venice.

executed before the bombing of Guernica, depicted the artist and model in the studio.[109]

Across the 1920s, Picasso painted a series of large-format, quasi-abstract studio pictures. The chaotic, monochromatic *Artist and His Model* (1926), which initiated the series, subverted rational space and experimented with flowing automatist line and bodily distortion.[110] Focusing on the encounter between artist and model, he envisaged the studio as an unfettered, polymorphous space of imagination and metamorphosis. Since he rarely worked from the model, the subject was primarily an archetype – an imaginary projection of artistic activity – that opened up endless pictorial possibilities and thus became a renewable genre like landscape.[111] Using a schematic Cubist syntax, Picasso painted a set of variations, culminating in *L'Atelier* (*The Studio*, 1928, fig.87).[112] In contrast to the New York *Studio* (1927–8), which depicts the artist painting a still life, *L'Atelier* reverses the composition and eliminates the artist. Instead, it shows dueling artworks that embody the rivalry between sculpture and painting: a sculptural bust at the left and a female portrait at the right.[113] *L'Atelier* radically reduces the studio to a ground zero of abstracted ideograms that emerge from an all-encompassing, white field. Only a few recognizable signs, such as the table and the painting within the painting, remain. Technical analysis has revealed that the canvas was modified during the painting process. Lines and details were eliminated, heightening the austerity of the canvas and thus dematerializing the studio.[114] Determined to possess *L'Atelier*, which was sold to Kahnweiler in 1929, Picasso reacquired it in 1934 in exchange for five paintings, attesting to its particular significance for him.[115]

EPILOGUE: THE FINAL ACT

After World War II, when Matisse and Picasso both lived in southern France, they grew closer. They saw each other regularly and conversed on various topics, including their legacies and artistic genealogies.[116] *Large Red Interior* (1948), one of Matisse's last major paintings, reprises the picture within a picture theme, though less radically than *Red Studio*. Dominated by tables with flowers and plants, this interior is not obviously a studio space. *The Pineapple* (1948) and a large still life drawing mirror the vegetation but read as interior decor rather than artworks. Unlike the staccato effect of *Red Studio*, where individual works jump out, *Large Red Interior* flows seamlessly. Matisse's relationship with his studio entered its final, immersive phase with his paper cutouts, which were assembled and displayed on the studio walls before becoming autonomous artworks. The walls now doubled as blank

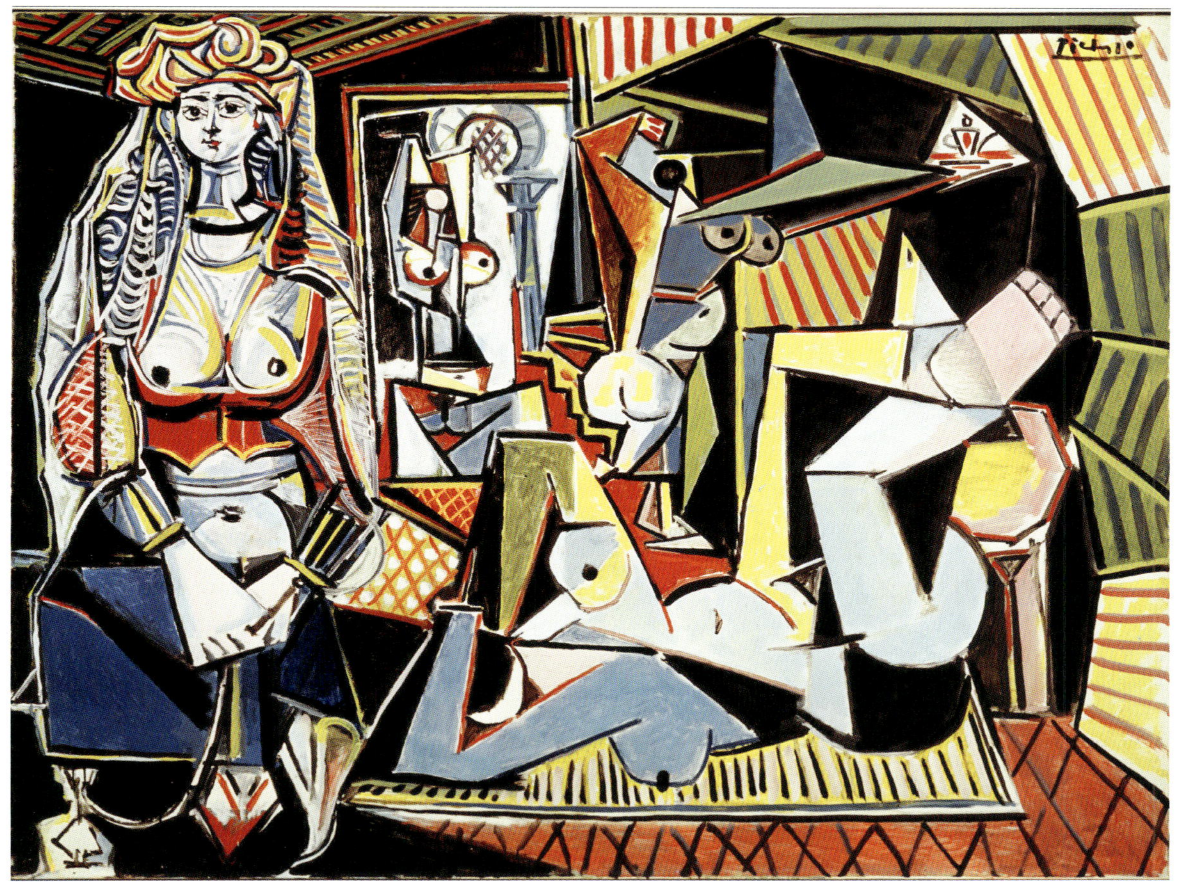

88. Pablo Picasso (after Delacroix), *Women of Algiers* (*Version 'O'*), 14 February 1955, oil on canvas, 114 × 146 cm, private collection.

slates for his artistic imagination and as supports for constructing his installations. To make his cutouts, Matisse carved colored forms with his scissors, thus merging drawing and painting. In these monumental late works, he achieved a new decorative synthesis and fluidity that freed him from his lifelong reliance on the model.

Although he did not attend Matisse's funeral, Picasso was deeply affected by his longtime rival's death on 3 November 1954. He worked through the devastating loss in his studio by taking up the odalisque theme, which was intimately associated with Matisse and Delacroix. From 13 December 1954 to 14 February 1955, Picasso painted 15 serial variations after Delacroix's *Women of Algiers* and made numerous drawings and prints.[117] Picasso's variations were a complex creative dialogue that linked past and present and was emblematic of the duality of the creative process, as well as a vehicle for measuring himself against past masters. Defending the significance of copies, he insisted that they revealed the personality of the artist making them and were never exact. He observed: 'A painter's atelier should be a laboratory. One doesn't do a monkey's job here: one invents. Painting is a *jeu d'esprit*.'[118] *Women of Algiers*, which obsessed Picasso, was the gateway for an intense, triangulated pictorial engagement with

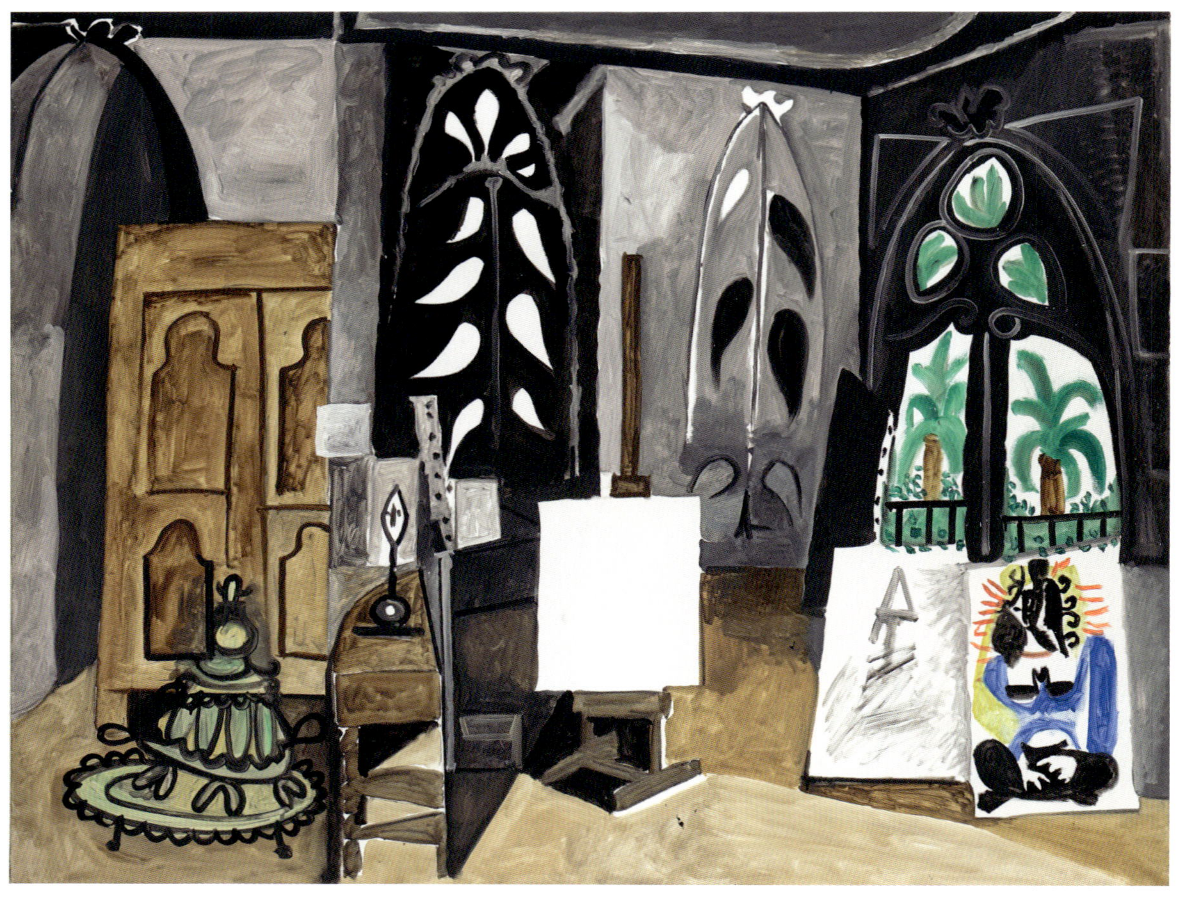

89. Pablo Picasso, *The Studio at La Californie, Cannes*, 30 March 1956, oil on canvas, 114 × 146 cm, Musée national Picasso-Paris, Paris.

Delacroix and Matisse. Delacroix was the wellspring and lodestar, encapsulating the colorist tradition across art history and connecting the Old Masters to the present.[119]

Picasso reinvented and transformed *Women of Algiers* serially, conceiving it as an ensemble rather than as a succession of individual canvases. The 15 variations (a–o) culminated in seven large-scale, multi-figure canvases. Picasso's variations deconstructed and cannibalized Delacroix's composition. He took possession of it and made it his own by recasting and rearranging the figures and literally upending the Cubist nude at the center. The exotic crouching or seated odalisque at the left metamorphosed into a towering evocation of Jacqueline, who became his second wife. In the final, most Matisse-like variation, Picasso introduced vibrant patterning, recalling Matisse's Nice interiors, and amalgamated color and line (fig.88). Leo Steinberg noted, 'Everything comes together in Canvas O . . . a synthesis on many levels'.[120] Picasso's *Women of Algiers* variations expanded his museum without walls to include Ingres's *Odalisque with Slave* (1839–40) and Velázquez's *Las Meninas*, thus thoroughly conflating harem and studio.

During the summer of 1955, Picasso moved to La Californie, a spacious Belle Époque mansion overlooking Cannes. He set up his studio in the large main salon on the ground floor and also entertained friends there. Between October and November 1955, he painted a series of vertical studio interiors that paid homage to Matisse's interiors.[121] Although he often portrayed the artist at work, unlike Matisse, Picasso rarely focused on the studio as subject. The La Californie studio paintings feature a plaster bust on a sculpture stand and a chair with artists' tools. The ornate central window, which links exterior and interior, and the profusion of patterning echo and emulate Matisse.[122] From late March to early April 1956, Picasso painted a group of horizontal canvases depicting the center of his studio, using a more somber palette that is reminiscent of Matisse's late interiors and odalisques. The first canvas, dated 30 March 1956 (fig.89), introduces the picture within a picture theme with a painting of a seated odalisque at the far right. The palm trees, exotic set-like interior and Moroccan dish recall Matisse's Nice studio. The most striking feature is the blank canvas on the easel at dead center – a gaping void waiting to be filled.[123] In the fourth canvas, this void was painted over in blue. Across these moving, commemorative canvases, Matisse's presence permeates Picasso's La Californie studio, continuing their pictorial dialogue.

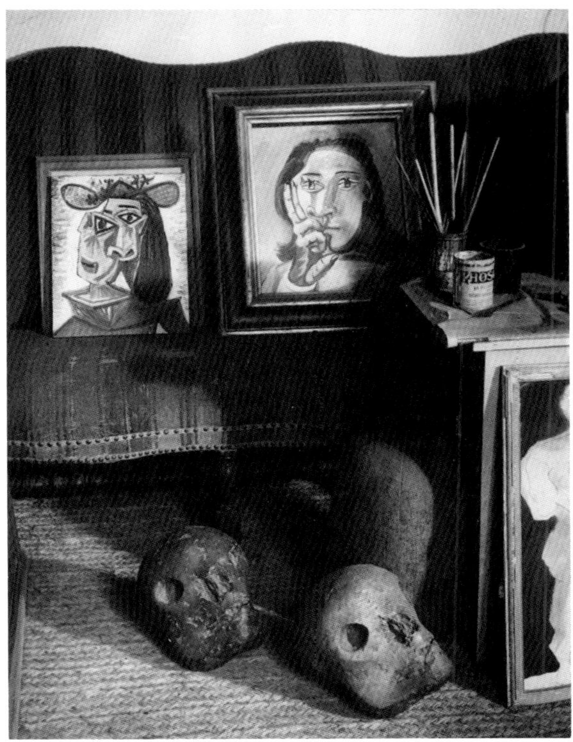

90. Brassaï, *Corner of the Studio des Grands-Augustins with Skulls*, 1943, gelatin silver print, 23.2 × 17.8 cm, Musée national Picasso-Paris, Paris.

CODA

The legendary studio where Picasso painted *Guernica* in a few feverish weeks in 1937 and lived and worked during the darkest days of World War II survives.[124] Classified as a public monument in 2014, the studio is inaccessible. However, it can be experienced vicariously in the mind's eye through photographs that capture it as a dynamic, fluid workspace where canvases were moved, rearranged and selectively displayed. Over four decades, Brassaï documented Picasso and his studios. Some of his most memorable images are those representing the empty, yet resonant, studio as material artifact and *lieu de mémoire* – notably *Corner of the Studio des Grands-Augustins with Skulls* (1943, fig.90).[125] Juxtaposing anguished portraits of Dora Maar with skulls and paintbrushes, this photograph is both artistic shrine and *memento mori*; it documents studio life and testifies to the studio's enduring role as a laboratory of creation and refracted self-portrait of the artist.

Abbreviations

Bazille 2016:
Frédéric Bazille (1841–1870) and the Birth of Impressionism, exh.cat., National Gallery of Art, Washington, DC, 2016

Corot 1996:
Corot, exh.cat., Metropolitan Museum of Art, New York, 1996

Delacroix Journal:
Delacroix, Eugène, *Journal*, 2 vols (M. Hannoosh, ed.), José Corti, Paris, 2009

Early Nice Years:
Henri Matisse: The Early Years in Nice, 1916–1930, exh.cat., National Gallery of Art, Washington, DC, 1986

Inventions of the Studio:
Cole, Michael, and Mary Pardo (eds), *Inventions of the Studio: Renaissance to Romanticism*, University of North Carolina Press, Chapel Hill, NC, 2005

Manet 1983:
Manet: 1832–1883, exh.cat., Metropolitan Museum of Art, New York, 1983

Manet Catalogue:
Rouart, Denis, and Georges Wildenstein, *Édouard Manet. Catalogue raisonné*, 2 vols, La Bibliothèque des Arts, Lausanne/Paris, 1975

'Old Masters':
Haskell, Francis,'The Old Masters in Nineteenth-Century French Painting', *Past and Present in Art and Taste: Selected Essays*, by Francis Haskell, Yale University Press, New Haven, CT/London, 1987, pp 90–115

Picasso/La Vie:
Robinson, William H., *Picasso and the Mysteries of Life: La Vie*, exh.cat., Cleveland Museum of Art, Cleveland, OH, 2012

Red Studio:
Temkin, Ann, and Dorthe Aagesen, *Matisse: The Red Studio*, exh.cat., Museum of Modern Art, New York, 2022

Robaut 1905:
Robaut, Alfred, *L'Oeuvre de Corot. Catalogue raisonné et illustré*, 4 vols, Floury, Paris, 1905

Robaut Cartons:
Robaut, Alfred, Cartons, 35 cartons, Cabinet des estampes, Bibliothèque nationale de France, Paris, on deposit at Département des peintures, Service d'étude et de documentation, Musée du Louvre, Paris

Robaut Documents:
Robaut, Alfred,'Documents sur Corot', ms., 3 vols, Cabinet des estampes, Bibliothèque nationale de France, Paris

'Studio Paintings':
FitzGerald, Michael,'The Studio Paintings', in *Picasso: The Artist's Studio*, exh.cat., Yale University Press, New Haven, CT/London, 2001, pp 15–61

Wildenstein *Monet:*
Wildenstein, Daniel, *Claude Monet. Biographie et catalogue raisonné*, 5 vols, Bibliothèque des Arts, Lausanne/Paris, 1974–1991

Notes

Unless otherwise indicated, translations are my own. Here, in my list of abbreviations, and in the bibliography, I have included the authors for exhibition catalogues when they are especially important – for instance, when the catalogue is by a single author.

INTRODUCTION: THE ARTIST'S STUDIO: THEME AND VARIATIONS

1. A.-J. du Pays, 'Atelier de M. Eugène Delacroix', *L'Illustration*, 25 September 1852, pp 205–7. The building (now no.58) survives; the studio was converted to an apartment.
2. Rachel Esner, 'In the Artist's Studio with *L'Illustration*', *RIHA Journal*, January–March 2013, http://www.riha-journal.org/articles/2013/2013-jan-mar/esner-illustration/.
3. Théophile Silvestre, 'Eugène Delacroix', *Histoire des artistes vivants français et étrangers. Études d'après nature*, E. Blanchard, Paris, 1856, p.42.
4. *Delacroix Journal*, vol.1, pp 1210–11.
5. See John Milner, *The Studios of Paris: The Capital of Art in the Late Nineteenth Century*, Yale University Press, New Haven, CT/London, 1988.
6. John Elderfield, *In the Studio*, vol.1: *Paintings*, Gagosian Gallery, New York, 2015, pp 12–44.
7. On the studio's origins, see *Inventions of the Studio*, pp 1–35; Rachel Esner, 'Nos artistes chez eux. L'Image des artistes dans la presse illustrée', in *L'Artiste en représentation. Images des artistes dans l'art du XIXe siècle* (A. Bonnet, ed.), Fage, Lyon, 2012, pp 139–49.
8. *Inventions of the Studio*; Elderfield, *In the Studio: Paintings*, pp 17–18.
9. Elderfield, *In the Studio: Paintings*, p.17.
10. Svetlana Alpers, 'The View from the Studio', in *The Vexations of Art: Velázquez and Others*, Yale University Press, New Haven, CT/London, 2005, pp 9–45, discusses various studio models.
11. Esner, 'Nos artistes chez eux', pp 139–49.
12. Besides Alpers and Elderfield (*In the Studio*), my thinking has been informed by: Daniel Buren, 'The Function of the Studio', trans. Thomas Repensek, *October*, vol.10, 1979, pp 51–8; Brian O'Doherty, *Studio and Cube*, Columbia University Press, New York, 2007; Philippe Hamon, 'Le topos de l'atelier', in *L'Artiste en représentation* (R. Démoris, ed.), Éditions Desjonquières, Paris, 1993, pp 126–44; and Giles Waterfield (ed.), *The Artist's Studio*, Hogarth Arts, Compton Verney, 2009, pp 1–41.
13. Charles Baudelaire, *The Painter of Modern Life and Other Essays* (J. Mayne, ed.), Phaidon, London, 1964, pp 60–61.

I THE ECHO CHAMBER: DELACROIX, MANET AND THE OLD MASTERS

1. *Delacroix Journal*, vol.1, p.138.
2. 'Old Masters', pp 90–115.
3. ibid., pp 109–10. Robert-Fleury depicted Cellini, Rubens, Murillo, Michelangelo, Titian, Rembrandt, Leonardo da Vinci, Tintoretto and Velázquez.
4. ibid., pp 92–3, 103.
5. ibid., pp 103–5.
6. ibid., pp 94, 99–100.
7. On Spanish influence, see *Manet/Velázquez: The French Taste for Spanish Painting*, exh.cat., Metropolitan Museum of Art, New York, 2003.
8. *Le Magasin pittoresque*, vol.17, 1849, pp 347–50, 380–82.
9. Sarah Betzer, 'Artist as Lover: Rereading Ingres's *Raphael and the Fornarina*', *Oxford Art Journal*, vol.38, no.3, December 2015, pp 313–41; Hélène Toussaint, 'Ingres et la Fornarina', *Bulletin du Musée Ingres*, September 1986, pp 63–74.
10. 'Old Masters', p.97.
11. Lee Johnson, *The Paintings of Eugène Delacroix: A Critical Catalogue*, 6 vols, Clarendon Press, Oxford, 1981–9, vol.3, pp 126–8, no.305.
12. Charles de Tolnay, '"Michel-Ange dans son atelier" par Delacroix', *Gazette des Beaux-Arts*, vol.59, January 1962, pp 43–52; Jack J. Spector, 'An Interpretation of Delacroix's *Michelangelo in His Studio*', in *Psychoanalytic Perspectives on Art* (M.M. Gedo, ed.), The Analytic Press, Hillsdale, NJ, 1985, pp 107–31; and Marc Gotlieb, 'Creation & Death in the Romantic Studio', *Inventions of the Studio*, pp 147–83.
13. *Manet Catalogue*, vol.1, p.44, no.25; Juliet Wilson-Bareau, 'Manet and Spain', in *Manet/Velázquez*, pp 206–8; Peter Rudd, 'Reconstructing Manet's "Velázquez in His Studio"', *Burlington Magazine*, vol.136, November 1994, pp 747–51.

14. Johnson, *Paintings*, vol.1, pp 17–18, no.21. Attributed to Carreño de Miranda, it was in the Duc d'Orléans's gallery.
15. ibid., vol.1, pp 208–9, no.L105; location unknown.
16. Eugène Delacroix, 'Essai sur les artistes célèbres: Raphaël', *Revue de Paris*, vol.11, February 1830, pp 138–50; *Delacroix Journal*, vol.2, pp 1482–88.
17. Gotlieb, 'Creation & Death', p.168, links it to a therapeutic conception in Romantic culture that Delacroix evoked in his 1830 essay.
18. Johnson, *Paintings*, vol.3, pp 127–28, fig.31. The dates of the painting and print are uncertain. Allan Doyle, 'Grasping the Antique: Michelangelo and the Erotics of Tradition', in *Reconsidering Gérôme*, exh.cat., J. Paul Getty Museum, Los Angeles, 2010, p.11.
19. *Artists by Artists: Sculpted Portraits in the Nineteenth Century*, exh.cat., Stuart Lochhead Sculpture, London, 2019, n.p.
20. The head is based on Michelangelo's self-portrait from his Florence *Pietà* (*c*.1547–55). ibid.
21. Delacroix made copies after the *Slaves*, the *Sistine Chapel*, the *Last Judgment* and *Night*.
22. De Tolnay, 'Michel-Ange', p.51, n.1.
23. Gotlieb, 'Creation & Death', p.166.
24. Michael Duffy, 'Michelangelo and the Sublime in Romantic Art Criticism', *Journal of the History of Ideas*, vol.56, no.2, 1995, pp 217–38.
25. David Wakefield (ed.), *Stendhal and the Arts*, Phaidon, London, 1973. Delacroix took extensive notes on Stendhal's *Histoire* (*Delacroix Journal*, vol.2, pp 1489–1504).
26. Claire Black McCoy, 'Made to Measure: Eugène Guillaume's Michelangelo', *Nineteenth-Century Art Worldwide*, vol.16, no.1, Spring 2017, p.33; Eugène Delacroix, 'Michel-Ange', *Revue de Paris*, vol.15, June 1830, pp 41–58; vol.16, July 1830, pp 164–78.
27. Duffy, 'Michelangelo', p.231; Gotlieb, 'Creation & Death', p.166.
28. De Tolnay, 'Michel-Ange', pp 43–4.
29. Delacroix, 'Michel-Ange', vol.15, p.46. Delacroix read Condivi's biography, which mentions the crisis.
30. Théophile Silvestre, *La Galerie Bruyas*, Imprimerie de J. Claye, Paris, 1876, p.305.
31. Delacroix, 'Michel-Ange', vol.16, pp 174–5.
32. De Tolnay, 'Michel-Ange', p.45.
33. Silvestre, *Galerie Bruyas*, p.297.
34. ibid., p.306.
35. Delacroix, 'Michel-Ange', vol.15, p.53.
36. De Tolnay, 'Michel-Ange', p.46.
37. ibid.
38. *Delacroix Journal*, vol.1, pp 459, 510, 512.
39. Johnson, *Paintings*, vol.3, pp 193–4, no.383; *Delacroix Journal*, vol.1, pp 416–17.
40. Margret Stuffmann, *Eugène Delacroix: Reflections: Tasso in the Madhouse*, exh.cat., Oskar Reinhart Collection Am Römerholz, Winterthur, 2008, p.62.
41. Stuffmann, *Delacroix: Reflections*, p.60.
42. For the inscriptions, see *Delacroix: An Exhibition of Paintings, Drawings, and Lithographs*, exh.cat., Arts Council, London, 1964, p.62, nos 167, 168.
43. *Dégrossir* is a sculptural term meaning to trim or rough out a form.
44. Stuffmann, *Delacroix: Reflections*, pp 13–15.
45. *Delacroix Journal*, vol.1, p.90.
46. ibid., vol.1, pp 617, 635.
47. Silvestre, *Galerie Bruyas*, p.335.
48. ibid., pp 307–8; *Michelangelo and His Genius*, Musée Fabre website. www.museefabre.fr.
49. Johnson, *Paintings*, vol.5, pp 50, 69, no.549. There is no oil study for the *Socrates*.
50. Cited in Étienne Moreau-Nélaton, *Delacroix raconté par lui-même*, 2 vols., Henri Laurens, Paris, 1916, vol.1, p.189.
51. Michèle Hannoosh, 'Delacroix and Sculpture', *Nineteenth-Century French Studies*, vol.35, no.1, Fall 2006, pp 95–109.
52. ibid., pp 96–7.
53. Cited in ibid., p.95.
54. ibid., pp 97, 105–6.
55. Stuffmann, *Delacroix: Reflections*, p.62.
56. Delacroix, 'Michel-Ange', vol.15, pp 57–8.
57. *Delacroix Journal*, vol.1, pp 542–3.
58. Stuffmann, *Delacroix: Reflections*, pp 30–31, no.5.
59. ibid., pp 52–4, no.14. Baudelaire, who wrote a poem about *Tasso in Prison*, recognized Delacroix's '*douleur morale*' ('moral sadness'). Rebecca M. Pauly, 'Baudelaire and Delacroix on Tasso in Prison: Romantic Reflections on a Renaissance Martyr', *College Literature*, vol.30, no.2, Spring 2003, pp 120–35.
60. Baudelaire, *Painter of Modern Life*, pp 1–40.
61. Étienne Moreau-Nélaton, *Manet raconté par lui-même*, 2 vols, Henri Laurens, Paris, 1926, vol.1, pp 21–2. Besides Velázquez, Manet copied Lippi, Delacroix, Titian, Tintoretto, Rembrandt and Rubens.
62. Manet's sources have been discussed in detail, but I focus here on his engagement with Velázquez and the central role of the studio.
63. *Manet* 1983, pp 45–6, no.1. Manet's admiration was reinforced by Delacroix's friendship with Baudelaire.
64. Bridget Alsdorf, *Fellow Men: Fantin-Latour and the Problem of the Group in Nineteenth-Century French Painting*, Princeton University Press, Princeton, NJ, 2013.
65. Wilson-Bareau, 'Manet and Spain', pp 203–20.
66. Antonin Proust, *Édouard Manet. Souvenirs*, Librairie Renouard, Paris, 1913, p.24. Manet and Proust made sketches of Velázquez's *Petits Cavaliers* after seeing *Barque of Dante*.
67. Wilson-Bareau, 'Manet and Spain', p.205, fig.9.2.
68. *Manet Catalogue*, vol.1, p.40, no.21. Manet made a watercolor and an etching based on the painting. Jean C. Harris, *Édouard Manet: The Graphic Work: A Catalogue Raisonné*, Alan Wofsy Fine Arts, San Francisco, 1990, pp 44–7, no.5.
69. Wilson-Bareau, 'Manet and Spain', p.206. Acquired as a Velázquez

in 1851; reattributed to Juan Bautista Martínez del Mazo, Velázquez's pupil and son-in-law. Wilson-Bareau compares it with *View of Saragasso* (1647), a joint work by Velázquez and Mazo.

70. On Faure's collecting, see Anthea Callen, 'Faure and Manet', *Gazette des Beaux-Arts*, vol.83, March 1974, pp 157–68.
71. *Manet Catalogue*, vol.1, p.44, nos 25, 26.
72. See *Manet* 1983, pp 46–8, no.2; *Manet Catalogue*, vol.2, p.164, no.454; Harris, *Graphic Work*, p.106, no.28.
73. Rudd, 'Reconstructing', pp 747–8.
74. *Manet Catalogue*, vol.2, p.58, no.68. The portrait is reversed in Manet's 1862 etching. Harris, *Graphic Work*, p.72, no.15.
75. Rudd, 'Reconstructing', pp 748–9, fig.14.
76. Jacques-Émile Blanche, *Propos de peintre, de David à Degas*, Émile-Paul Frères, Paris, 1919, p.152.
77. Rudd, 'Reconstructing', pp 750–51.
78. Cited in Moreau-Nélaton, *Manet raconté*, vol.1, pp 71–2.
79. Cited in Wilson-Bareau, 'Manet and Spain', p.231.
80. Scott Allan, 'Faux Frère: Manet and the Salon, 1879–82', in *Manet and Modern Beauty: The Artist's Last Years*, exh.cat., J. Paul Getty Museum, Los Angeles, 2019, pp 36–8.
81. Juliet Wilson-Bareau, 'Édouard Manet dans ses ateliers', *Ironie*, no.161, January–February 2012, http://interrogationcritiqueludique.blogspot.com/2012/10/ironie-n161-janvierfevfriefr-2012.html.
82. Juliet Wilson-Bareau (ed.), *Manet by Himself*, Chartwell Books, Edison, NJ, 2001, p.9.
83. Michael Wilson, *Manet at Work*, exh.cat., National Gallery, London, 1983, pp 4–14.
84. Devi Ormond and Catherine Schmidt Patterson, 'The Making of a *Parisienne*: Manet's Methods and Materials', in *Manet and Modern Beauty*, pp 147–59.
85. For photographs of the buildings and of the Saint-Pétersbourg interior, see Juliet Wilson-Bareau, *Manet, Monet and the Gare Saint-Lazare*, exh.cat., National Gallery of Art, Washington, DC, 1998.
86. Wilson-Bareau, *Manet/Gare Saint-Lazare*, pp 9–10, 184, n.5; Wilson-Bareau, 'Manet ateliers'.
87. Émile Zola, 'Préface', in *Exposition des oeuvres de Édouard Manet. Catalogue*, A. Quantin, Paris, 1884, p.10.
88. Théodore Duret, *Histoire de Édouard Manet et de son œuvre*, Bernheim Jeune, Paris, 1919, pp 86–9.
89. Juliet Wilson-Bareau, 'The Salon des Refusés: A New View', *Burlington Magazine*, vol.149, May 2007, p.312. Legros's other paintings were exhibited at the Salon. *Portrait of Manet* was relegated to the Salon des Refusés, with Manet's rejected canvases, including *Déjeuner sur l'herbe*.
90. Alsdorf, *Fellow Men*, pp 139–41.
91. *Manet Catalogue*, vol.1, p.140, no.153; Carol Jane Grant, 'Eva Gonzalès (1849–1883): An Examination of the Artist's Style and Subject Matter', PhD diss., Ohio State University, Columbus, OH, 1994, p.111.
92. Moreau-Nélaton, *Manet raconté*, vol.1, pp 112–13.
93. *La Posada* (c.1865–6) depicts a matador in a similar pose. *Manet Catalogue*, vol.2, p.188, no.534.
94. Cited in Moreau-Nélaton, *Manet raconté*, vol.1, p.113. On Manet's revisions, see *Discover Manet & Eva Gonzalès*, exh.cat., National Gallery, London, 2022, pp 81–4. For propriety, Gonzalès posed in a small salon in the familial apartment (Wilson-Bareau, 'Manet ateliers').
95. Emily A. Beeny, 'Manet and the Eighteenth Century', in *Manet and Modern Beauty*, p.103, compares it to self-portraits by female artists, such as Vigée-Lebrun and Labille-Guiard.
96. Gloria Groom, 'Foregrounding Manet's Backgrounds', in *Manet and Modern Beauty*, p.71.
97. *Manet* 1983, pp 280–85, no.106. Zola defended *Olympia* as Manet's masterpiece and 'the total expression of his temperament' (p.282).
98. Cited in ibid., p.282.
99. ibid., pp 248–52, no.94; Therese Dolan, 'A Model Complicated by an Artist: Manet's *Portrait of the Poet Zacharie Astruc*', in *Women in Impressionism: From Mythical Feminine to Modern Woman*, exh.cat., Ny Carlsberg Glpytotek, Copenhagen, 2006, pp 135–55.
100. Dolan, 'Model Complicated', p.136, notes that the witty but inexact Titian quotation is typical of Manet's modus operandi.
101. ibid., p.147.
102. Wilson-Bareau, *Manet/Gare Saint-Lazare*, pp 143–50; Wilson-Barreau, 'Manet ateliers'.
103. Cited in Moreau-Nélaton, *Manet raconté*, vol.2, pp 8–10.
104. Gaston La Touche, 'Édouard Manet. Souvenirs intimes', *Le Journal des Arts*, vol.15, January 1884, cited in Wilson-Bareau, 'Manet ateliers'.
105. Cited in ibid.
106. Wilson-Bareau, *Manet/Gare Saint-Lazare*, pp 43–50.
107. *Manet and Modern Beauty*, pp 279–80, no.8.
108. On the frequently hostile responses, see Adolphe Tabarant, *Manet. Histoire catalographique*, Éditions Montaigne, Paris, 1931, pp 277–83.
109. Wilson-Bareau, 'Manet ateliers'.
110. Blanche, *Propos de peintre*, pp 140–46.
111. *Manet and Modern Beauty*, pp 273–4, no.1. Zola used the same strategy to defend Manet.
112. *Manet Catalogue*, vol.1, p.222, nos 276, 277; *Manet* 1983, pp 405–7, no.164.
113. Duret, *Histoire de Manet*, p.156.
114. *Manet Catalogue*, vol.1, p.32, no.2.
115. *Manet* 1983, pp 405–7, no.164.
116. Moreau-Nélaton, *Delacroix raconté*, vol.2, pp.193–5, 204–5.
117. Sébastien Allard and Côme Fabrice, *Delacroix*, exh.cat., Metropolitan Museum of Art, New York, 2018, pp 167–73.
118. Blanche, *Propos de peintre*, pp.149–52.
119. Nina Maria Athanassaglou Kallmyer, 'Cézanne and Delacroix's Posthumous Reputation', *Art Bulletin*, vol.87, no.1, March 2005, p.111.
120. Théophile Silvestre, *Eugène Delacroix. Documents nouveaux*, Lévy Frères, Paris, 1864, pp 8–11.

121. *Catalogue de la vente de Eugène Delacroix, Hôtel Drouot*, J. Claye, Paris, 1864, pp vii–xv.
122. Moreau-Nélaton, *Delacroix raconté*, vol.2, p.221.
123. Silvestre, *Eugène Delacroix*, pp 19–20.
124. Moreau-Nélaton, *Delacroix raconté*, vol.2, p.221.
125. 'Delacroix by Carrier-Belleuse', *Artists by Artists*, n.p., visible in Albertini's painting.
126. Zola, 'Préface', pp 7–19.
127. Duret, *Histoire de Manet*, pp 201–12.
128. Callen, 'Faure and Manet', p.169. Faure lent 30 works.
129. Moreau-Nélaton, *Manet raconté*, vol.2, pp 104–5.
130. Duret, *Histoire de Manet*, pp 209–18.

2 ABSENCE AND PRESENCE: COROT'S STUDIO REVISITED

1. *Delacroix Journal*, vol.1, p.365.
2. Patricia Mainardi, 'Corot entre deux chaises', in *Corot, un artiste et son temps. Actes des colloques organisés au Musée du Louvre* (V. Pomarède, C. Stefani and G. de Wallens, eds), Klinksieck, Paris, 1998, pp 157–71.
3. Anthea Callen, *The Art of Impressionism: Painting Technique & the Making of Modernity*, Yale University Press, New Haven, CT/London, 2000, pp 1–14; Oskar Bätschmann, *The Artist in the Modern World: The Conflict between Market and Self-Expression*, Dumont, Cologne, 1997.
4. Philippe Junod, 'L'Atelier comme autoportrait', in *Chemins de traverse. Essais sur l'histoire des arts*, Infolio, Gollion, 2007, pp 285–304.
5. Dominique Horbez, *Corot et les peintres de l'école d'Arras*, La Renaissance du Livre, Tournai, 2004.
6. On the absent artist and empty studio, see Pierre Georgel, *La Peinture dans la peinture*, exh.cat., Musée des Beaux-Arts, Dijon, 1983, pp 184–5.
7. Gary Tinterow, *Corot* 1996, pp 409–18.
8. Robaut Cartons, vol.33; Robaut Documents, vol.1, pp 39 (A–H), 41; vol.2, pp 44, 47.
9. Anne Roquebert, 'Annexe', in *Corot, un artiste*, pp 107–8, 113.
10. Robaut 1905, vol.1, pp 316–17, 323.
11. Robaut Cartons, vol.33, no.109.
12. Horbez, *Corot/Arras*, p.41.
13. David Ogawa, 'Alfred Robaut, Étienne Moreau-Nélaton, and Writing Corot', *Word and Image*, vol.22, October–December 2006, pp 327–39.
14. Charles Asselineau, 'Intérieurs d'Atelier: C. Corot', *L'Artiste*, September 1851, pp 53–5.
15. ibid., pp 54–5.
16. Michèle Hannoosh, 'Théophile Silvestre's *Histoire des artistes vivants*: Art Criticism and Photography', *Art Bulletin*, vol.88, no.4, 2006, pp 729–55.
17. Théophile Silvestre, 'Corot', in *Histoire des artistes vivants français et étrangers. Études d'après nature*, E. Blanchard, Paris, 1856, pp 85–104.
18. ibid., p.100; Hannoosh, 'Silvestre's *Histoire*', p.735.
19. Silvestre, *Histoire*, pp 92, 94.
20. ibid., p.97.
21. Henri Dumesnil, *Corot. Souvenirs intimes*, Rapilly, Paris, 1875.
22. O'Doherty, *Studio and Cube*, pp 18–19.
23. Dumesnil, *Corot*, pp 15–16.
24. ibid., pp 100–02.
25. Robaut Documents, vol.1, pp 35–7.
26. Madeleine Hours, 'Figures de Corot. Étude photographique et radiographiquee', *Bulletin du Laboratoire du Musée du Louvre*, vol.7, 1962, pp 3–39; conservation reports, *The Artist's Studio*, 14 July 1991, and *Agostina*, 15 January 2013, National Gallery, Washington, DC
27. Robaut Cartons, vol.27.
28. Étienne Moreau-Nélaton, *Corot raconté par lui-même*, 2 vols, Henri Laurens, Paris, 1924, vol.1, p.13.
29. Lorenz Eitner, *French Paintings of the Nineteenth Century*, National Gallery of Art, Washington, DC, 2000, pp 23–9.
30. Tinterow, *Corot* 1996, pp 122–3, R370.
31. Robaut 1905, vol.2, pp 134–5.
32. Eitner, *French Paintings*, pp 71–2.
33. David Ogawa, 'Conditions of Beholding: Images of Femininity in the Work of Jean-Baptiste-Camille Corot', PhD diss., Brown University, Providence, RI, 1999, pp 173–87.
34. Hélène Toussaint, *Hommage à Corot: Peintures et dessins des collections françaises*, exh.cat., Orangerie des Tuileries, Paris, 1975, pp 119–20.
35. ibid., p.122.
36. Ogawa, 'Conditions' and Eitner, *French Paintings*, provide the fullest analysis. See also Peter Schmunk, 'Music and the Art of Corot', *SECAC Review*, vol.14, no.4, 1999, p.362; Anthony F. Janson, 'Corot: Tradition and the Muse', *Art Quarterly*, vol.1, Autumn 1978, pp 294–317 (for a Freudian reading).
37. *Catalogue des tableaux, études, esquisses, dessins, et eaux-fortes par Corot, dressé par M. Alfred Robaut*, sale cat., Hôtel Drouot, Paris, 1875, no.134.
38. Dumesnil, *Corot*, pp 82–3.
39. Robaut 1905: R1557, 1558 1559, 1559bis, 1560 and 1561, dated *c.*1865–70. The Karlsruhe painting is a variant of R1559bis; *Camille Corot. Natur und Traum*, exh.cat., Staatliche Kunsthalle, Karlsruhe, 2012, pp 219–22, 470, no.117. *Young Woman Playing a Mandolin in the Studio* (R2148bis); *Young Girl Holding a Palette* (R1552); *Woman Reading in the Studio* (R1570); and *Lady in Blue* (R1427). All 'R' numbers here refer to the cataloguing numbers given in Robaut 1905.
40. Jean-Baptiste-Camille Corot, *L'Atelier de Corot*, sale cat., Christie's, New York, 23 April 2003, pp 62–3, no.40; Tinterow, *Corot* 1996, pp 318–19.
41. The landscape in the Washington and Louvre versions resembles *Italian Dance* (R1678). The landscape in the Baltimore and Karlsruhe

versions is *Ville d'Avray: A Cluster of Trees* (R291). Tinterow, *Corot* 1996, pp 318–20.

42. Left to right: *Rome: Fountain of the Académie de France* (R79); unidentified; *Two Windmills on the Butte de Picardie, near Versailles* (R86); unidentified; *Blonde Gascon* (R459bis); and unidentified. ibid., pp 319–20.
43. *Corot en Suisse*, exh.cat., Musée Rath, Geneva, 2010, p.165, no.92.
44. David Ogawa, 'L'Atelier de Corot', in *Impressionist and Modern Paintings, Drawings, and Sculpture*, sale cat., Christie's, New York, 9 November 1994, pp 24–9; Germain Bazin, *Corot*, Pierre Tisné, Paris, 1951, p.132; Tinterow, *Corot* 1996, pp 326–7.
45. Robaut Cartons, vol.27, fol.58.
46. Bazin, *Corot*, pp 48, 132.
47. Moreau-Nélaton, *Corot raconté*, vol.2, pp 4–5.
48. Schmunk, 'Music and Corot', pp 354–63; Kermit S. Champa, *The Rise of Landscape Painting in France: Corot to Monet*, exh.cat., Currier Museum of Art, Manchester, NH, 1991, pp 31–41, n.40; pp 52–3. Dumesnil, *Corot*, pp 76–81, notes Corot's comparisons of music and painting.
49. Cited in Champa, *Rise of Landscape*, pp 36–7.
50. ibid., p.38, suggests that touch makes Corot modern.
51. Hours, 'Figures de Corot', pp 4–5.
52. Bazin, *Corot*, p.54.
53. Tinterow, *Corot* 1996, pp 316–17.
54. Toussaint, *Hommage à Corot*, p.123.
55. Robaut Cartons, vol.27, fol.60.
56. Eitner, 'Young Girl Reading', *French Paintings*, pp 75–8. On the reader theme, see *The Secret Armoire: Corot's Figure Paintings and the World of Reading*, exh.cat., Oskar Reinhart Collection Am Römerholz, Winterthur, 2011, pp 55–71.
57. Robaut Cartons, vol.27, fol.56, identified as *Gouvieux, près Chantilly*. Robaut 1905, vol.2, pp 282–3, lists five landscapes with that title.
58. Robaut 1905, vol.3, pp 112–13.
59. Robaut Cartons, vol.27, fol.59.
60. Moreau-Nélaton, *Corot raconté*, vol.1, p.11.
61. Robaut 1905, vol.3, pp 110–11 (R1552).
62. Bazin, *Corot*, p.56.
63. Tinterow, *Corot* 1996, pp 375–8.
64. The model is Emma Dobigny, who also posed for Degas. ibid.
65. *Corot en Suisse*, p.66, fig.9. Cuvelier and Léandre Grandguillaume launched the *cliché-verre* technique.
66. Justine Moeckli, 'Corot et la photographie', *Corot en Suisse*, pp 60–69.
67. Horbez, *Corot/Arras*, pp 34–7.
68. ibid., pp 38–41.
69. Nathalie Michel-Szelechowska, 'Camille Corot et la famille Dutilleux. Une commune émulation artistique', in *Corot dans la lumière du Nord* (M.-P. Botte, ed.), Silvana Editoriale, Milan, 2013, pp 34–43.
70. ibid., pp 54–5, no.8.
71. ibid., pp 50–51, no.6.
72. ibid., pp 36–7, 52–3, no.7 (Musée municipal, Ville d'Avray). The other version, illustrated in Robaut 1905, vol.1, p.255, depicts Corot in a white smock, with a helmet suspended from the easel.
73. Robaut Documents, vol.1, p.10.
74. ibid., p.39 (A–H).
75. ibid., p.41.
76. *Le Monde illustré*, 27 February 1875, pp 140, 142.
77. *L'Illustration*, no.1671, 6 March 1875, pp 157–8; Robaut Cartons, vol.33.
78. Robaut's annotations denounce Fichot for falsifying and denaturing his 'original' drawing and criticize the caricatural smoke swirling from Corot's pipe while he paints (Robaut Cartons, vol.33).
79. ibid., based on the previous drawing.
80. Moreau-Nélaton, *Corot raconté*, vol.2, pp 79–80, discusses Corot's patronage and reproduces a photograph of his portrait placed below a crucifix (fig.246).
81. Robaut 1905, vol.4, pp 298–324, lists 122 images made during his lifetime.
82. *Corot Sale*, 1875, nos 885 and 887 included 200 photographs '*d'après nature*' and 130 of artworks.
83. Robaut 1905, vol.4, no.109.
84. ibid., no.104, lists a photograph (*c*.1872–3) of Corot in the studio (not illus.).
85. ibid., no.78, engraved 1872.
86. Moreau-Nélaton describes Corot posing on 2 January 1874. Moreau-Nélaton, *Corot raconté*, vol.2, p.81. See also Robaut Documents, vol.2, p.85.
87. Robaut 1905, vol.4, only lists Masson's small study, no.117 (not illus.).

3 THE VIRTUAL STUDIO: DAUBIGNY, MONET AND BAZILLE

1. Étienne Moreau-Nélaton, *Daubigny raconté par lui-même*, H. Laurens, Paris, 1925, p.77.
2. Émile Taboureux, 'Claude Monet', *La Vie moderne*, June 1880, p.380.
3. Kirstin Ringelberg, *Redefining Gender in American Impressionist Studio Paintings: Work Place/Domestic Place*, Ashgate, Farnham, 2010, pp 5–6.
4. Alpers, 'View from the Studio', pp 37–9, 44.
5. Callen, *Art of Impressionism*, pp 1–14; Anthea Callen, *The Work of Art: Plein-Air Painting and Artistic Identity in Nineteenth-Century France*, Reaktion Books, London, 2015, pp 33–103.
6. Milner, *Studios of Paris*, pp 39–44.
7. Paul Hayes Tucker, *The Impressionists at Argenteuil*, exh.cat., National Gallery of Art, Washington, DC, 2000, pp 25–6, 90.
8. John Rewald, *The History of Impressionism*, Museum of Modern Art, New York, 1973, pp 284–5.

9. Tucker, *Impressionists at Argenteuil*, pp 92–4.
10. Taboureux, 'Monet', p.380.
11. Tucker, *Impressionists at Argenteuil*, pp 36–7.
12. Robert L. Herbert, 'Method and Meaning in Monet', *Art in America*, vol.67, no.5, September 1979, pp 90–108; Callen, *Art of Impressionism*, pp 1–14.
13. Dianne W. Pitman, 'Overlapping Frames', in *Monet & Bazille: A Collaboration*, exh.cat., High Museum of Art, Atlanta, 1999, p.60.
14. Michael Duffy, *The Influence of Charles-François Daubigny (1817–1878) on French Plein-Air Landscape Painting*, Edwin Mellen Press, Lewiston, NY, 2010.
15. Lynne Ambrosini, 'Leader of the School of Impressionism', in *Daubigny, Monet, Van Gogh: Impressions of Landscape*, exh.cat., Taft Museum of Art, Cincinnati, 2016, pp 28–9.
16. Callen, *Art of Impressionism*, pp 113–17.
17. Melissa McQuillan, *Impressionist Portraits*, Thames & Hudson, London, 1986, pp 7–26.
18. Alison Strauber, 'At Home in the Studio', in *Interior Portraiture and Masculine Identity in France, 1789–1914* (T. Balducci, H.B. Jensen and P.J. Warner, eds), Ashgate, Farnham, 2011, pp 121–34.
19. Michael Clark, 'Tales of the Riverbank: Daubigny's River Scenes', in *Daubigny, Monet*, pp 69, 158, n.14.
20. *Le Tour de Marne* (1865), text by Émile de la Bédollière, with 30 photographs by Rousset.
21. Bonnie L. Grad, 'Le Voyage en Bateau: Daubigny's Visual Diary of River Life', *The Print Collector's Newsletter*, vol.11, no.4, September–October 1980, pp 123–7; *Entre ciel et terre. Camille Pissarro et les peintres de la vallée de l'Oise*, exh.cat., Musée Tavet-Delacour, Pontoise, 2003, pp 38–48.
22. Moreau-Nélaton, *Daubigny raconté*, p.77, fig.52 facing p.78; Clark, 'Daubigny's River Scenes', pp 69–72.
23. Charles-François Daubigny, *Le Voyage en bateau*, préface by Frédéric Henriet, Delâtre, Paris, 1862.
24. Phillip Dennis Cate, 'Visions of Boating in French Printmaking: From Daubigny to the Pont-Aven School', in *Impressionists on the Water*, exh.cat., Fine Arts Museums of San Francisco, San Francisco, 2013, pp 78–83.
25. Frédéric Henriet, *Le Paysagiste aux champs*, A. Lévy, Paris, 1876, pp 78–9.
26. Daniel Raskin, 'Charles-François Daubigny, le poète du paysage fluvial', *Reflets de la Seine impressionniste*, exh.cat., Atelier Grognard, Rueil-Malmaison, 2008–9, pp 22–3.
27. Henriet, *Paysagiste*, pp 77–80.
28. Clark, 'Daubigny's River Scenes', pp 69–72.
29. Cate, 'Visions of Boating', p.83.
30. Duffy, *Influence of Daubigny*, pp 71–3, 83–5.
31. Robert and Anne Hellebranth, *Charles-François Daubigny, 1817–1878 (Supplément)*, s.n., France, *c.*1996, no.220.
32. ibid., no.36. Daubigny's *Le Botin II* (*c.*1868–70), formerly in a private collection, was recently purchased by the Musée d'Orsay.
33. Clark, 'Daubigny's River Scenes', pp 69–72. On the transfer drawings, see Ashley Dunn, 'Charles-François Daubigny', *Metropolitan Museum of Art Bulletin*, vol.76, no.2, Fall 2018, p.62.
34. Letter from Charles-François Daubigny to Frédéric Henriet, August 1860, cited in Madeleine Fidell-Beaufort and Janine Bailly-Herzberg, *Daubigny*, Geoffroy-Dechaume, Paris, 1975, p.52; Duffy, *Influence of Daubigny*, pp 72–3.
35. Frances Fowle, 'Auvers-sur-Oise as an Artist's Colony: From Daubigny to Van Gogh', in *Daubigny, Monet*, pp 93–103.
36. Nienke Bakker, 'In Daubigny's Footsteps', in *Daubigny, Monet*, pp 105–24. Van Gogh's letter to Theo van Gogh, 23 July 1890, includes a sketch (illus., ibid., pp 126–7).
37. Moreau-Nélaton, *Daubigny raconté*, p.129, fig.112.
38. Maite van Dijk, 'Daubigny and the Impressionists in the 1860s', in *Daubigny, Monet*, pp 45–9, citing Monet's letters to Eugène Boudin (p.46).
39. ibid., p.57.
40. Paul Hayes Tucker, *Monet at Argenteuil*, Yale University Press, New Haven, CT/London, 1982, pp 89–124.
41. Cited in Clark, 'Daubigny's River Scenes', p.74.
42. Frédéric Henriet, 'Les Paysagistes contemporains', *Gazette des Beaux-Arts*, January–June 1874, pp 255–70, illus. p.265.
43. Christopher Lloyd, 'Coastal Adventures, Riparian Pleasures', in *Impressionists on the Water*, pp 26, 41, n.34.
44. Tucker, *Monet at Argenteuil*, p.87.
45. On boating as elite leisure, see Robert L. Herbert, *Impressionism: Art, Leisure, & Parisian Society*, Yale University Press, New Haven, CT/London, 1988, pp 234–6.
46. Wildenstein, *Monet*, nos 323, 390–3.
47. ibid., no.391, photographed c.1915. The early provenance of no.390 is unknown.
48. Tucker, *Impressionists at Argenteuil*, p.138.
49. Clark, 'Daubigny's River Scenes', pp 74–5; Tucker, *Impressionists at Argenteuil*, pp 26–8.
50. Tucker, *Monet at Argenteuil*, pp 112–13.
51. Taboureux, 'Monet', pp 380–82.
52. Clark, 'Daubigny's River Scenes', p.77.
53. Tanya Paul, 'A Marvel of Intense Poetry: Monet's *Mornings on the Seine*', in *Monet and the Seine: Impressions of a River*, exh.cat., Museum of Fine Arts, Houston, 2014, pp 41–51.
54. Maurice Guillemot, 'Claude Monet', *La Revue illustrée*, no.7, 15 March 1898, n.p.
55. Cited in Clark, 'Daubigny's River Scenes', p.78.
56. *Monet's Years at Giverny: Beyond Impressionism*, exh.cat., Metropolitan Museum of Art, New York, 1978, p.25.
57. *Monet/Giverny*, p.32.
58. George T.M. Shackelford, *Monet: The Late Years*, exh.cat., Kimbell Art Museum, Fort Worth, TX, 2019, pp 17–20.

59. Paul Hayes Tucker, 'Monet Public and Private', in *Claude Monet: Late Work*. exh.cat., Gagosian Gallery, New York, 2010, pp 16–39; illus., p.17.
60. *Monet: Late Years*, p.137, fig.162.
61. Marcel Proust, 'Splendors', *Le Figaro*, 15 June 1907, cited in *Monet: Late Years*, p.12. Although Proust never visited Giverny, Monet was a model for Proust's painter, Elstir, in *Remembrance of Things Past*. See Heather McPherson, *Fin-de-Siècle Faces: Portraiture in the Age of Proust*, UAB Visual Arts Gallery, Birmingham, AL, 1988, pp 11–12.
62. Kermit Swiler Champa, 'A Complicated Codependence', in *Monet & Bazille*, pp 67–95.
63. Kimberly A. Jones, 'The Studio on the Rue La Condamine', in *Bazille* 2016, pp 164–8.
64. ibid., pp 159–61. It is unclear whether Bazille or Renoir painted the study.
65. Letter from Frédéric Bazille to his father, 1 January 1870, *Frédéric Bazille. Correspondance* (D. Vatuone, ed.), Les Presses du Languedoc, Montpellier, 1992, p.182, no.127. On Manet, see Michel Schulman, *Frédéric Bazille, 1841–70. Catalogue raisonné: peintures, dessins, pastels, aquarelles*, Éditions de l'Amateur, Paris, 1995, p.207.
66. François-Bernard Michel, *Frédéric Bazille: réflexions*, Grasset, Paris, 1992, pp 33–4. Bruyas owned the 1849 version.
67. Letter from Frédéric Bazille to his mother, [22 December 1864], in Bazille, *Correspondance*, pp 100–101, no.61. Champa, 'Complicated Codependence', pp 71–3, associates Bazille's preoccupation with dress and studio furnishings with self-feminizing.
68. Jones, *Bazille* 2016, p.50, most likely fall 1865.
69. ibid., pp 48–50.
70. Michel, *Bazille*, p.117.
71. Letter from Frédéric Bazille to his mother, [late February 1867], in Bazille, *Correspondance*, pp 134–5, no.88.
72. Cited in Schulman, *Bazille catalogue*, p.146, no.27.
73. Jones, *Bazille* 2016, p.238.
74. Described in an 1867 letter from Frédéric Bazille to his parents, cited in François Daulte, *Frédéric Bazille et son temps*, Pierre Cailler, Geneva, 1952, p.58.
75. Stanislas Colodiet, 'Still Life with Heron', in *Bazille* 2016, pp 96–101.
76. Gaston Poulain, *Bazille et ses amis*, La Renaissance du Livre, Paris, 1932, pp 102–4.
77. Colodiet, 'Still Life', p.99, shown at the 1876 Impressionist exhibition.
78. ibid., n.6.
79. Jones, *Bazille* 2016, p.236, no.33.
80. Letter from Frédéric Bazille to his father, 11 May 1867, in Schulman, *Bazille catalogue*, p.357, no.167.
81. Letter from Frédéric Bazille to his father, [late November 1867], in Bazille, *Correspondance*, pp 145–6, no.96.
82. In December 1869, the original address changed from 9 rue de la Paix to 9 rue La Condamine.
83. Letter from Frédéric Bazille to his mother, [late December 1867], in Bazille, *Correspondance*, pp 148–9, no.98.
84. Jones, 'Rue La Condamine', pp 164–5; Alsdorf, *Fellow Men*, pp 144–9.
85. Jones, 'Rue La Condamine', pp 164–8.
86. The drawing's date and circumstances are unknown.
87. Bazille depicted Monet in *Improvised Field Hospital* (1865); *Man with a Pipe* (1869) probably depicts Astruc. *Bazille* 2016, pp 228, 230.
88. François Daulte, *Frédéric Bazille et les débuts de l'impressionisme, catalogue raisonné de l'oeuvre peint*, La Bibliothèque des Arts, Paris, 1992, p.66.
89. See Dianne W. Pitman, *Bazille: Purity, Pose, and Painting*, Pennsylvania State University Press, University Park, PA, 1998, pp 184–7. Zola and Sisley have been proposed as possible models.
90. On the X-radiograph, see *Bazille* 2016, pp 74–7. A male figure reclines, listening. It probably influenced Degas's painting of Mme Manet playing the piano and Manet sprawled on a sofa.
91. Pitman, *Bazille*, p.186.
92. Buren, 'Function of the Studio', pp 51–8.
93. See Margaret MacDonald, and Grischka Petri, *The Paintings of James McNeill Whistler: A Catalogue Raisonné*, University of Glasgow, Glasgow, 2020, http://whistlerpaintings.gla.ac.uk, YMSM 062 and 063; Stephanie L. Strother, *Whistler Paintings and Drawings at the Art Institute of Chicago*, Art Institute of Chicago, Chicago, 2020, n.p., cat.8., publications.artic.edu. There are two versions: in Chicago and Dublin. Whistler owned photographs of *Las Meninas*.
94. Cited in Strother, *Whistler Paintings*, cat.8. Whistler envisaged a 3 × 1.8 or 2.1 m canvas.
95. Kimberly Muir, in Strother, *Whistler Paintings*, cat.8. Vestiges of the figure are visible to the naked eye.
96. Margaret Flora MacDonald, 'James McNeill Whistler: An Artist on Artists', *Visual Culture in Britain*, 2015, pp 200–22.
97. Melissa Berry, *The Société des Trois in the Nineteenth Century*, Routledge, New York, 2018. Whistler, Fantin-Latour and Alphonse Legros formed the 'Société des Trois'.
98. See Aileen Ribeiro, 'Fashioning White in the Work of Whistler and His Contemporaries', in *The Woman in White: Joanna Hiffernan and James McNeill Whistler*, exh.cat., National Gallery of Art, Washington, DC, 2021, pp 157–66.
99. Whistler made multiple studies for *Symphony in White no.3*, which preceded *Artist in His Studio. Woman in White*, pp 102–7, pls 37–40.
100. Strother, *Whistler Paintings*, cat.8.
101. Whistler lived at no.7 from March 1863 to February 1867, and he then moved to no.2 Lindsey Row. Deanna Marohn Bendix, *Diabolical Designs: Paintings, Interiors, and Exhibitions of James McNeill Whistler*, Smithsonian Institution Press, Washington, DC, 1995, pp 63, 86.
102. ibid., pp 194–200.
103. John Siewert, 'Interior Motives: Whistler's Studio and Symbolist Mythmaking', in *Palaces of Art: Whistler and the Art Worlds of*

Aestheticism (L. Glazer and L. Merrill, eds), Smithsonian Institution Press, Washington, DC, 2013, pp 81–92.

104. Strother, *Whistler Paintings*, cat.8.
105. Thomas Robert Way, *Memories of James McNeill Whistler the Artist*, John Lane, London, 1912, p.24.
106. Elizabeth Robbins Pennell and Joseph Pennell, *The Whistler Journal*, J.B. Lippincott, Philadelphia, 1921, p.116. His pose derives from *Artist in His Studio*.
107. Bendix, *Diabolical Designs*, pp 64–72.
108. Way, *Memories*, p.28.
109. ibid., pp 62–4. Whistler had a large light-filled studio at 13 Tite Street, with flesh-colored walls in the 1880s.
110. Jacques-Émile Blanche, *Portraits of a Lifetime: The Late Victorian Era, The Edwardian Pageant, 1870–1914* (W. Clement, ed.), Coward-McCann, New York, 1938, pp 73–4.
111. Gustave Geffroy, *La vie artistique*, vol.1, E. Dentu, Paris, 1892, pp 74–80.
112. Bendix, *Diabolical Designs*, p.94.
113. Cited in Strother, *Whistler Paintings*, cat.8.

4: IMPROMPTU STUDIOS: FROM BERTHE MORISOT TO MARIE LAURENCIN

1. Cited in Anne Higonnet, *Berthe Morisot*, HarperCollins, New York, 1990, p.52.
2. Cited in ibid., p.203.
3. Whitney Chadwick, *Women, Art, and Society*, Thames & Hudson, London 2020, pp 238–43.
4. Ringelberg, *Redefining Gender*, pp 24–30.
5. Edmond Duranty, 'L'Atelier,' in *Le Pays des arts*, G. Charpentier, Paris, 1881, pp 182–3.
6. Charlotte Yeldham, *Women Artists in Nineteenth-Century France and England*, 2 vols, Garland Publishing, New York, 1984, vol.1, pp 40–58.
7. Tamar Garb, *Sisters of the Brush: Women's Artistic Culture in Late Nineteenth-Century Paris*, Yale University Press, New Haven, CT/London, 1994, pp 70–104.
8. Yeldham, *Women Artists*, vol.1, pp 42–3, 51–3.
9. Griselda Pollock, *Vision and Difference: Femininity, Feminism, and Histories of Art*, Routledge, London, 1988.
10. Higonnet, *Morisot*, pp 13–14.
11. Ringelberg, *Redefining Gender*, p.77.
12. Anne Higonnet, *Berthe Morisot's Images of Women*, Harvard University Press, Cambridge, MA, 1992, pp 46, 56–8.
13. Yeldham, *Women Artists*, vol.1, p.65.
14. Garb, *Sisters of the Brush*, pp 26–32.
15. ibid., pp 3–18, situates the Union in the context of diversification and expanding exhibition venues outside the Salon.
16. ibid., pp 37–8.
17. Caterina Y. Pierre, *'Genius Has No Sex': The Sculpture of Marcello (1836–1879)*, Éditions de Penthes, Pregny-Geneva/Infolio, Gollion, 2010, offers the fullest account.
18. *Marcello. Adèle d'Affry, Duchesse de Castiglione Colonna*, exh.cat., Musée d'art et d'histoire, Fribourg, 2014, pp 34–5, 43–5. She received a modest pension but relied on selling sculpture to support herself.
19. Pierre, *'Genius Has No Sex,'* p.39. She obtained a permit from the police to wear male attire.
20. *Marcello*, pp 95–103.
21. Pierre, *'Genius Has No Sex'*, p.47.
22. Caterina Y.Pierre, 'Sculpter à contre-courant. Images de femmes dans l'œuvre de Marcello,' in *Marcello*, pp 65–76 ; Pierre, *'Genius Has No Sex,'* p.171.
23. Higonnet, *Morisot*, pp 33–4.
24. *Marcello*, pp 48–9, 105–13. While completing *La Pythie*, she rented a studio in Rome and painted with Ernest Hébert and Fortuny.
25. Pierre, *'Genius Has No Sex,'* pp 89–91.
26. Cited in Caterina Y. Pierre, 'Marcello's Heroic Sculpture,' *Woman's Art Journal*, vol.22, no.1, 2001, p.18. On the museum, see *Marcello*, pp 16–21. Her studio is preserved in the Château d'Affry, Givisiez.
27. *Marcello*, pp 37–8.
28. Marcello, cited in ibid., p.37.
29. *Un soir chez la princesse Mathilde. Une Bonaparte et les arts*, exh.cat., Palais Fesch Musée des Beaux-Arts, Ajaccio, 2019, esp. Paul Perrin, 'Mathilde, "princesse artiste",' pp 85–9.
30. Nolween Piquant, 'Mathilde artiste. Une princesse entre le salon et le Salon,' in *Un soir chez la princesse*, pp 91–5. She exhibited as 'S.A.I. Madame la Princesse Mathilde, élève de M. Eugène Giraud.'
31. Piquant, 'Mathilde artiste,' p.94.
32. *Un soir chez la princesse*, pp 96–9, nos 41–4.
33. ibid., pp 96–8, no.43.
34. Cited in ibid., p.97.
35. ibid., pp 173–4.
36. ibid., pp 99–101, nos 45, 46.
37. ibid., pp 99–100.
38. ibid., pp 101–2, no.47.
39. Jean-Yves Tadié, 'Proust et la princesse Mathilde. Une ligne mystérieuse,' in *Un soir chez la princesse*,' pp 269–70.
40. Letter from Joseph Guichard to Cornélie Morisot, cited in Higonnet, *Morisot*, p.19.
41. Charles Stuckey, *Berthe Morisot, Impressionist*, Hudson Hills, New York, 1987, p.19.
42. Higonnet, *Morisot*, pp 34–5.
43. ibid., pp 88–9.
44. Jacques-Émile Blanche, 'Les Dames de la grande-rue,' *Dates*, Émile-Paul Frères, Paris, 1920, pp 21–2.
45. Higonnet, *Morisot*, p.89.
46. Letter from Edma Pointillon to Berthe Morisot, 15 March 1869, cited in Higonnet, *Morisot*, p.52.
47. ibid., pp 21–9.

48. ibid., pp 170–71.
49. Julie Manet, *Growing up with the Impressionists: The Diary of Julie Manet* (R. de Boland Roberts and J. Roberts, trans. and eds), Sotheby's Publications, New York, 1987, p.12.
50. Higonnet, *Morisot*, p.171.
51. ibid., pp 202, 213.
52. Marianne Mathieu, *Berthe Morisot*, 1841–1895, exh.cat., Musée Marmottan, Paris, 2012, p.156.
53. Higonnet, *Morisot*, pp 189–90.
54. Tamar Garb, *The Painted Face: Portraits of Women in France 1814–1914*, Yale University Press, New Haven, CT/London, 2007, p.12, notes women's difficulty in making self-portraits.
55. Higonnet, *Morisot's Images of Women*, pp 200, 204–6.
56. ibid., pp 204–8.
57. ibid., pp 208–9. For the painting, see Mathieu, *Berthe Morisot*, no.66.
58. Sylvie Patry, 'Femmes au travail', in *Berthe Morisot*, exh.cat., Musée d'Orsay, Paris, 2019, pp 127–8.
59. On the conflation of femininity and Impressionist technique, see Tamar Garb, 'Berthe Morisot and the Feminizing of Impressionism', in *Critical Readings in Impressionism and Post-Impressionism* (M.T. Lewis, ed.), University of California Press, Berkeley, 2007, pp 191–201.
60. Cited in Higonnet, *Morisot*, p.146.
61. ibid., pp 215–16.
62. Anna Klumpke, *Rosa Bonheur, sa vie, son oeuvre*, Flammarion, Paris, 1908.
63. Christophe Brouard, 'Rosa Bonheur et les maîtres anciens. La "vraie grammaire de l'art"', in *Rosa Bonheur (1822–1899)*, exh.cat., Musée d'Orsay, Paris, 2022, pp 34–8; Catherine Hewitt, *Art Is a Tyrant: The Unconventional Life of Rosa Bonheur*, Icon, London, 2020, pp 89–91.
64. Theodore Stanton (ed.), *Reminiscences of Rosa Bonheur*, Appleton & Co., New York, 1910, pp 19–20.
65. On its reception, see Hewitt, *Art Is a Tyrant*, pp 121–3.
66. Dore Ashton, *Rosa Bonheur: A Life and a Legend*, Viking, New York, 1981, pp 70, 90–97.
67. A.-J. du Pays, , 'L'Atelier de Mlle Rosa Bonheur', *L'Illustration*, 1 May 1852, pp 283–4.
68. Hewitt, *Art Is a Tyrant*, pp 157–8.
69 Eugène de Mirecourt, *Rosa Bonheur*, Achille Faure, Paris, 1867, pp 48–9.
70. On Bonheur's social circle, see Patricia Bouchenot-Déchin, 'Vous avez dit "sauvage". Ampleur de Rosa Bonheur', in *Rosa Bonheur*, pp 48–53.
71. Baschet, cited in Ashton, *Bonheur/Life and Legend*, p.96.
72. Anon., 'Rosa Bonheur', *Cosmopolitan Art Journal*, vol.2, no.4, September 1858, pp 193–4.
73. Hewitt, *Art Is a Tyrant*, p.161; Ashton, *Bonheur/Life and Legend*, pp 96–9.
74. On reproductive prints, see Michel Pons, 'Les oeuvres de Rosa Bonheur révélées par l'estampe et la photographie', in *Rosa Bonheur*, pp 196–202.
75. Ashton, *Bonheur/Life and Legend*, pp 104–6.
76. Hewitt, *Art Is a Tyrant*, pp 158–61.
77. Patricia Bouchenot-Déchin, 'L'Atelier de plein air de Rosa Bonheur à By-Thomery ou "La nature pour atelier"', in *Rosa Bonheur*, p.152.
78. Milner, *Studios of Paris*, pp 233–4.
79. Hewitt, *Art is a Tyrant*, pp 214–15, 223–4.
80. Rosa Bonheur, 'Fragments of My Autobiography', trans. Lucie Ponsard, *The Magazine of Art*, 1902, p.534.
81. Hewitt, *Art Is a Tyrant*, p.223; Ashton, *Bonheur/Life and Legend*, pp 124–5.
82. Ashton, *Bonheur/Life and Legend*, pp 150–57; illus. p.151.
83. Cited in Hewitt, *Art Is a Tyrant*, p.18.
84. Stanton, *Reminiscences*, p.xvi, illus. facing p.312.
85. Ashton, *Bonheur/Life and Legend*, p.75.
86. Stanton, *Reminiscences*, pp xiv, 250–51, illus. facing p.260.
87. ibid., pp 259–61, signed by both artists.
88. ibid., pp xvi, 251, illus. facing p.312.
89. Klumpke donated the portrait to the Metropolitan Museum in 1922. A photograph (1898) depicts Klumpke working on it in the studio, illus. in Klumpke, *Rosa Bonheur*, p.71.
90. Higonnet, *Morisot's Images*, pp 61–83.
91. Ashton, *Bonheur/Life and Legend*, pp 182–7. Prices for Bonheur's art remained robust.
92. Daniel Marchesseau, *Marie Laurencin*, Fernand Hazan, Paris, 1981; *Marie Laurencin: Artist and Muse*, exh.cat., Birmingham Museum of Art, Birmingham, AL, 1989.
93. Marie Laurencin, *Le carnet des nuits* [1942], Pierre Cailler, Geneva, 1956, p.16.
94. Marchesseau, *Laurencin*, pp 23–5.
95. Heather McPherson, 'Marie Laurencin: An Undividedly Feminine Psyche', in *Laurencin/Artist and Muse*, p.16.
96. Marchesseau, *Laurencin*, pp 26–7. Roché introduced her work to collectors and negotiated contracts. Roché, cited in Diane Zorzi, '5 choses à savoir sur Marie Laurencin', *Le Magazine des enchères*, n.p. magazine.interenchères.com.
97. McPherson, 'Laurencin', pp 16–18.
98. Marchesseau, *Laurencin*, p.26.
99. ibid., p.54.
100. Flora Groult, *Marie Laurencin*, Mercure de France, Paris, 1987, p.225.
101. ibid., pp 254–5.
102. Guillaume Apollinaire, *Les peintres cubistes*, cited in McPherson, 'Laurencin', p.23.
103. ibid., pp. 23–5.
104. The Nagano Laurencin Museum, which holds 600 works, closed in 2011; it reopened in Tokyo in 2017. See *Marie Laurencin, 1883–1956*, exh.cat., Musée Marmottan Monet, Paris, 2013.
105. Chadwick, *Women, Art, and Society*, pp 305–7.

5 THE REFRACTED STUDIO: MATISSE AND PICASSO

1. Henri Matisse, 'Interview with André Verdet', cited in Jack Flam, *Matisse on Art*, University of California Press, Berkeley, CA, 1995, p.212.
2. Cited in Anne Baldassari, *Picasso and Photography: The Dark Mirror*, exh.cat., Museum of Fine Arts, Houston, 1997, p.7.
3. Picasso studied at La Llotja in Barcelona and at the Academy of San Fernando in Madrid (1895–7). Matisse studied at the École des Beaux-Arts and worked in Gustave Moreau's studio (1892–8). *Picasso: The Early Years, 1892–1906*, exh.cat., National Gallery of Art, Washington, DC, 1997, pp 24–7; Alfred Barr, *Matisse: His Art and His Public*, Museum of Modern Art, New York, 1951, pp 14–15.
4. Peter Galassi, *In the Studio*, vol.2: *Photographs*, exh.cat., Gagosian Gallery, New York, 2015, pp 33–4, notes that Picasso's and Matisse's careers are inconceivable without their studio photographs.
5. Anne Baldassari, *Picasso photographe, 1901–1916*, Éditions de la Réunion des Musées Nationaux, Paris, 1994, p.25.
6. On Picasso's collaboration with photographers, see Baldassari, *Picasso photographe* and *Picasso & the Camera*, exh.cat., Gagosian Gallery, New York, 2014.
7. Ellen McBreen and Helen Burnham, *Matisse in the Studio*, exh.cat., Museum of Fine Arts, Boston, 2017; *Henri Matisse, une palette d'objets*, exh.cat., Art Lys, Paris/Musée Matisse, Nice, 2016.
8. Claudine Grammont, 'Matisse and Picasso, the Comedy of the Model', in *Matisse & Picasso. La Comédie du modèle*, exh.cat., Musée Matisse, Nice, 2018, pp 163–9.
9. McBreen, *Matisse in the Studio*, pp 13–43.
10. 'Studio Paintings', pp 17–18.
11 Fernande Olivier, *Loving Picasso: The Private Journal of Fernande Olivier*, trans. Christine Baker and Michael Raeburn, Harry N. Abrams, New York, 2001, p.139.
12. Jack Flam, *Matisse and Picasso: The Story of Their Rivalry and Friendship*, Icon, Cambridge, MA, 2003, pp 15–16.
13. ibid., pp 24–5.
14. Yve-Alain Bois, *Matisse and Picasso*, exh.cat., Kimbell Art Museum, Fort Worth, TX, 1998, pp 11–23.
15. Flam, *Matisse and Picasso*, pp 54–6.
16. Cited in ibid., p.45.
17. *Yo Picasso: Self Portraits*, exh.cat., Museu Picasso, Barcelona, 2013; Kirk Varnedoe, 'Picasso's Self-Portraits', in *Picasso and Portraiture: Representation and Transformation*, exh.cat., Museum of Modern Art, New York, 1996, pp 111–79.
18. John Klein, *Matisse Portraits*, Yale University Press, New Haven, CT/London, 2001, pp 128–30. *Self-Portrait in Striped Jersey* (1906) is the major exception.
19. Hilary Spurling, *The Unknown Matisse: A Life of Henri Matisse: The Early Years, 1869–1908*, University of California Press, Berkeley, CA, 1998, p.222; Klein, *Matisse Portraits*, pp 50–54.
20. *Becoming Picasso: Paris 1901*, exh.cat., Courtauld Gallery, London, 2013, pp 108–10.
21. *Picasso/La Vie*, p.41, fig.23.
22. Baldassari, *Picasso photographe*, pp 43, 47, fig.23, resembles *Self-Portrait in Top Hat* (1901).
23. Cited in *Yo Picasso*, p.63.
24. Isabel Cendoya, 'The Photographic Self-Portrait in Picasso's Oeuvre', in *Yo Picasso*, pp 96–7.
25. Baldassari, *Picasso photographe*, pp 39–43. Picasso was painting a sort of Holy Family while friends admired his works. Marilyn McCully, 'Picasso in the Studio', in *Picasso: Painting the Blue Period*, exh.cat., Phillips Collection, Washington, DC, 2021, pp 11–13.
26. See Susan Behrends Frank, 'The Blue Room Reconsidered', in *Painting the Blue Period*, pp 24–51, for the fullest account; John Richardson and Marilyn McCully, *A Life of Picasso*, vol.1, *The Early Years, 1881–1906*, Random House, New York, 1991, pp 225–6. Duncan Phillips titled it *The Blue Room*.
27. Frank, 'Blue Room', pp 28–9.
28. Patricia Favero and Sandra Webster-Cook, 'Hidden Layers and Meaning: Moments of Transition in Picasso's Early Blue Period', in *Painting the Blue Period*, pp 263–9. Technical analysis dates it to autumn 1901.
29. *Picasso/La Vie* is the fullest account.
30. ibid., pp 21–3, 43–4. The earliest study is dated 2 May 1903.
31. ibid., pp 11–12. Picasso and Junyent painted each other. Junyent may have purchased *La Vie* to finance Picasso's move to Paris.
32. Picasso made multiple portraits of Casagemas and attributed the melancholy of the Blue Period to his death. ibid., pp 64–5.
33. Varnedoe, 'Picasso's Self-Portraits', pp 111, 133–4. Picasso's oeuvre is heavily autobiographical, making determining what constitutes a self-portrait tricky.
34. Baldassari, *Picasso photographe*, pp 93–133.
35. John Richardson, *A Life of Picasso, 1907–1917: The Painter of Modern Life*, vol.2, Random House, New York, 1996, p.285.
36. 'Studio Paintings', pp 27–31.
37. Richardson, *Life of Picasso, 1907–1917*, pp 338–41.
38. Pierre Daix, *Picasso: The Cubist Years, 1907–16: A Catalogue Raisonné of the Paintings and Related Works*, New York Graphic Society, Boston, 1979, p.333, no.763.
39. Richardson, *Life of Picasso, 1907–1917*, pp 384–7.
40. Varnedoe, 'Picasso's Self-Portraits', pp 143–5.
41. 'Studio Paintings', p.27.
42. Pierre Schneider, *Matisse*, Rizzoli, New York, 1984, pp 424–38.
43. Cited in ibid., p.429.
44. In 1908, Matisse set up his teaching academy in the Couvent des Oiseaux, which soon moved to the nearby Couvent du Sacré-Coeur. *Red Studio*, p.15.

45. Michael P. Mezzatesta, *Henri Matisse: Sculptor/Painter*, exh.cat., Kimbell Art Museum, Fort Worth, TX, 1984, pp 40–41; Jack Flam, *Matisse, The Man and His Art, 1869–1918*, Cornell University Press, Ithaca, NY, 1986, p.103.
46. *Red Studio*, pp 15–21. It cost 11,000 francs, which was a sizable investment.
47. Elderfield, *In the Studio: Paintings*, pp 36–7.
48. Flam, *Matisse, the Man*, pp 295–6.
49. *Red Studio*, pp 38–9. The proposed price was 30,000 francs.
50. Barr, *Matisse, His Art and His Public*, pp 151–4; Hilary Spurling, *Matisse the Master: A Life of Henri Matisse, The Conquest of Color, 1909–1954*, Alfred A. Knopf, New York, 2005, pp 83–4.
51. *Red Studio*, diagram, p.80. *Pink Studio* depicts the southwest corner and a garden view through a window. *Red Studio* depicts the southeast portion and edge of a doorway.
52. *Red Studio*, p.41. Matisse submitted *Manilla Shawl*; it was replaced by *Pink Studio* days later.
53. Hilary Spurling, 'Material World: Matisse, His Art and His Textiles', in *Matisse, His Art and His Textiles: The Fabric of Dreams*, exh.cat., Royal Academy of Arts, London, 2004, pp 14–33.
54. *Red Studio*, pp 43–5.
55. Henri Matisse, 'The Path of Color', in Flam, *Matisse on Art*, p.178.
56. *Red Studio*, p.47; Anne Baldassari, *Icônes de l'art moderne. La Collection Chtchoukine*, exh.cat., Fondation Louis Vuitton, Paris, 2016, pp 75, 82.
57. Flam, *Matisse on Art*, pp 37–43.
58. Flam, *Matisse, the Man*, pp 301–3; the painting in progress, is illus. p.303, fig.300.
59. On Matisse's working method, see ibid., p.175.
60. Distemper (a quick-drying technique using dry pigment mixed water and glue) was mostly used for large-scale decoration and sets.
61. *Red Studio*, pp 48–50.
62. Flam, *Matisse, The Man*, p.306, illus. p.309, fig.306.
63. ibid., pp 306–7.
64. *Red Studio*, p.55; Anny Aviram, Michael Duffy, Abed Haddad and Caroline Hoover, 'Painting the Red Studio: An Investigation', in ibid., pp 188–208. Technical evidence indicates that it was painted in two distinct phases.
65. A 1911 photograph shows *Large Nude*, the doorway and *Interior with Aubergines*, extending the view beyond what *Red Studio* shows. *Red Studio*, p.23, fig.II.12, pp 57–8.
66. ibid., pp 59–64; Flam, *Matisse, The Man*, p.321.
67. *Red Studio*, p.73.
68. My understanding of *Red Studio* is indebted to the MOMA Member Roundtable: 'Secrets of the Red Studio', 24 May 2022. Ann Temkin, noting Matisse's use of Venetian red (also known as brick red), likened it to a wall. See also Flam, *Matisse, the Man*, pp 318–21.
69. 'Painting Red Studio', *Red Studio*, pp 188–208.
70. Cited in Baldassari, *Icônes de l'art moderne*, p.73. Eugène Druet photographed the blue version. Matisse sent Shchukin the photograph and a watercolor of *Harmony in Red*. Flam, *Matisse, the Man*, pp 230–32, illus. p.231, fig.229.
71. Matisse, 'Notes of a Painter', pp 40–41; Flam, *Matisse, The Man*, p.232.
72. Cited in *Red Studio*, pp 85–7.
73. Cited in ibid., pp 177–87.
74. Cited in ibid., p.178.
75. Cited in ibid., p.181.
76. ibid., pp 90–93, overshadowing Picasso's 13 paintings.
77. Arthur B. Davies and Walter Kuhn, organizers of the Armory exhibition, saw the exhibition at the Grafton Galleries. ibid., p.94.
78. *Red Studio*, pp 103–13. It was acquired by the Museum of Modern Art in New York in 1949.
79. Flam, *Matisse, the Man*, pp 375–6, 397, 402. ibid., p.399, fig.398, reproduces a sketch of Matisse seated with his palette.
80. Jack Flam, *Matisse in Transition: Around Laurette*, exh.cat., Norton Museum of Art, West Palm Beach, FL, 2006.
81. Flam, *Matisse, the Man*, pp 437–41; *Lorette Reclining* (1916), illus., p.445, fig.449.
82. X-radiographs show that the model and pictures were originally lower; the balcony grillwork was painted out. Object File, Phillips Collection and Conservation Report November 2009 by Elizabeth Steele.
83. Flam, *Matisse in Transition*, p.18.
84. Jean Laude, 'Les "ateliers" de Matisse', *Colóquio Artes*, vol.18, June 1974, pp 20–22.
85. Grammont, *La Comédie du modèle*, pp 16–17. Matisse generally used hired models.
86. See *Early Nice Years*.
87. Flam, *Matisse, the Man*, p.477; fig.491 shows the portrait in progress.
88. Klein, *Matisse Portraits*, p.184.
89. Spurling, *Matisse, the Master*, pp 205–6.
90. Jack Cowart, *Early Nice Years*, pp 30–32; figs 29, 30, 32.
91. Hilary Spurling, 'Material World: Matisse, His Art and His Textiles', pp 28–9.
92. Letter from Henri Matisse to his daughter, Marguerite Duthuit, 29 November 1943, cited in *Matisse in the Studio*, p.14.
93. *Matisse in the Studio*, pp 16–17.
94. Matisse, 'Testimonial', 1951, in Flam, *Matisse on Art*, pp 207–8.
95. Cited in Cowart, *Early Nice Years*, pp 32–3.
96. *Matisse in the Studio*, pp 126–7, illus. fig.108. Matisse excised the painted floral decoration.
97. See the diagram in *Early Nice Years*, p.36, fig.36.
98. Cowart, *Early Nice Years*, pp 36–7. Matisse constructed an awning and sometimes hung curtains or shades.
99. Picasso's classicizing idiom coexisted and alternated with Cubism.
100. *Olga Picasso*, exh.cat., Musée national Picasso-Paris/Gallimard, Paris, 2017, offers the fullest account.

101. ibid., illus., p.115, fig.69; p.123, fig.70; p.112, fig.86, (March–June 1920).
102. John Richardson, *A Life of Picasso: The Triumphant Years, 1917–1932*, vol.3, Alfred A. Knopf, New York, 2007, p.297.
103. Brassaï, *The Artists of My Life*, trans. Richard Miller, Viking Press, New York, 1982, p.156. *Picasso's Palette* (1932) shows paint cans and tubes, mixing trays and cigarette butts strewn across the floor (illus. p.160).
104. On Brassaï's photographs, see John Richardson, *A Life of Picasso: The Minotaur Years, 1933–1943*, vol.4, Alfred A. Knopf, New York, 2021, pp 13–17, 31–2.
105. Picasso set up a vast sculpture studio in the stables at Boisgeloup outside Paris. ibid., pp 13–17.
106. André Breton, 'Picasso dans son élément', *Minotaure*, no.1, 1933, pp 13–14.
107. For an overview, see 'Studio Paintings'; Dore Ashton, 'Picasso in His Studio', in *Pablo Picasso: L'Atelier*, exh.cat., Peggy Guggenheim Collection, Venice, 1996, pp 119–49.
108. Renée Riese Hubert, 'The Encounter of Balzac and Picasso', *Dalhousie French Studies*, vol.5, October 1983, pp 38–54.
109. Richardson, *Minotaur Years*, pp 129–33, 136–7, illus. p.137.
110. 'Studio Paintings', pp 36–42.
111. Michel Leiris, 'The Artist and His Model', in *Picasso in Retrospect* (R. Penrose and J. Golding, eds), Praeger, New York, 1973, p.244.
112. Angelica Zander Rudenstine, *Peggy Guggenheim Collection, Venice*, Harry N. Abrams, New York, 1985, pp 617–22; Ashton, *Picasso in His Studio*, pp 133–4.
113. Rudenstine, *Guggenheim Collection*, pp 621–2.
114. ibid., p.620, fig.b; ultra-violet and infra-red reflectography reveal the original composition.
115. Picasso lent *L'Atelier* to Alfred Barr's 1939 retrospective and perhaps sold it to ensure its safety. ibid., p.617.
116. Françoise Gilot, *Life with Picasso*, Doubleday, New York, 1989.
117. Susan Grace Galassi, *Picasso's Variations on the Masters: Confrontations with the Past*, Abrams, New York, 1996, pp 127–47; Leo Steinberg, 'The Algerian Women and Picasso at Large', in *Other Criteria: Confrontations with Twentieth-Century Art*, Oxford University Press, New York, 1972, pp 125–234.
118. Cited in Dore Ashton, *Picasso on Art*, Viking, New York, 1972, p.51.
119. Galassi, *Picasso's Variations*, pp 129, 132–3.
120. Steinberg, 'The Algerian Women', p.223.
121. Bois, *Matisse and Picasso*, p.231.
122. 'Studio Paintings', pp 148, 150.
123. Bois, *Matisse and Picasso*, p.236.
124. Richardson, *Minotaur Years*, pp 129–30. Visitors climbed a spiral staircase to the attic studio, which was formerly a weaving workshop.
125. Steinberg, 'The Skulls of Picasso', in *Other Criteria*, pp 115–23.

Select Bibliography

STUDIO HISTORIOGRAPHY

Alpers, Svetlana, 'The View from the Studio', in *The Vexations of Art: Velázquez and Others*, Yale University Press, New Haven, CT/London, 2005, pp 9–45

Alsdorf, Bridget, *Fellow Men: Fantin-Latour and the Problem of the Group in Nineteenth-Century French Painting*, Princeton University Press, Princeton, NJ, 2013

Bätschmann, Oskar, *The Artist in the Modern World: The Conflict Between Market and Self-Expression*, Dumont, Cologne, 1997

Bonnet, Alain (ed.), *L'Artiste en représentation. Images des artistes dans l'art du XIXe siècle*, Fage, Lyon, 2012

Buren, Daniel, 'The Function of the Studio', trans. Thomas Repensek, *October*, vol.10, 1979, pp 51–58

Cole, Michael, and Mary Pardo (eds), *Inventions of the Studio: Renaissance to Romanticism*, University of North Carolina Press, Chapel Hill, NC, 2005

Démoris, René, (ed.), *L'Artiste en représentation*, Éditions Desjonquières, Paris, 1993

Elderfield, John, *In the Studio*, vol.1: *Painting*, exh.cat., Gagosian Gallery, New York, 2015

Esner, Rachel, 'In the Artist's Studio with *L'Illustration*', *RIHA Journal*, January–March 2013, http://www.riha-journal.org/articles/2013/2013-jan-mar/esner-illustration/

Esner, Rachel, 'Nos artistes chez eux. L'Image des artistes dans la presse illustrée', *L'Artiste en représentation. Images des artistes dans l'art du XIXe siècle* (A. Bonnet, ed.), Fage, Lyon, 2012, pp 139–49.

Hamon, Philippe, 'Le topos de l'atelier', in *L'Artiste en représentation* (R. Démoris, ed.), Éditions Desjonquières, Paris, 1993, pp 126–44

Junod, Philippe, 'L'Atelier comme autoportrait', in *Chemins de traverse. Essais sur l'histoire des arts*, Infolio, Gollion, 2007, pp 285–304

La Peinture dans la peinture, exh.cat., Musée des Beaux-Arts, Dijon, 1983

Milner, John, *The Studios of Paris: The Capital of Art in the Late Nineteenth Century*, Yale University Press, New Haven, CT/London, 1988

O'Doherty, Brian, *Studio and Cube*, Columbia University Press, New York, 2007

Silvestre, Théophile, *Histoire des artistes vivants français et étrangers: Études d'après nature*, E. Blanchard, Paris, 1856

Waterfield, Giles (ed.), *The Artist's Studio*, Hogarth Arts, Compton Verney, 2009

I THE ECHO CHAMBER: DELACROIX, MANET AND THE OLD MASTERS

Artists by Artists: Sculpted Portraits in the Nineteenth Century, exh.cat., Stuart Lochhead Sculpture, London, 2019

Baudelaire, Charles, *The Painter of Modern Life and Other Essays* (J. Mayne, trans. and ed.), Phaidon, London, 1964

Betzer, Sarah, 'Artist as Lover: Rereading Ingres's *Raphael and the Fornarina*', *Oxford Art Journal*, vol.38, no.3, December 2015, pp 313–41

Blanche, Jacques-Émile, *Propos de peintre, de David à Degas*, Émile-Paul Frères, Paris, 1919

Callen, Anthea, 'Faure and Manet', *Gazette des Beaux-Arts*, vol.83, March 1974, pp 157–68

Catalogue de la vente de Eugène Delacroix, Hôtel Drouot, J. Claye, Paris, 1864

De Tolnay, Charles, '"Michel-Ange dans son atelier" par Delacroix', *Gazette des Beaux-Arts*, vol.59, January 1962, pp 43–52

Delacroix, exh.cat., Metropolitan Museum of Art, New York, 2018

Delacroix: An Exhibition of Paintings, Drawings, and Lithographs, exh.cat., Arts Council, London, 1964

Delacroix, Eugène, 'Essai sur les artistes célèbres: Raphaël', *Revue de Paris*, vol.11, February 1830, pp 138–50

Delacroix, Eugène, *Journal*, 2 vols (M. Hannoosh, ed.), José Corti, Paris, 2009

Delacroix, Eugène, 'Michel-Ange', *Revue de Paris*, vol.15, June 1830, pp 41–58; vol.16, July 1830, pp 164–78

Discover Manet & Eva Gonzalès, exh.cat., National Gallery, London, 2022

Dolan, Therese, 'A Model Complicated by an Artist: Manet's *Portrait of the Poet Zaccharie Astruc*', in *Women in Impressionism: From Mythical Feminine to Modern Woman*, exh.cat., Ny Carlsberg Glyptotek, Copenhagen, 2006, pp 135–55

Doyle, Allan, 'Grasping the Antique: Michelangelo and the Erotics of Tradition', in *Reconsidering Gérôme*, exh.cat., J. Paul Getty Museum, Los Angeles, 2010, pp 7–21

Duffy, Michael, 'Michelangelo and the Sublime in Romantic Art Criticism', *Journal of the History of Ideas*, vol.56, no.2, 1995, pp 217–38

Du Pays, A.-J., 'Atelier de M. Eugène Delacroix', *L'Illustration*, 25 September 1852, pp 205–7

Duret, Théodore, *Histoire de Édouard Manet et de son œuvre*, Bernheim Jeune, Paris, 1919

Eugène Delacroix: Reflections: Tasso in the Madhouse, exh.cat., Oskar Reinhart Collection Am Römerholz, Winterthur, 2008

Gotlieb, Marc, 'Creation & Death in the Romantic Studio', in *Inventions of the Studio, Renaissance to Romanticism* (M. Cole and M. Pardo, eds), University of North Carolina Press, Chapel Hill, NC, 2005, pp 147–83

Grant, Carol Jane, 'Eva Gonzalès (1849–1883): An Examination of the Artist's Style and Subject Matter', PhD diss, Ohio State University, Columbus, OH, 1994

Hannoosh, Michèle, 'Delacroix and Sculpture', *Nineteenth-Century French Studies* vol.35, no.1, Autumn, 2006, pp 95–109

Harris, Jean C., *Édouard Manet: The Graphic Work: A Catalogue Raisonné* (rev. ed.), Alan Wofsy Fine Arts, San Francisco, 1990

Haskell, Francis, 'The Old Masters in Nineteenth-Century French Painting', *Past and Present in Art and Taste: Selected Essays*, by Francis Haskell, Yale University Press, New Haven, CT/London, 1987, pp 90–115

Johnson, Lee, *The Paintings of Eugène Delacroix: A Critical Catalogue*, 6 vols, Clarendon Press, Oxford, 1981–9

Kallmyer, Nina Maria Athanassaglou, 'Cézanne and Delacroix's Posthumous Reputation', *Art Bulletin*, vol.87, no.1, March 2005, pp 111–29

Manet, 1832–1883, exh.cat., Metropolitan Museum of Art, New York, 1983

Manet and Modern Beauty: The Artist's Last Years, exh.cat., J. Paul Getty Museum, Los Angeles, 2019

Manet at Work, exh.cat., National Gallery, London, 1983

McCoy, Claire Black, 'Made to Measure: Eugène Guillaume's Michelangelo', *Nineteenth-Century Art Worldwide*, vol.16, no.1, Spring 2017, pp 29–54

Moreau-Nélaton, Étienne, *Delacroix raconté par lui-même*, 2 vols, Henri Laurens, Paris, 1916

Moreau-Nélaton, Étienne, *Manet raconté par lui-même*, 2 vols, Henri Laurens, Paris, 1926

Pauly, Rebecca M., 'Baudelaire and Delacroix on Tasso in Prison: Romantic Reflections on a Renaissance Martyr', *College Literature*, vol.30, no.2, 2003, pp 120–35

Proust, Antonin, *Édouard Manet. Souvenirs*, Librarie Renouard, Paris, 1913

Rouart, Denis, and Georges Wildenstein, *Édouard Manet. Catalogue raisonné*, 2 vols, La Bibliothèque des Arts, Lausanne/Paris, 1975

Rudd, Peter, 'Reconstructing Manet's "Velázquez in His Studio"', *Burlington Magazine*, vol.136, November 1994, pp 747–51

Silvestre, Théodore, *Eugène Delacroix. Documents nouveaux*, Lévy Frères, Paris, 1864

Silvestre, Théodore, *La Galerie Bruyas*, Imprimerie de J. Claye, Paris, 1876

Spector, Jack J., 'An Interpretation of Delacroix's *Michelangelo in His Studio*', in *Psychoanalytic Perspectives on Art* (M.M. Gedo, ed.), The Analytic Press, Hillsdale, NJ, 1985, pp 107–31

Tabarant, Adolphe, *Manet. Histoire catalographique*, Éditions Montaigne, Paris, 1931

Toussaint, Hélène, 'Ingres et la Fornarina', *Bulletin du Musée Ingres*, September 1986, pp 63–74

Wakefield, David (ed.), *Stendahl and the Arts*, Phaidon, London, 1973

Wilson-Bareau, Juliet, 'Édouard Manet dans ses ateliers', *Ironie*, no.161, January–February 2012, http://interrogationcritiqueludique.blogspot.com/2012/10/ironie-n161-janvierfevfriefr-2012.html.

Wilson-Bareau, Juliet, 'Manet and Spain', in *Manet/Velázquez: The French Taste for Spanish Painting*, exh.cat., Metropolitan Museum of Art, New York, 2003, pp 203–57

Wilson-Bareau, Juliet (ed.), *Manet by Himself*, Chartwell Books, Edison, NJ, 2001

Wilson-Bareau, Juliet, *Manet, Monet, and the Gare Saint-Lazare*, exh.cat., National Gallery of Art, Washington, DC, 1998

Wilson-Bareau, Juliet, 'The Salon des Refusés: A New View', *Burlington Magazine*, vol.149, May 2007, pp 309–19

Zola, Émile, 'Préface', in *Exposition des oeuvres de Édouard Manet. Catalogue*, A. Quantin, Paris, 1884, pp 7–19

2 ABSENCE AND PRESENCE: COROT'S STUDIO REVISITED

Asselineau, Charles, 'Intérieurs d'atelier: C. Corot', *L'Artiste*, 15 September 1851, pp 53–5

Bazin, Germain, *Corot*, Pierre Tisné, Paris, 1951

Catalogue des tableaux, études, esquisses, dessins et eaux-fortes par Corot, dressé par M. Alfred Robaut, sale cat., Hôtel Drouot, Paris, 26 May–9 June 1875

Champa, Kermit S., *The Rise of Landscape Painting in France: Corot to Monet*, exh.cat., Currier Museum of Art, Manchester, NH, 1991

Claude Monet: Late Work, Gagosian Gallery, New York, 2010

Corot, exh.cat., Metropolitan Museum of Art, New York, 1996

Corot dans la lumière du Nord, Silvana Editoriale, Milan, 2013

Corot en Suisse, exh.cat., Musée Rath, Geneva, 2010

Dumesnil, Henri, *Corot. Souvenirs intimes*, Rapilly, Paris, 1875

Eitner, Lorenz, *French Paintings of the Nineteenth Century*, National Gallery of Art, Washington, DC, 2000, pp 70–78

Esner, Rachel, 'Nos artistes chez eux. L'Image des artistes dans la presse illustrée', in *L'Artiste en représentation. Images des artistes dans l'art du XIXe siècle* (J. Bonnet, ed.), Fage, Lyon, 2012, pp 139–49

Gaillot, Édouard, *La vie secrète de Jean-Baptiste-Camille Corot*, Éditions Occitania, Paris, 1934

Hannoosh, Michèle, 'Théophile Silvestre's *Histoire des artistes vivants*: Art History and Photography', *Art Bulletin*, vol.88. no.4, 2006, pp 729–55

Hommage à Corot: Peintures et dessins des collections françaises, exh.cat., Orangerie des Tuileries, Paris, 1975

Horbez, Dominique, *Corot et les peintres de l'école d'Arras*, La Renaissance du Livre, Tournai, 2004

Horbez, Dominique, *Corot et les peintres du Nord*, Les Éditions de l'Amateur, Paris, 2014

Hours, Madeleine, 'Figures de Corot. Étude photographique et radiographique', *Bulletin du Laboratoire* du *Musée du Louvre*, vol.7, 1962, pp 3–39

Janson, Anthony F., 'Corot: Tradition and the Muse', *Art Quarterly*, Autumn 1978, pp 294–317

La Peinture dans la peinture, exh.cat., Musée des Beaux-Arts, Dijon, 1983

Moreau-Nélaton, Étienne, *Corot raconté par lui-même*, 2 vols, Henri Laurens, Paris, 1924

Morton, Mary, et al., *Corot: Women*, exh.cat., National Gallery of Art, Washington, DC, 2018

Ogawa, David, 'Conditions of Beholding: Images of Femininity in the Work of Jean-Baptiste-Camille Corot', PhD diss., Brown University, Providence, RI, 1999

Ogawa, David, 'Alfred Robaut, Étienne Moreau-Nélaton, and Writing Corot', *Word and Image*, vol.22, no.4, October–December 2006, pp 327–39

Pomarède, Vincent, Chiara Stefani and Gérard de Wallens (eds), *Corot, un artiste et son temps. Actes des colloques organisés au Musée du Louvre*, Klincksieck, Paris, 1998

Robaut, Alfred, Cartons, 35 cartons, Cabinet des estampes, Bibliothèque nationale de France, Paris, on deposit at Département des peintures, Service d'étude et de documentation, Musée du Louvre, Paris

Robaut, Alfred, 'Documents sur Corot', ms, 3 vols, Cabinet des estampes, Bibliothèque nationale de France, Paris

Robaut, Alfred, *L'Oeuvre de Corot. Catalogue raisonné et illustré*, 4 vols, Floury, Paris, 1905

Schmunk, Peter, 'Music and the Art of Corot', *SECAC Review*, vol.13, no.4, 1999, pp 354–63

The Secret Armoire: Corot's Figure Paintings and the World of Reading, exh.cat., Oskar Reinhart Collection Am Römerholz, Winterthur, 2011

3 THE VIRTUAL STUDIO: DAUBIGNY, MONET AND BAZILLE

Bajou, Valérie, *Frédéric Bazille, 1841–1870*, Édisud, Aix-en-Provence, 1993

Bazille Frédéric, *Frédéric Bazille. Correspondance* (D. Vatuone, ed.), Les Presses du Languedoc, Montpellier, 1992

Bendix, Deanna Marohn, *Diabolical Designs: Paintings, Interiors, and Exhibitions of James McNeill Whistler*, Smithsonian Institution Press, Washington, DC, 1995

Blanche, Jacques-Émile, *Portraits of a Lifetime: The Late Victorian Era, The Edwardian Pageant, 1870–1914*, (W. Clement, ed.), Coward-McCann, New York, 1938

Callen, Anthea, *The Art of Impressionism: Painting Technique & the Making of Modernity*, Yale University Press, New Haven, CT/London, 2000

Callen, Anthea, *The Work of Art: Plein-Air Painting and Artistic Identity in Nineteenth-Century France*, Reaktion Books, London, 2015

Claude Monet: Late Work, Gagosian Gallery, New York, 2010

Daubigny, Charles-François, *Le Voyage en bateau*, préface by Frédéric Henriet, Delâtre, Paris, 1862

Daubigny, Monet, Van Gogh: Impressions of Landscape, exh.cat., Taft Museum of Art, Cincinnati, 2016

Daulte, François, *Frédéric Bazille et les débuts de l'impressioninisme, catalogue raisonné de l'oeuvre peint*, La Bibliothèque des Arts, Paris, 1992

Daulte, François, *Frédéric Bazille et son temps*, Pierre Cailler, Geneva, 1952

Duffy, Michael, *The Influence of Charles-Francois Daubigny (1817–1878) on French Plein-Air Landscape Painting*, Edwin Mellen Press, Lewiston, NY, 2010

Duffy, Michael, 'Landscape Painting & the Floating Studio: Constructing Visual Sensation and Picturesque Travel from Daubigny's "Le Botin"', *SECAC Review*, vol.14, no.1, 2001, pp 21–9

Entre ciel et terre. Camille Pissarro et les peintres de la vallée de l'Oise, exh.cat., Musée Tavet-Delacour, Pontoise, 2003

Fidell-Beaufort, Madeleine, and Janine Bailly-Herzberg, *Daubigny*, Geoffroy-Dechaume, Paris, 1975

Frédéric Bazille (1841–1870) and the Birth of Impressionism, exh.cat., National Gallery of Art, Washington, DC, 2016

Geffroy, Gustave, *La Vie artistique*, vol.1, E. Dentu, Paris, 1892

Grad, Bonnie L., 'Le Voyage en Bateau: Daubigny's Visual Diary of River Life', *The Print Collector's Newsletter*, vol.11, no.4, September–October 1980, pp 123–7

Guillemot, Maurice, 'Claude Monet', *La Revue illustrée*, no.7, 15 March 1898, n.p.

Hellebranth, Robert, and Anne Hellebranth, *Charles-François Daubigny, 1817–1878 (Supplément)*, s.n., France, *c.*1996

Henriet, Frédéric, *Le Paysagiste aux champs*, A. Lévy, Paris, 1876

Henriet, Frédéric, 'Les Paysagistes contemporains', *Gazette des Beaux-Arts*, January–June 1874, pp 255–70

Herbert, Robert L., *Impressionism: Art, Leisure, and Parisian Society*, Yale University Press, New Haven, CT/London, 1988

Herbert, Robert L., 'Method and Meaning in Monet', *Art in America*, vol.16, no.5, September 1979, pp 90–108

Impressionists on the Water, exh.cat., Fine Arts Museums of San Francisco, San Francisco, 2013

MacDonald, Margaret Flora, 'James McNeill Whistler: An Artist on Artists', *Visual Culture in Britain*, 2015, pp 200–22

MacDonald, Margaret, and Grischka Petri, *The Paintings of James McNeill Whistler: A Catalogue Raisonné*, University of Glasgow, Glasgow, 2020, http://whistlerpaintings.gla.ac.uk

McQuillan, Melissa, *Impressionist Portraits*, Thames & Hudson, London, 1986

Michel, François-Bernard, *Frédéric Bazille: réflexions*, Grasset, Paris, 1992

Monet: The Late Years, exh.cat., Kimbell Art Museum, Fort Worth, TX, 2019

Monet & Bazille: A Collaboration, exh.cat., High Museum of Art, Atlanta, 1999

Monet and the Seine: Impressions of a River, exh.cat., Museum of Fine Arts, Houston, 2014
Monet's Years at Giverny: Beyond Impressionism, exh.cat., Metropolitan Museum of Art, New York, 1978
Moreau-Nélaton, Étienne, *Daubigny raconté par lui-même*, Henri Laurens, Paris, 1925
Pennell, Elizabeth Robbins, and Joseph Pennell, *The Whistler Journal*, J.B. Lippincott, Philadelphia, 1921
Pitman, Dianne, *Bazille: Purity, Pose, and Painting in the 1860s*, Pennsylvania State University Press, University Park, PA, 1998
Poulain, Gaston, *Bazille et ses amis*, La Renaissance du Livre, Paris, 1932
Raskin, Daniel,'Charles-François Daubigny, le poète du paysage fluvial', in *Reflets de la Seine impressionniste*, exh.cat., Atelier Grognard, Rueil-Malmaison, 2008–9
Rewald, John, *The History of Impressionism*, Museum of Modern Art, New York, 1973
Schulman, Michel, *Frédéric Bazille, 1841–1870. Catalogue raisonné: peintures, dessins, pastels, aquarelles*, Éditions de L'Amateur, Paris, 1995
Siewert, John,'Interior Motives: Whistler's Studio and Symbolist Mythmaking', in *Palaces of Art: Whistler and the Art Worlds of Aestheticism* (L. Glazer and L. Merrill, eds), Smithsonian Institution Scholarly Press, Washington, DC, 2013, pp 81–92
Strauber, Alison,'At Home in the Studio', in *Interior Portraiture and Masculine Identity in France, 1789–1914* (T. Balducci, H.B. Jensen and P. J. Warner, eds), Ashgate, Farnham, 2011, pp 121–34
Strother, Stephanie L., *Whistler Paintings and Drawings at the Art Institute of Chicago*, Art Institute of Chicago, Chicago, 2020, publications.artic.edu
Taboureux, Émile,'Claude Monet', *La Vie moderne*, June 1880, pp 380–82
The Woman in White: Joanna Hiffernan and James McNeill Whistler, exh. cat., National Gallery of Art, Washington, DC, 2020
Tucker, Paul Hayes, *The Impressionists at Argenteuil*, exh.cat., National Gallery of Art, Washington, DC, 2000
Tucker, Paul Hayes, *Monet at Argenteuil*, Yale University Press, New Haven, CT/London, 1982
Way, Thomas Robert, *Memories of James McNeill Whistler, the Artist*, John Lane, London, 1912
Wildenstein, Daniel, *Claude Monet. Biographie et catalogue raisonné*, 5 vols, Bibliothèque des Arts, Lausanne-Paris, 1974–1991

4 IMPROMPTU STUDIOS: BERTHE MORISOT TO MARIE LAURENCIN

Ashton, Dore, *Rosa Bonheur: A Life and a Legend*, Viking, New York, 1981
Berthe Morisot, exh.cat., Musée d'Orsay, Paris, 2019
Berthe Morisot, 1841–1895, exh.cat., Musée Marmottan, Paris, 2012
Blanche, Jacques-Émile,'Les Dames de la grande-rue', *Dates*, Émile-Paul Frères, Paris, 1920, pp 16–24
Chadwick, Whitney, *Women, Art, and Society*, Thames & Hudson, London, 2020
Du Pays, A.-J.,'L'Atelier de Mlle Rosa Bonheur', *L'Illustration*, 1 May 1852, pp 283–4
Duranty, Edmond,'L'Atelier', in *Le Pays des arts*, G. Charpentier, Paris, 1881, pp 131–207
Garb, Tamar,'Berthe Morisot and the Feminizing of Impressionism', in *Critical Readings in Impressionism and Post-Impressionism* (ed., M.T. Lewis), University of California Press, Berkeley, 2007, pp 19–201
Garb, Tamar, *The Painted Face: Portraits of Women in France, 1814–1914*, Yale University Press, New Haven, CT/London, 2007
Garb, Tamar, *Sisters of the Brush: Women's Artistic Culture in Late Nineteenth-Century Paris*, Yale University Press, New Haven, CT/London, 1994
Groult, Flora, *Marie Laurencin*, Mercure de France, Paris, 1987
Hewitt, Catherine, *Art Is a Tyrant: The Unconventional Life of Rosa Bonheur*, Icon, London, 2020
Higonnet, Anne, *Berthe Morisot*, HarperCollins, New York, 1990
Higonnet, Anne, *Berthe Morisot's Images of Women*, Harvard University Press, Cambridge, MA, 1992
Klumpke, Anna Elizabeth, *Rosa Bonheur, sa vie, son œuvre*, Flammarion, Paris, 1908
Laurencin, Marie, *Le carnet des nuits* [1942], Pierre Cailler, Geneva, 1956
Manet, Julie, *Growing up with the Impressionists: The Diary of Julie Manet* (R. de Boland Roberts and J. Roberts, eds), Sotheby's Publications, New York, 1987
Marcello. Adèle d'Affry, Duchesse de Castiglione Colonna, exh.cat., Musée d'art et d'histoire, Fribourg, 2014
Marchesseau, Daniel, *Marie Laurencin*, Fernand Hazan, Paris, 1981
Marie Laurencin, 1883–1956, exh.cat., Musée Marmottan Monet, Paris, 2013
Marie Laurencin: Artist and Muse, exh.cat., Birmingham Museum of Art, Birmingham, AL, 1989
Mirecourt, Eugène de, *Rosa Bonheur*, Achille Faure, Paris, 1867
Pierre, Caterina Y., *'Genius Has No Sex': The Sculpture of Marcello (1836–1879)*, Éditions de Penthes, Pregny-Geneva/Infolio, Gollion, 2010
Pierre, Caterina Y.,'Marcello's Heroic Sculpture', *Woman's Art Journal*, vol. 22, no.1, Spring–Summer 2001, pp 14–20
Pollock, Griselda, *Vision and Difference: Femininity, Feminism, and Histories of Art*, Routledge, London, 1988
Ringelberg, Kirstin, *Redefining Gender in American Impressionist Studio Paintings: Work Place/Domestic Place*, Ashgate, Farnham, 2010
Rosa Bonheur (1822–1899), exh.cat., Musée d'Orsay, Paris, 2022
Stanton, Theodore (ed.), *Reminiscences of Rosa Bonheur*, Appleton & Co., New York, 1910
Stuckey, Charles, *Berthe Morisot, Impressionist*, Hudson Hills, New York, 1987
Un soir chez la Princesse Mathilde. Une Bonaparte et les arts, exh.cat., Palais Fesch Musée des Beaux-Arts, Ajaccio, 2019
Yeldham, Charlotte, *Women Artists in Nineteenth-Century France and England*, 2 vols, Garland Publishing, New York, 1984

5 THE REFRACTED STUDIO: MATISSE AND PICASSO

Ashton, Dore, *Picasso on Art*, Viking, New York, 1972

Baldassari, Anne, 'Le Rose et le noir', in *Icônes de l'art moderne. La Collection Chtchoukine*, exh.cat., Fondation Louis Vuitton, Paris, 2016

Baldassari, Anne, *Picasso and Photography: The Dark Mirror*, exh.cat., Museum of Fine Arts, Houston, 1997

Baldassari, Anne, *Picasso photographe, 1901–1916*, Éditions de la Réunion des Musées Nationaux, Paris, 1994

Barr, Alfred, *Matisse: His Art and His Public*, Museum of Modern Art, New York, 1951

Becoming Picasso: Paris 1901, exh.cat., Courtauld Gallery, London, 2013

Bois, Yve-Alain, *Matisse and Picasso*, exh.cat., Kimbell Art Museum, Fort Worth, TX, 1998

Brassaï, *The Artists of My Life*, trans. R. Miller, Viking Press, New York, 1982

Breton, André, 'Picasso dans son élément', *Minotaure*, no.1, 1933, pp 10–22

Butor, Michel, *Les ateliers de Picasso. L'Alambic des formes*, Images Modernes, Paris, 2003

Daix, Pierre, *Picasso: The Cubist Years, 1907–16: A Catalogue Raisonné of the Paintings and Related Works*, New York Graphic Society, Boston, 1979

Devenir Matisse, 1890–1911, exh.cat., Silvana Editoriale, Milan, 2019

Elsen, Albert E., *The Sculpture of Henri Matisse*, Harry N. Abrams, New York, 1972

Flam, Jack, *Matisse, the Man and His Art, 1869–1918*, Cornell University Press, Ithaca, NY, 1986

Flam, Jack, *Matisse and Picasso: The Story of Their Rivalry and Friendship*, Icon, Cambridge, MA, 2003

Flam, Jack, *Matisse in Transition: Around Laurette*, exh.cat., Norton Museum of Art, West Palm Beach, FL, 2006

Flam, Jack, *Matisse on Art*, University of California Press, Berkeley, CA, 1995

Galassi, Peter, *In the Studio: Photographs*, vol.2, exh.cat., Gagosian Gallery, New York, 2015

Galassi, Susan Grace, *Picasso's Variations on the Masters: Confrontations with the Past*, Abrams, New York, 1996

Gillot, Françoise, *Life with Picasso*, Doubleday, New York, 1989

Grammont, Claudine, 'Matisse and Picasso, the Comedy of the Model', *Matisse & Picasso: La comédie du modèle*, exh.cat., Musée Matisse, Nice, 2018

Henri Matisse: The Early Years in Nice, 1916–1930, exh.cat., National Gallery of Art, Washington, DC, 1986

Henri Matisse, une palette d'objets, exh.cat., Art Lys, Paris/Musée Matisse, Nice, 2016

Hubert, René Riese, 'The Encounter of Balzac and Picasso', *Dalhousie French Studies*, vol.5, October 1983, pp.38–54

Klein, John, *Matisse Portraits*, Yale University Press, New Haven, CT/London, 2001

L'Atelier des combles, exh.cat., Musée Picasso, Antibes, 2008

Laude, Jean, 'Les "Ateliers" de Matisse', *Colóquio Artes*, 18 June 1974, pp 16–25

Matisse comme un roman, exh.cat., Centre Pompidou, Paris, 2020

Matisse, His Art and His Textiles: The Fabric of Dreams, exh.cat., Royal Academy of Arts, London, 2004

McBreen, Ellen, and Helen Burnham, *Matisse in the Studio*, exh.cat., Museum of Fine Arts, Boston, 2017

Mezzatesta, Michael P., *Henri Matisse: Sculptor/Painter*, exh.cat., Kimbell Museum of Art, Fort Worth, TX, 1984

Olga Picasso, exh.cat., Musée national Picasso-Paris/Gallimard, Paris, 2017

Olivier, Fernande, *Loving Picasso: The Private Journal of Fernande Olivier*, trans. C. Baker and M. Raeburn, Harry N. Abrams, New York, 2001

Pablo Picasso: L'Atelier, exh.cat., Peggy Guggenheim Collection, Venice, 1996

Penrose, Roland, and John Golding (eds), *Picasso in Retrospect*, Praeger, New York, 1973

Picasso: Painting the Blue Period, exh.cat., The Phillips Collection, Washington DC, 2021

Picasso: The Early Years, 1892–1906, exh.cat., National Gallery of Art, Washington, DC, 1997

Picasso and Portraiture: Representation and Transformation, exh.cat., Museum of Modern Art, New York, 1996

Picasso & the Camera, exh.cat., Gagosian Gallery, New York, 2014

Richardson, John, and Marilyn McCully, *A Life of Picasso*, vol.1: *The Early Years, 1881–1906*, Random House, New York, 1991

Richardson, John, *A Life of Picasso, 1907–1917*, vol.2: *The Painter of Modern Life*, Random House, New York, 1996

Richardson, John, *A Life of Picasso*, vol.3: *The Triumphant Years, 1917–1932*, Alfred A. Knopf, New York, 2007

Richardson, John, *A Life of Picasso*, vol.4: *The Minotaur Years, 1933–1943*, Alfred A. Knopf, New York, 2021

Robinson, William H., *Picasso and the Mysteries of Life: La Vie*, exh.cat., Cleveland Museum of Art, Cleveland, OH, 2012.

Rudenstine, Angelika Zander, *Peggy Guggenheim Collection, Venice*, Harry N. Abrams, New York, 1985

Schneider, Pierre, *Matisse*, Rizzoli, New York, 1984

Spurling, Hilary, *Matisse the Master: A Life of Henri Matisse, The Conquest of Color, 1909–1954*, Alfred A. Knopf, New York, 2005

Spurling, Hilary, *The Unknown Matisse: A Life of Henri Matisse, The Early Years, 1869–1908*, University of California Press, Berkeley, CA, 1998

Steinberg, Leo, 'The Algerian Women and Picasso at Large', in *Other Criteria: Confrontations with Twentieth-Century Art*, Oxford University Press, Oxford, 1972, pp 125–234

Steinberg, Leo, 'The Skulls of Picasso', in *Other Criteria: Confrontations with Twentieth-Century Art*, Oxford University Press, Oxford, 1972, pp 115–23

Yo Picasso: Self-Portraits, exh.cat., Museu Picasso, Barcelona, 2013

Image Credits

Fig.70: © Art Resource, NY © Succession Picasso/DACS, London, 2023; Fig.71: Artwork: © Succession H. Matisse/ DACS 2023. Photo: Archives Henri Matisse, all rights reserved; Fig.77: Artwork: © Succession H. Matisse/ DACS 2023. Photo: © Tate, London /Art Resource, NY; Fig.79: Artwork: © Succession H. Matisse/ DACS 2023. Photo: © The Museum of Modern Art/Licensed by SCALA / Art Resource, NY; Fig.80: Artwork: © Succession H. Matisse/ DACS 2023. Photo: The Phillips Collection, Washington DC. Acquired 1940; Fig.81: Artwork: © Succession H. Matisse/ DACS 2023. Photo: Philippe Migeat. Digital Image: © CNAC/MNAM, Dist. RMN-Grand Palais/Art Resource, NY; Fig.82: Artwork: © Succession H. Matisse/ DACS 2023. Photo: Musée Matisse, Le Cateau-Cambrésis, France Phaidon Press / Bridgeman Images; Fig.83: Artwork: © Succession H. Matisse/ DACS 2023. Photo: © Paris Musées, musée d'Art moderne, Dist. RMN-Grand Palais / image ville de Paris/Art Resource, NY; Fig.85: Artwork: © Succession H. Matisse/ DACS 2023. Photo: bpk Bildagentur / Museum Berggruen/ Nationalgalerie/ Staatliche Museen, Berlin/ Art Resource, NY. Photo: Jens Ziehe; Figs 24, 25, 64: Author's own; Fig.29: Baltimore Museum of Art, The Cone Collection formed by Dr. Claribel Cone and Miss Etta Cone of Baltimore, Maryland. Photo: Mitro Hood; Fig.49: Barnes Foundation; Figs 38, 40, 41: Bibliothèque Nationale de France; Fig.42: Bonhams; Figs 7, 21, 30: © Christie's Images/Bridgeman Images; Fig.69: © Christie's Images/Bridgeman Images © Fondation Foujita/ADAGP, Paris and DACS, London, 2023; Fig.68: Photo: Ville de Grenoble/ Musée de Grenoble: J.L. Lacroix. © Fondation Foujita/ ADAGP, Paris and DACS, London, 2023; Fig.74: Cleveland Museum of Art, Gift of the Hanna Fund 1945.24. © Succession Picasso/ DACS, London, 2023; Fig.14: The Chrysler Museum of Art, Norfolk, VA. Gift of Walter P. Chrysler, Jr.; Figs 1, 34, 39, 61: Creative Commons; Fig.63: Digitized by Google; Figs 4, 19, 31, 37, 53: © Erich Lessing/ Art Resource, NY; Figs 10, 11: © Fitzwilliam Museum/ Bridgeman Images; Fig.56: Friends of American Art Collection; Fig.78: Getty Images News via Getty Images; Fig.44: Gift of Theodore De Witt, 1923; Fig.5: Harvard Art Museums; Fig.17 Historic Images/ Alamy Stock Photo; Fig.20: Kunsthalle Bremen. Photo: Marcus Meyer ARTOTHEK; Fig.32: © Lyon MBA-Photo: Alin Basset; Fig.66: Mairie de Bordeaux, Musée des Beaux-Arts. Photo:

F. Deval; Fig.67: Image © Metropolitan Museum of Art, NY. Gift of the artist, in memory of Rosa Bonheur, 1922. Image source: Art Resource, NY; Fig.55: Robert Lehman Collection, 1975; Fig.54: Mr. and Mrs. H. Marlatt Fund; Figs 57, 58: © Musée d'art et d'histoire, Fribourg/ Primula Bosshard; Fig.12: Musée Fabre, Montpellier. Photo: Frédéric Jaulmes; Fig. 62: Musée Marmottan Monet, Paris; Fig.76: Museum of Modern Art (MoMA), New York, USA © Succession Picasso/DACS, London, 2023/ Bridgeman Images; Fig.86: Digital image © Museum of Modern Art/Licensed by SCALA/Art Resource, NY. © Succession Picasso/DACS, London, 2023. Fig.18: © National Gallery, London/ Art Resource, NY; Fig.47: National Gallery of Art, Washington, Ailsa Mellon Bruce, Collection; Fig.33: National Gallery of Art, Washington, Collection Mr. and Mrs. Paul Mellon; Fig.27: National Gallery of Art, Washington, Widener Collection; Figs 22, 23: National Gallery of Art Library, Gift of R. Horace Gallatin; Fig.36: Nationalmuseum, Stockholm; Fig.46: Neue Pinakothek, Munich, Germany/ Bridgeman Images; Fig. 13: Oskar Reinhart Collection 'Am Römerholz', Winterthur; Fig.73: The Phillips Collection, Washington, DC. Acquired 1927. © Succession Picasso/ DACS, London, 2023; Fig.8: Piasa, Paris; Fig.2: Prado, Madrid, Spain/ Bridgeman Images; Fig.45: Princeton University Art Museum, Gift of Harry A. Brooks, Class of 1935, and Mrs. Brooks; Fig.9: Private Collection Liszt Collection/ Bridgeman Images; Fig. 51: Purchased with funds provided by Mr. and Mrs. Frank H. Woods in memory of Mrs. Edward Harris Brewer; Fig.15: © RMN-Grand Palais/Art Resource, NY; Fig.60: © RMN-Grand Palais/Art Resource, NY. Photo: Daniel Arnaudet; Fig.35: © RMN-Grand Palais/ Art Resource, NY. Photo: Jean-Gilles Berizzi; Figs 59, 65: © RMN-Grand Palais/ Art Resource, NY. Photo: Gérard Blot; Figs 6, 16: © RMN-Grand Palais/ Art Resource, NY. Photo: Bulloz; Fig.50: RMN-Grand Palais/Art Resource, NY. Photo: Christian Jean; Fig.28: © RMN-Grand Palais/ Art Resource. Photo: René Gabriel Ojéda; Fig.3: RMN-Grand Palais/ Art Resource, NY. Photo: Patrice Schmidt; Fig.72: © RMN-Grand Palais / Art Resource, NY. © Succession Picasso/ DACS, London, 2023; Fig.75: © RMN-Grand Palais/Art Resource, NY. © Succession Picasso/ DACS, London, 2023; Fig. 89: © RMN-Grand Palais/ Art Resource, NY. © Succession Picasso/ DACS, London, 2023; Fig.90: © RMN-Grand Palais /Art Resource, NY. © Succession Picasso/ DACS, London, 2023. © Estate Brassai-RMN; Fig.87: Peggy Guggenheim Foundation, Venice, Italy © Succession Picasso/DACS, London, 2023 / Bridgeman Images; Fig.48: Rijksmuseum Kröller-Müller, Otterloo, Netherlands/ Bridgeman Images; Fig.26: Scala/ Art Resource, NY; Fig.88: Scala/ Art Resource, NY. © Succession Picasso/DACS, London, 2023; Fig.52: © Virginia Museum of Fine Arts, Richmond. Collection of Mr. and Mrs. Paul Mellon. Photo: Travis Fullerton; Fig.43: Wadsworth Atheneum Museum of Art, Hartford, CT. Bequest of Anne Parrish Titzell. Photo: Allen Phillips. Paul Mellon 83.4. Photo: Travis Fullerton; Fig.39: Wikipedia Commons

Index

Note: italic page numbers indicate figures; page numbers followed by n refer to notes.